WANTING WHAT'S BEST

WANTING WHAT'S BEST

PARENTING, PRIVILEGE, AND BUILDING A JUST WORLD

SARAH W. JAFFE

CHICAGO

Copyright © 2022 by Sarah W. Jaffe
All rights reserved
Published by Parenting Press
An imprint of Chicago Review Press Incorporated
814 North Franklin Street
Chicago, Illinois 60610
ISBN 978-1-64160-767-4

Library of Congress Control Number: 2021951979

Cover design: Jonathan Hahn
Cover photographs: BRO.vector / Shutterstock
Typesetting: Nord Compo

Printed in the United States of America
5 4 3 2 1

To Alice

CONTENTS

PROLOGUE

A FEW WEEKS after giving birth to my daughter, I joined the parent listserv for Park Slope, Brooklyn. I lived a few miles south of that neighborhood, but I knew it was famous for having a high concentration of families. I thought I could get free hand-me-down baby gear. I also thought that I might be able to meet "like-minded people." (I thought very little about what I meant by that.)

The administrators of the listserv placed me on an email list with other parents who had babies born in the same month as mine— September 2017. Each day, I got a message telling me the location of the daily meetup, which was usually a café where I would find a table of women (and the occasional man) with babies the same age as my own.

Everyone at these meetings had some things in common: we had forty-five dollars to spend on annual dues for a parent listserv, and we had either the kind of jobs that gave you parental leave or partners with the kind of jobs that allow you to be a one-income family in Brooklyn. Everyone lived in Park Slope or its surrounding neighborhoods, some of the most expensive real estate in the country. Most were White. The meetings were generally pleasant and calm affairs, with small talk about our babies' birthdays, names, birth weights, and sleep schedules.

The listserv itself was a different story. There, lengthy, anxiety-filled emails would spawn thirty-part threads dissecting every aspect of raising a baby, and how and why we might get it wrong. I ran a search for the word *worried* from the September 2017 Babies listserv and found that the word had been used in eighty-two different email chains in contexts ranging from "Baby Rolling on Tummy in Sleep—Help!" to "Nursery Carpet??"

I certainly wasn't immune to the worry. When my daughter was a month old, I brought her to her pediatrician convinced that she had a bruise on her head. It had actually been a shadow, just a trick of afternoon light. But having seen what I thought was a large purple patch of swelling skin on her temple, I couldn't fully unsee it—not until I'd been told, for sure, that there was nothing there.

Worry, to a large extent, defined what parenting was for me. Certainly, it seemed to be what good parents did. The other major topic on the listserv was finding the best, whether that be doctors, daycares, on-the-go snacks, or teething necklaces. Eggo waffles were the best for holding peanut butter (better than Van's waffles). Someone's pediatrician had told her that it was best to start potty training at "2.4 years." The Yoyo stroller was the best for the subway (better than the Zoe XL1, which got stuck on sidewalk bumps).

I went back to work when my daughter was six weeks old, though I mostly worked from home, and at odd hours that still allowed for the occasional 10:00 AM café meetup. My life at work and my life as a parent began to give me a sense of whiplash. I worked as an attorney at a nonprofit law firm that brought lawsuits on behalf of children in foster care. Our office manager, in a play on the industry nickname for corporate law firms (BigLaw) joked that we practiced "SadLaw." It was that kind of gallows humor that I leaned upon to get through stomach-turning tasks. One of my job responsibilities was to read child fatality reports about children who died after their state's government knew that they were already in danger. When I finished a day of reading those reports to see a typical question on the Park Slope Parents listserv ("If you skip the iron-fortified cereal, do you worry about your baby getting enough iron?"), I would simultaneously think, *What a thing to worry about! Do you want to know what kids we should actually worry about?* and *Hmmm, I wasn't worrying about that but . . . maybe I should be?*

One day in the fall of 2018 my work world and my parenting world seemed coincidentally to be in conversation with each other. For work, I was reading the case file of Edward, a little boy in New York City foster care. When he'd been removed from his parents' care at age three, an underpaid city employee had made some quick calls to a list of foster parents in order to find one with an open bed. The first foster parent to answer her phone spoke Spanish exclusively, but she had room in her home and agreed she could be home that afternoon. Hours later, Edward was delivered to her door. It appeared to trouble no one that Edward had spent his whole life up until that point in an English-speaking household, that his parents only spoke English, or that his caseworker hadn't heard him speak at all. He spent months in the Spanish-speaking home before a different caseworker realized that he had a serious speech delay, which was only being exacerbated by the fact that his caretaker spoke a language that he couldn't understand. But since he was a foster child on Medicaid, the waiting list to even get him evaluated for much-needed speech services stretched on for months.

As I was reading Edward's case file, my phone was buzzing with messages from parents on the Park Slope Parents group discussing their own babies' speech. At that time, our babies were just a little over a year old, an age when normally developing children may not speak at all yet. But some of the parents wondered if they should get their baby an evaluation. (One mother confessed that she already had gotten a speech evaluation, and that the evaluator had been "basically looking cross-eyed" at her.)

The gap between Edward and the Park Slope kids couldn't have been clearer. It felt almost like a fable about the children in the city I lived in, a fable with a chilling moral: Some children get to speak while others do not. And who can least afford to wait will wait the longest.

Snowplow Parenting

In the last five years there's been an explosion of books and articles about the problems with "snowplow" parenting. (It's also called "lawnmower parenting," "concerted cultivation," or "hyperintense" parenting.) It begins with getting speech evaluations for your normally developing one-year-old and eventually leads to being a parent who calls your child's professor to argue over their grades. Snowplow parents view their duty as a parent to seek every possible advantage for their child and remove all obstacles from their child's path.

After observing years of this behavior from the parents of eighteen-year-old students, Julie Lythcott-Haims, a former dean at Stanford, published one of the first books critical of snowplow parenting. Her 2015 *How to Raise an Adult: Break Free of the Overparenting Trap and Prepare Your Kid for Success* is essentially a plea to parents to let their children experience failure so that they are better prepared for the real challenges of college and life. The book makes a convincing case that parents who obsessively clear every obstacle from their children's paths are setting them up for a host of issues. Lythcott-Haims also briefly addresses the impact of what she calls "overparenting" on the parents themselves, describing today's parents as "scared, not to mention exhausted, anxious, and depressed." The "snowplow" metaphor wasn't in common use yet, but the behavior Lythcott-Haims discusses is the same.

The most infamous example of snowplow parenting is the Varsity Blues scandal: thirty-three wealthy people were criminally charged for bribing and cheating to get their kids into college. That scandal quickly became a symbolic flash point: many writers saw it as an event that exemplified something disturbing about today's parenting culture.

The idea that there is something deeply wrong with modern parenthood didn't start with Varsity Blues—both Judith Warner's 2005 *Perfect Madness: Motherhood in the Age of Anxiety* and Kim Brooks's 2018 *Small Animals: Parenthood in the Age of Fear* capture the frenzied state that has defined parenting for them (and the parents in their social circle) in the twenty-first century. Both books discuss a culture of parenting defined by all-consuming anxiety: about your children's physical safety and about their prospects in life. Brooks writes of her own parenting experience that there was "an endless expanse of products and services for a concerned parent to buy. But strangely, the more I bought, the more I did, the more there was, it seemed, to buy or do; perhaps because fear tends to feed on itself, drawing parents into an ever-accelerating arms race of devotion."

This kind of parenting is harmful for children and exhausting for parents. Most of the books and articles about overparenting only discuss the harm to the overparented children themselves. But that's only half the story.

The other half, the part that this book attempts to address, is, What does it mean for our future, and our children's future, for the kids who need the least to get the most, and the kids who need the most to get the least? And, for those of us who are in a position to do something about it, what should we do?

INTRODUCTION

I T'S HARD TO BE A PARENT in the United States in the 2020s. As of this
writing, it is the only high-income country in the world that does not
offer paid leave to new parents (and one of only a handful that don't
among all countries on the planet). In most states, daycare costs more
than the average mortgage payment or public college tuition. Our
schools are chronically underfunded, and our college admission process is reminiscent of the *Hunger Games*. Our country's lack of a safety
net can leave even comfortably middle-class families decimated by an
unexpected expense or a medical crisis. This was all true before the
pandemic, which exacerbated many of the aforementioned problems.
As Anne Helen Petersen writes in *Can't Even: How Millennials Became
the Burnout Generation* (a book that's essentially a long catalog of
all the ways that modern life burns us out), parenting before the
pandemic felt "exhausting and impossible, now it's *more* exhausting
and impossible."

We also live in a culture that tells us that the solution to these
problems is simple: we just need to try harder. The pervasive cultural
message is that we, as individual parents, are the only ones responsible

for how our kids "turn out." We have no cultural conception of child-rearing as a communal activity, and little acknowledgment that all members of a society benefit when its children have food to eat, places to sleep, loving adults to care for them, and schools to educate them. The rules of being a parent in this country are simple: You owe your own children everything. You owe other children nothing.

It's little wonder that parents tend to close their eyes, put their heads down, and just try to get through the difficult task of raising children in a country that pays lip service to "family values" and then does little to help actual families. Collective action takes time, and time is in short supply.

And so, divisions within our society have widened, and keep widening. Many academics and journalists have chronicled that the class divide today isn't really between the top 1 percent and everybody else: it's between roughly the top 10 or 20 percent of income earners and everybody else. And the outcomes for children in this country born to those in the top brackets look very, very different from children born to those in the bottom.

Of course, the idea that there was ever a time when every class was on an even playing field is a myth. Accumulating wealth has been dramatically easier for White families throughout this country's history. It's always been the case that if you were born into wealth, it was easier to become wealthy yourself. But many already-existing inequities have worsened in recent decades. In his 2015 book *Our Kids: The American Dream in Crisis*, Robert Putnam chronicles how, over the latter half of the twentieth century his hometown of Port Clinton, Ohio, went from a "passable embodiment of the American Dream" to a "split-screen American nightmare . . . in which kids from the wrong side of the tracks that bisect the town can barely imagine the future that awaits the kids from the right side of the tracks." Putnam contends that what has happened in that town is a microcosm of changes across the United States that have dramatically decreased class mobility.

Writer and Brookings Institution fellow Richard V. Reeves made a similar point in 2017's *Dream Hoarders: How the American Upper Middle Class Is Leaving Everyone Else in the Dust, Why That Is a Problem, and What to Do About It.* Reeves is British and came to the United States, in part, because he found the class consciousness of his home country "depressing." Yet instead of a land of equal opportunity for all, he found the United States to be "more calcified by class than Britain, especially toward the top." The chief difference he found between the two countries was that "most of the people on the highest rung in America are in denial about their privilege." His book is a close look at how families in the top 20 percent of income earners (basically, any family who writes down six or more figures on the "total household income" line of their tax return) are amassing advantages for their own children while children in the lower income brackets get less and less. In the *Atlantic* Matthew Stewart described modern upper-middle-class parents as having "mastered the old trick of consolidating wealth and passing along privilege at the expense of other people's children," usually while either living in denial that they're doing it or buying into the self-justifying myth that it's the only way.

The pandemic has brought these divisions to the fore. On Saturday mornings in 2019 I would take my daughter to a free library story time, where any child could walk in, sit on the rug, and sing "Itsy Bitsy Spider." During the pandemic, we would still go sing, but at a thirty-dollar outdoor music class, where attendance was capped at six and we all spread our blankets as far from each other as possible. Children whose parents couldn't afford that thirty dollars weren't there. It's long been the case that children in wealthy families have more experienced teachers; during the pandemic, they were, by and large, the only children who saw their teachers in person at all. And it gets far worse: of the few hundred children who have died of COVID-19 in the United States, 75 percent of them were Black, Hispanic, or Indigenous children.

Our country's disturbing combination of extreme income inequality and lack of a safety net also leaves all but the very wealthiest families in a constant state of fear that any mistake will consign their child to a life of diminished prospects. This fear of what the future will bring gives our actions in the present a frantic urgency—it's part of what's at the root of all the "worry" about waffles and strollers that I encountered among my parent peer group. Philip Cohen, a sociologist at the University of Maryland, told the *New York Times* that snowplow parenting is born out of economic anxieties: "As the gap between rich and poor increases, the cost of screwing up increases. The fear is they'll end up on the other side of the divide."

I don't discount that fear. Among my interviewees, this fear is particularly potent for parents who themselves are the first generation of their family to experience any semblance of economic stability. But I also think that allowing that fear to dictate our major parenting decisions is to tacitly accept the most narrow and depressing vision for all our children's future.

In trying to grapple with how to think about all of this differently, I talked to parents (and in the final chapter, a few people without kids) from all around the country. Primarily, I talked to parents who live in cities or suburbs. I talked to single parents, foster and adoptive parents, and people in both opposite-sex and same-sex relationships. Though I sought to include parents from various backgrounds in this book, this is a parenting/self-help nonfiction book, not a sociology text. I won't pretend that these parents are a representative sample of any particular group. Writers and podcasters are certainly overrepresented in the coming pages, since I often sought interviews with people after reading or listening to their insights about a given issue. But there are plenty of parents featured who don't live public lives, and don't publicly write or speak about their parenting choices. With every person I interviewed, I tried to have frank, honest conversations about how they make parenting decisions that are guided by their deepest values rather than fear.

The parents I spoke with also had certain things in common: they all spoke English. They all had a working Internet connection and an email address. They were willing to spend hours of time talking to me without being paid. In other words, I talked to people with some degree of privilege. Many of them had real struggles. But they weren't about to get evicted, and they knew where their next meal was coming from. They were often exhausted and spread thin, but they also had some time and money left over after they'd met their needs for immediate survival. They weren't all in the top 20 percent of income earners, but all were in the top 50 percent. They were on the "right side of the divide."

That's who I imagine is reading this book too. It's aimed at parents who have the privilege of making choices. I myself am only able to write this book because of a list of privileges. I am White, cis, straight, expensively educated, neurotypical, able-bodied, healthy, and a US citizen. I don't know exactly what generation of college student I am (fifth, I think?), but I do know that every relative I've met from the generations above me has been to college. The very thing that inspired me to write the book was a parenting "norm" I saw all around me, which of course isn't a "norm" at all—it's a kind of parenting only practiced by a tiny slice of humanity during a tiny slice of human history.

Race and Class

This book isn't aimed only at White parents who have White kids. But it's both impossible and dishonest to write a book about inequality without acknowledging that, in the United States, White supremacy plays a major role in determining who gets ahead and who gets left behind. Whether I was researching labor legislation for childcare workers, school funding, college admissions, or wealth accumulation, I found a history that included the purposeful exclusion and subjugation of people of color.

Growing up in the 1990s in Seattle, a majority White city (and in an even Whiter neighborhood), I, like a lot of White kids in my generation, thought of racism primarily about being "mean" or "nice" to people who "looked different from me." Not being actively "mean" to someone because of their skin color was sufficient to be "not racist."

Of course, that was a cop-out. And while certainly plenty of White people still think that way, there is a much wider-spread understanding that racism is structural, not about words and feelings. But the cultural norms of privileged White parents often lead us to act in a way that worsens racial disparities, and that further advantages our (often also White) kids. As a White parent of a White kid, I had to do the painful but necessary work to really grapple with that fact and to realize that, while my parenting decisions feel deeply personal, they are shaped by the racist society in which I'm raising my daughter.

So I hope that any reader of any race can find something interesting or inspiring in the pages ahead, but I write with a particular sense of urgency for White parents with White kids, who are committed to the work of raising antiracist children and acting in antiracist ways themselves. This book is primarily about actions: what we do, not what we say. It's not a book about how to talk to your kids about racism or White supremacy, though I include some of those books in the Further Reading sections at the end of some of the chapters. Ibram X. Kendi, whose bestselling 2019 book *How to Be an Antiracist* brought the term *antiracist* into popular culture, repeatedly emphasizes that antiracism work is about outcomes, not about feelings. It doesn't matter what is "in your heart"; Kendi writes, "One either allows racial inequities to persevere, as a racist, or confronts racial inequities, as an antiracist."

So while I believe that talking with children about race is important, it's central to the idea of antiracism itself that being an antiracist person is about more than having the right kinds of conversations or reading the right books. After George Floyd's murder, the Park Slope Parents listserv was suddenly ablaze with mostly White parents urgently requesting recommendations of "books about racism/tolerance for this age group?" I don't discount the power of reading books, having tough conversations, or putting up Black Lives Matter signs on the lawn. But our actions say a lot more—how we treat people of color whom we may work with and whom our kids go to school with, for instance.

Is this just a book for rich parents? The short answer is no. The longer answer is similar to the distinction I made about White parents: that while this book isn't only written for, or about, wealthy families, those families' actions are particularly consequential. We like to vilify the top 1 percent as the drivers of inequality in this country. But, as Richard V. Reeves explores deeply in his book, people in the top 20 percent of income earners (a bracket I count myself in) are continuing to do OK for ourselves while leaving everyone else further and further behind.

Most of us don't have enough money to pay $50,000 for a stand-in student to take the ACT in our child's place, much less pay $6.5 million to the college in a bribe for admission (as one Varsity Blues family did). And we mostly don't want to—most wealthy families "play by the rules" when we're seeking advantages for our kids. But the Varsity Blues scandal nonetheless serves a useful purpose when thinking about how wealth interacts with our parenting choices: it can put to rest the idea that hyperintense parenting is *only* driven by the fear that our children will end up destitute, that if we just had a little bit more money we'd be able to relax. Two of the parents involved in the scandal, Felicity Huffman and William H. Macy, have a combined net worth of around $45 million; Lori Loughlin and Mossimo Giannulli are worth nearly double that. In the chapter on college I write about how many parents view their child's college degree as a shield against downward mobility. But downward mobility isn't a real concern, or at least not a reasonable one, if you have that kind of money. Yet dozens of the wealthiest parents were willing to cross both ethical and legal lines to make sure their child got into their desired school.

Parents with very few financial resources often instinctively understand that finding a private work-around within a system is less beneficial than trying to improve the system itself. In my career as a public interest attorney, I've met many parents living below the poverty line who are extremely invested in making systems work for everyone, even when they haven't worked well for them. One of those parents was Kasha Phillips-Lewis, a single mother of a ten-year-old who lives in the New York City shelter system. She'd spent fourteen years in foster care in Georgia before aging out of the system. At the beginning of the pandemic, she and her daughter were featured in a *New York Times* article about how the Department of Education hadn't provided Wi-Fi or computers to families in the shelter system, even though all their classes were being held online. After the story ran, she received offers of Chromebooks, music lessons, and money by people who were moved by her situation.

Kasha declined them all. She did not want a privately funded work-around. She did not want charity. She wanted to hold her school system to the promise it had made to its students. I reached out to her for an interview for an article about remote learning, and asked her, in several different ways, why she turned those offers down, and she said that she was "tired of agencies and politicians saying pretty words." She added, "I didn't want my daughter and other children to get screwed because no one called them on their B.S."

Most readers of this book will have financial resources somewhere between that of a Hollywood couple and that of a woman who grew up in foster care and lives in the shelter system. I don't expect every parent to identify with every interview, or to feel like every suggested action is something their family can do. The interviews depict people with vastly different amounts of resources and privilege. But all of them are thinking about how to do more than just get "the best" for their own kid.

The Chapters Ahead

In the first half of the book, I'll look at three systems: our childcare system, our K–12 school system, and our higher education system. Roughly, this follows an age progression—the childcare chapter will focus on families with kids ages birth to five, the schools chapter on families with kids ages five to eighteen, and the higher education chapter on families with adult children ages eighteen and up.

In each chapter I'll try to answer two basic questions: First, what choices should individual parents make? Second, what collective action can we take to make these systems work better for everyone?

I don't imagine that any reader will need much convincing that, currently, those three systems aren't working well. I certainly had some sense of that before I started writing this book. In brief, our country's childcare system is one in which care work is devalued, where workers have few protections or rights, and, paradoxically, where care is also priced out of reach for most families. Our school system has astonishing levels of racial and economic segregation and a shocking level of resource inequality between even schools in the same district. There are stark inequities in higher education in who gets access to the kinds of schools that educate their students and lead to a career. Meanwhile, an explosion of for-profit schools has left the poorest students saddled with serious debt and a degree that doesn't open any doors.

The parents I spoke to are not satisfied with this status quo, and they're doing more than just griping about it. They're changing it and offering concrete actions for how we can change it too.

In chapter 4 I interview parents who undertook major activism efforts in service of their communities. Parents and other advocates in

Portland, Oregon, got a ballot initiative passed that will provide free universal early childhood education for all three- and four-year-old children in the city; the staff providing the care at these programs will get at least eighteen dollars per hour. In Evanston, Illinois, two parents successfully won a campaign to change their school district's PTA funding structure, ensuring that all the schools in their district will share parent donations equally. That chapter also includes conversations with parents who are involved in quieter, ongoing forms of activism work: working with mutual aid groups, raising their own food to reduce their environmental impact, or working to improve their local foster care system.

The focus of the last chapter is wealth, legacy, and inheritance—some of the big questions when we contemplate the end of our lives and of our parenting journey. What legacy do we want to leave behind, beyond (we hope) raising "good people"?

No one individual, or one family, can solve a systemic problem. But collective action, particularly when it's undertaken by people with privilege, creates change. And, also, our individual choices matter. Decisions about childcare, schools, and how we use our time and money may not feel like political decisions, but they are. They either further calcify inequality, contributing to a system where only a few can thrive, or take a small step toward dismantling it. Something I heard repeatedly throughout interviews was that the parents also felt better—more relaxed, less frazzled and exhausted—when they were thinking about more than just how to get "the best" for their own child. Approaching parenting through that lens is bad for society; it's also exhausting for the individual parent.

Many books about how to teach your child to be a "good person" are narrowly focused on what happens in our own homes—teaching our children to share toys, not hit, say please and thank you. This book isn't trying to replace any of that advice, or to discount the importance of teaching those things. But our children are also watching, and learning, from how we make bigger-picture choices. How we treat the people who care for them tells them how they should behave as a boss. Where we send them to school teaches them about their place in the world. How we spend our time and money sends them more powerful messages about how to spend theirs than any lecture ever could.

The writer Courtney Martin beautifully summarized the question at the center of this book in a passage that has rung in my head since I read it. Instead of being so focused on getting "the best," she asks, "What if, instead, what is healthy for your child—not 'best,' but healthy—is to receive no end of love and only proportional resources, and to witness parents trying to fumble their way toward closing the gap between their values and their actions each and every exhausting day?"

No end of love, but only proportional resources. And every decision guided not by getting the best, but by living out your values. What would we do differently if that was our goal?

1

CHILDCARE

IN JANUARY 2020 a Menlo Park mother's nearly two-thousand-word ad seeking a "household manager/cook/nanny" went viral. Among the laundry list of requirements were that the nanny would "ski on an intermediate level," "research the latest developments in food science," have "experience driving in other countries," "do calisthenics," and "correctly quantify how much fish to purchase for five people." "Is this the most demanding ad for a nanny ever?" the *Guardian* asked. *Jezebel* suggested that the mother behind the ad seemed to be seeking a "chef, accountant, travel agent, math teacher, and personal trainer, like the iPhone of people."

There are many differences between the writer of that ad and the average parent seeking childcare arrangements. (Most parents don't have a "pool cottage" for their nanny to live in, for one.) But one difference that struck me when I read it was the ad-writer's clarity about her role: she was an employer. An exacting (and perhaps terrifying) manager of her "household staff."

For most parents, it goes more like this: A child shows up in your house. If you ever want to go anywhere (like to your job) again, you need childcare. All the options are hideously expensive and/or don't provide the needed time coverage. And then . . . you figure out the least-bad option, usually without thinking much about the structural forces that have created this impossible situation.

We still talk about whether parents (particularly mothers) "choose" to work or to stay home with their children, but for the vast majority of families, there is very little "choice" involved. Almost a quarter of children in the United States live with a single parent who is the household's sole income earner. For parents in partnered relationships, a combination of stagnating wages and increased costs for everything, from groceries to healthcare, has made it much harder for this generation of parents to get by on one income. But parents can also feel forced *not* to work: a report from the Center for American Progress from a few years ago found that 2 million American parents were forced to quit a job, not take a job, or "greatly change" their job because of childcare issues. Some parents are in the financial position to work, or not work, purely out of personal choice. But they're a small minority. Our country's current lack of subsidized care means that even relatively well-off families can be in a catch-22: they can neither afford to live on one parent's income nor afford the childcare needed for both parents to work. The $250–$300 checks that millions of families began receiving in 2021 through the Child Tax Credit provision in the American Rescue Plan did not change that fundamental calculation: nowhere in the country does $300 come close to covering the cost of full-time childcare. (The childcare provisions in the Build Back Better bill are likely to have a dramatic impact on many families' ability to afford childcare—that bill, and its limitations, are discussed in the conclusion of this chapter. As of this writing, the bill has passed in the House but not in the Senate.)

When we first had our daughter, I spent a lot of time staring at calendars (to figure out the minimum number of hours of care that we'd need) and our bank account balance, trying to make the numbers work. It was a math problem without a good solution. The Department of Health and Human Services considers a family to have "affordable" childcare if their childcare costs don't exceed 7 percent of their income. Prior to 2022, there has been no state in the country in which a family making their state's median income can find affordable full-time daycare by this metric for a child under four years old. (Infant care—that is, care for children between the ages of six weeks to one year—is even more expensive.) Of course, for families with more than one child, the costs are even more extreme. One mother I spoke to referred to the daycare costs for her two young children as "the house we'll never live in." Childcare costs, Elliot Haspel writes in his book *Crawling Behind: America's Childcare Crisis and How to Fix It*, "is a problem for the three-quarters of Americans who makes less than $100,000 a year," and "absurdly, it's a problem for a decent number who make six-figures."

Yet one of the most maddening things about this country's childcare crisis is that the high costs for families have not corresponded to high wages for caretakers. Childcare workers, particularly at daycare centers, are notoriously underpaid. The Economic Policy Institute found that childcare providers are twice as likely as other workers to live below the poverty line. The median hourly wage for childcare workers in the United States is $12.27 per hour. Though nannies sometimes fare slightly better than childcare professionals who work in a daycare setting (national averages hover closer to sixteen dollars per hour for nannies), it is still a profession with no room for advancement, usually no benefits, and no job security.

Childcare worker wages are so low in large part due to the roots of domestic work in this country, and who does and doesn't garner respect in our society. Sheila Bapat, an author and activist, summarized the current status of childcare in an interview: "The roots of domestic work are deeply connected to the history of slavery in the U.S. It's no accident that a vast majority of domestic workers were African American women to begin with, and increasingly now, immigrant women of color." Undocumented workers are overrepresented in this workforce. In part because of who typically performs the job, our society has little respect for the work of childcare; it is considered a "low-skill job," a baffling designation to any person who's tried it. I've done plenty of things that are traditionally thought of as "hard work": I've gone to law school, studied for the bar exam, and practiced law in the busiest family court in the country. None of them were as hard as my first job: camp counselor at an understaffed day camp. That job was also my lowest paying ($6.80 an hour).

I've been a nanny (for a summer) and a frequent babysitter, and when I had my daughter I still had clear memories of both the exhausting work and the awkwardness of seeing a family's usually private dynamics. So when I began the process of finding childcare for my daughter, I felt like I had some window into the difficulty of the work. But it wasn't really the same job. For me, providing childcare had always been a temporary job, not a job on which I was trying to support my own family.

Megan Stack deeply explores the issues around childcare in *Women's Work: A Reckoning with Work and Home*, a book that is part-memoir, part-journalism and looks unflinchingly at the complicated ethical questions that she faced as a White American woman who employed domestic workers while she lived in India and China. Even in her attempt to tell the workers' stories and allow them to take center stage, she frequently acknowledges the fundamental power imbalance between herself and the women she employed. The experience of employing people to provide childcare and household help, she writes, is one in which she "held a dismaying amount of power over vulnerable people, and that meant grappling with ethics, finances, schedules, and personalities."

I wanted to talk to parents who were in the thick of this "grappling." In privileged parenting circles, the predominant question that we're encouraged to ask is whether a given childcare arrangement will maximize our child's potential (preferably for as low a cost as possible). Will our nanny teach our child a second language? Will our daycare offer a rigorous (but still play-based) curriculum that will have them reading by the time they're three? A striking thing about the Menlo Park nanny ad was how extensively it documented the criteria for the nanny while saying nothing about what the parent herself would bring to the table—nothing about the pay, the benefits, or the working conditions of what was clearly a very demanding job. This chapter talks about that second half of the equation. What kind of employer will we be if we're using a nanny? How will we find out if our daycare treats its employees well? These are the questions we need to encourage each other to ask.

I spoke with parents who used three childcare situations: nannies, daycares, and family care. The three situations presented some similar, interrelated issues. I also spoke with some of the people who provide childcare, as well as some experts in the field. I wanted to answer two questions: First, what can individual families do to make sure they're acting legally and morally when making childcare choices? Second, what collective solutions should we be pushing for that will change the current paradigm and create a care infrastructure that will eventually benefit our children's children?

Daycare

Because of our country's lack of childcare infrastructure, most parents have very little "choice" when choosing a daycare. Even before the pandemic caused thousands of childcare centers across the country to close, daycare for families was hard to come by. Low-income families who both meet the strict income cutoffs and can navigate what one article called the "maddening bureaucracy" of getting subsidized childcare are relegated to only the facilities that actually take those vouchers; they mostly do not get the luxury of touring various programs and finding the one that best meets their child's needs. The childcare system is thus deeply segregated by race and class. That segregation is, as one article put it, "due to a fractured system in which many low-income children are in publicly funded programs with strict income cut-offs, while higher-income children are in private programs that are unaffordable for working families." (Chapter 4 discusses a program in Oregon that's looking to change that fractured system, creating a publicly funded childcare option for all three- and four-year-old children.)

Yet even among families who make too much to qualify for subsidized care and can (often with great difficulty) afford to pay for a daycare spot in a private program, competition for those spots has become absurd. In Seattle, for instance, families may get on waiting lists for a daycare before they're even pregnant; some daycares include an option for "trying to conceive" on the form that asks for their child's name, age, and birthdate. If a family gets off the waiting list before they're ready to use the daycare's services (perhaps because they don't yet have a child) it's not uncommon for them to pay for months just to hold their spot, spending thousands of dollars just to hold onto their chance to spend thousands more.

Tiffany Koyama Lane, a Portland parent, has a story that exemplifies the problems with talking about "choice" in childcare. When she was pregnant with her older son, she found a preschool program that seemed perfectly in line with her values. Its teachers were unionized, and it had low staff turnover. Tiffany is a teacher herself, and those qualities were important to her. "I got on the waitlist when I was pregnant; my son is now five and half years old—and I'm still on the waitlist," she tells me. "They contacted me recently and said, 'Are you still interested?'" She laughed, "It's literally been six years. . . . I said, 'I don't even live [in the same neighborhood]. You can take me off this list.'"

Meanwhile, for the daycare workers themselves, it is underpaid work with little security. Rhian Evans Allvin, the CEO of the National Association for the Education of Young Children, succinctly described our country's problem with daycare: "Parents can't pay more, and early childhood educators can't earn less." (The Build Back Better bill, if it passes with its current provisions, would change this calculation and is discussed at the end of this chapter.)

Tracy and Matt
Midwestern City

Tracy and Matt (who asked that their last names not be used nor their city named) have a seven-year-old son and a similar story to Tiffany: "Shortly after I got pregnant," Tracy says, "I made my spreadsheet—I had things in columns: the cost, the distance from our house." They planned to use the spreadsheet to compare their various daycare options and figure out which one made the most sense. But when they went to a childcare fair when she was still pregnant, they were told by one daycare representative that if they wanted a spot, they "should have already been on the waitlist a month ago." They quickly discarded the detailed spreadsheet and turned their attention to simply finding a program with space.

As it happened, the only reason they were able to secure a daycare spot at all when their son was an infant was through fortunate happenstance; a new daycare center was opening at just the right time that gave priority spots to employees at Matt's company. (Tracy works as a university administrator, and Matt works in biotech.) They jumped at the spot in what I'll call Daycare A. The center was in the opposite direction from both of their workplaces, which led to complicated family logistics since they'd made the choice, for both environmental and financial reasons, to have one car rather than two.

When their son was two years old, they finally got off the waiting list at a daycare that was within walking distance of Tracy's work. At the time that they went to tour their new option, Tracy had recently worked on putting together programming for her university that focused on labor rights and had attended a speech by Ai-jen Poo, the head of the National Domestic Workers Alliance, that had gotten her thinking about the wages of childcare workers. So, when she toured Daycare B, she asked the director how much the workers there made. The answer was the federal minimum wage—$7.25 an hour. She asked about benefits and got a response to this effect: "We don't give benefits, but we have lots of love—we just love what we do."

Tracy then wrote an email to the director of Daycare A, where their son was already enrolled, asking the same questions. The head of the school wrote her back a heartfelt response, which she got permission to share with me. The response began, "As a teacher with more than 20 years in this field, from the bottom of my heart, THANK YOU for being concerned with how centers treat their teachers." The center director said in a text message on which I was included that she didn't recall any other parent having asked that question, though she was quick to acknowledge that "the cost of childcare is so high that many families aren't able to care about things like that (at least in a way that they can do something about it)."

The wages and benefits at Daycare A were, as Tracy said, "not great, but significantly better." Despite the appeal of Daycare B's location and cheaper cost, they decided to stay with Daycare A, even though Daycare B would have cost their family about $300 less a month. A combination of their family's economic privilege (which both Tracy and Matt were quick to acknowledge) and their other decisions (including forgoing a second car) had put them in a position to make that choice.

While not every family could, or would, make the same choice as Matt and Tracy, all parents can ask about the pay and benefits for staff when they're touring a daycare, and use that information when deciding what waitlists to get onto (usually, the only real "decision" that most parents ever get). Most daycare operators are trying to do right by both their employees and the families they serve on very tight margins. But if parents with options were consistently choosing centers that better compensated their employees, that could shift operator's incentives to provide better compensation.

Here are some questions to ask a daycare provider:

- What is the hourly wage for starting workers? Do they receive cost of living wages?
- What benefits are offered?
- Are workers offered paid vacation time?
- Are workers offered opportunities for professional development?
- What is worker turnover like?

Nannies

Domestic help is a poorly regulated industry; one prominent activist has called the labor force "invisible" and the industry "the Wild West." When figuring out how to structure employment agreements, parents are often simply relying on word-of-mouth and prevailing community norms when it comes to figuring out a fair hourly wage, paid time off, and other benefits.

For the past decade, the organization Hand in Hand has attempted to fill that gap by giving employers some guidance about what it looks like to have your home be, as they put it, a "workplace you can be proud of."

Tatiana Bejar
The Rockaways, NY

Tatiana Bejar is an organizer with Hand in Hand and is the mother of two teenagers. She has been an organizer for decades who has thought deeply about why domestic work is so devalued and what we can do to fix it.

The problems with the devaluation of domestic work, Tatiana told me, are not unique to the United States. Typically, domestic workers are women from groups with less political and economic power than the families who employ them. In the United States, nannies are mostly women of color; recent immigrants are overrepresented in the workforce. In Lima, Peru, where Tatiana grew up, domestic workers were mostly Indigenous young women who had grown up in rural areas. They would then come to the city as teenagers to live and provide care for city-dwelling families. How those workers were treated varied greatly depending on the families who employed them. "Because of the lack of regulations, and because of the racism and sexism, it was very easy for employers to be very abusive. There was no accountability at all," Tatiana says. She recalls going to friends' houses and being shocked at how they spoke to their domestic workers. At some homes, domestic workers were not permitted to sit at a table—any table—to eat a meal. "My parents always set examples on how to respect and treat a worker at home—they both were teachers, so we were not wealthy, but they were very clear that they needed to provide a good salary with benefits, a full month's vacation, a bonus once or twice a year." A central idea of Hand in Hand is that people's homes are expressions of their political ideologies. "My parents were always politically left leaning," Tatiana says. "But it really becomes very abstract unless you use your home as a center of your own political actions."

Tatiana and her coworkers at Hand and Hand educate employers and facilitate conversations between domestic employers and domestic employees. The most difficult conversations, in her opinion, are the ones she has with those who employ nannies or housekeepers. She asks employers to consider "how you are recognizing not only the value of the person in your home, but also . . . how does the way you treat your

domestic employee express your feminist values? How are you building the solidarity that begins at home?" Hand in Hand's advice about
employing a domestic worker starts from a generous premise: "Most
of us want to do the right thing when we hire a childcare provider,
housecleaner, or home attendant. We just don't know how." The organization has extensive resources for families, such as sample contracts
for families to use when setting up various arrangements, including
a nanny share (in which two or more families use the same nanny
for childcare, which can be a lower-cost option), and guides to having difficult conversations (what to do if your childcare provider is
repeatedly late, or how to approach changing a job description after
you've already hired someone).

Legal Obligations

New York State passed the first Domestic Workers' Bill of Rights in
2010; Hawaii and California passed their own laws in 2013. Other
states and cities have followed suit, though most jurisdictions still
have no such law.

Getting those laws on the books in any state was the culmination
of over eighty years of effort from activists. In 1933 Zipporah Elizabeth Moman, a Black educator and activist from Mississippi, wrote a
pointed letter to President Roosevelt, noting that the average wages of
the domestic workers who raised children and cleaned homes in her
area was "$3.50 a week" (less than $100 a week in today's money).
She inquired, "Does this mean a living wage? If not, what protection
do they have?" Enclosed with the letter was a proposed "Code of Fair
Competition for Personal and Domestic Workers" with astonishingly
modest demands of a workweek not to exceed fifty-six hours, one
week of paid vacation per year, and a minimum wage of $14.40 per
week (averaging out to twenty-five cents an hour—less than five dollars in today's money).

Moman was neither the first nor the last activist seeking to get domestic workers the same protections as other members of the workforce. But throughout the New Deal era, and thereafter, domestic workers were repeatedly left out of the laws that provided legal protections to other categories of workers. The racist motivation behind their exclusion was impossible to miss. Nannies and cleaners (who were primarily Black women) and farm laborers (who were primarily Black and Latino men) were two groups explicitly *not* covered by various pieces of federal legislation, including the Social Security Act, that granted important rights to other workers. The omission famously led then-president of the NAACP Charles Hamilton Houston to describe the law as a "sieve with the holes just big enough for the majority of Negroes to fall through." In 1968 an Atlanta-based Black domestic worker, Dorothy Lee Bolden, formed the National Domestic Worker's Union of America, which pursued both local and national legislation. She also ran a training program that, as her obituary stated, taught domestic workers to "ask, diplomatically, for vacation time or higher wages."

While most states still have very few laws about domestic work, there are (finally) some laws that protect this workforce. One crucial piece of making your home a "workplace you can be proud of" is thus simply understanding, and meeting, your legal obligations to your nanny.

Gabriela Siegel is an attorney with the nonprofit advocacy organization Make the Road New York. She specializes in representing domestic workers in legal disputes and has seen dozens of cases where things have gone very, very wrong between a nanny and an employer. I talked with Gabriela in order to understand the most common ways that families, inadvertently or purposefully, break the law when employing someone in their home.

Under federal law, nannies are nonexempt employees, which means that an employer is required to pay them by the hour. (Legally, that hourly rate needs to be at least your state's minimum wage, though most areas have an "expected rate" for nannies that is significantly higher than that.) Gabriela frequently sees employers who, instead of paying by the hour, pay their nannies a fixed weekly rate. Using that method can quickly lead to wage theft; Gabriela explains that when you have a fixed rate, "it's not clear what the base hourly rate is." Knowing the "base rate" is important because any work over forty hours should be paid at a rate of time and a half. If the base rate of pay is eighteen dollars per hour, for instance, that would mean that the forty-first hour worked that week, and any additional hours beyond that, should be compensated at a rate of twenty-seven dollars per hour. Gabriela also cautioned employers to be aware that nannies often count on being paid for the agreed-upon hours. It's not a legal requirement to pay your nanny for their full workday if you happen to come home two hours early, but, as Gabriela puts it, "don't come home early, not pay them for that time, and think you've done them a favor."

The other legal requirement that applies no matter what state you're in is to pay "on the books." If you pay a domestic employee more than $2,100 a year, you and the nanny are *each* obligated to pay 7.65 percent of their earned income toward Social Security and Medicare taxes. Some states have additional tax requirements. To avoid shorting their take-home pay, some employers may choose to pay the nanny's portion of those taxes, or to at least pay a higher base wage. Care.com offers a free calculator that allows you to compare a nanny's weekly gross pay to their net pay once these taxes have been taken out. A nanny making twenty dollars per hour for a forty-hour workweek, for instance, would have a gross pay of $800 but net only about $650, depending on what additional deductions the state requires—meaning that the "real" rate would be closer to between sixteen to seventeen dollars an hour if the employer isn't covering both portions of the taxes.

Even though employers who pay on the books can claim a modest childcare credit on their own taxes, and have the peace of mind that comes from being safe from fines or (theoretically) imprisonment if they are audited, astonishingly few employers do it—one economist estimated that only about 5 percent of families who use in-home childcare pay all the required taxes. In different ways, employers and nannies are both disincentivized from having on-the-books arrangements. For employers, paying on the books requires both extra money and extra paperwork. For some nannies, being paid on the books threatens their very survival, making them ineligible for the benefits that make it possible to live on their low salaries, such as food stamps or housing assistance. A nanny who is paid on the books will qualify for unemployment insurance if her employer lets her go, as well as Social Security when she wants to retire, but those potential future benefits don't help her with day-to-day survival in the present. One mother wrote in *Slate* that she had interviewed over sixty nannies, many of whom turned down the job *because* it was on the books. She was, she writes, turned down by "women who were earning part-time degrees and qualified for tuition assistance" and those "who needed affordable health care and housing for their own families" since on-the-books pay would jeopardize those benefits without providing enough income to make the trade worth it.

Many employers mistakenly believe that an undocumented worker cannot be paid on the books. An undocumented nanny *can* be paid on the books; they can apply for an Individual Taxpayer Identification Number—for obvious reasons, something that many undocumented workers were reticent to do, particularly during the Trump presidency. Employing an undocumented person is still illegal, but employing an undocumented person and paying them off the books is illegal twice over.

The pandemic brought into sharp relief the risk that both employers and employees face when they haven't complied with this law. Many families asked their nannies to stop coming into work once stay-at-home orders were issued in March 2020. Nannies who had been paid on the books (and, crucially, who weren't undocumented) had the option of applying for unemployment and qualifying for additional federal funds. Those who were paid under the table were reliant on their employer's willingness to continue paying them. Many parents *did* pay their nannies to stay home. But of course, many didn't— sometimes because they had lost their own jobs, but often because they didn't feel obligated to do so.

The requirement to pay on the books often gets conflated or confused with a separate legal obligation: in forty-one states, you're required to give your nanny a pay stub that lays out the pay period, hourly rate (and any overtime wages), and the taxes taken out. The pandemic also highlighted the necessity of that requirement: nannies who had pay stubs were able to use those pay stubs to qualify for vaccination once vaccines became available to caregivers.

In sum, these are the legal requirements of employing a nanny in almost every state:

- Pay your nanny hourly, for all the hours they work.
- Pay at least minimum wage (which varies by state), and pay time-and-a-half for any hours worked over forty within a given seven-day period.
- Pay on the books.
- Provide a pay stub (in most states).

If you live in one of nine states (Oregon, Illinois, New York, California, New Mexico, Nevada, Connecticut, Massachusetts, and Hawaii) or the cities of Philadelphia or Seattle, there are additional laws that pertain to domestic employers. Some statutes entitle domestic workers to the most basic level of protections, including freedom from hiring discrimination and sexual or racial harassment; others have more detailed requirements. The Nevada Domestic Workers' Bill of Rights includes the right of employees to receive a written agreement, in their own language, that outlines, among other things, their job responsibilities and a notice period before they can be terminated. Seattle's bill of rights specifies that employees must get a half-hour break every five hours; if the conditions of their employment make that break impossible (for instance, they're providing care to a small child who never stops moving), they are entitled to additional compensation. Any employer who lives in those jurisdictions should start by reading those statutes.

"Part of the Family"

Gabriela, the attorney who represents domestic workers, tells me that while meeting the legal requirements is important, she finds that the most pervasive problem, and the hardest pill for her clients to swallow, is the disrespect that they endure from their employers. Even in cases where an employer has been underpaying their employee for years, she says, "wage theft is not something that brings people in the door. Unfortunately, that's often baked into low-wage work." Instead, when her clients come to see her, they often will begin by telling her a story that doesn't involve a legal issue: "It's stuff that's not actually actionable or illegal—stuff like 'she just spoke to me so disrespectfully and had no regard for me.'" Gabriela typically finds that such disrespectful treatment will go hand in hand with things that are legally actionable: the nanny was underpaid or that they employers weren't following other laws—but the low pay wasn't what had led the nanny to seek legal advice. (That fact, she clarifies, was not an excuse for parents to underpay but be polite to their nanny, and thus hope to get away with it.)

When I spoke to nannies, I heard the same thing. Though fair pay was, of course, an absolute necessity, it wasn't the only factor in their job satisfaction. Several nannies said that one of the most important things their employer could do was simply listen and be willing to have a conversation. Lilly, a nanny in Minneapolis, recalls an interaction with a former employer that left a bad taste in her mouth. She had nannied for the same family starting when she was eighteen. After five years of working for them, Lilly, then age twenty-three, asked for a raise. She did so via email, which she wanted to do in order to keep the conversation professional. The family responded that they would "think about it." Lilly said that she really would have preferred if they had instead said that they would "talk about it" with her. Years later, she says, it wasn't so much the lack of the raise (though Hand in Hand best practice suggests that employers should provide, at a minimum, annual cost of living raises). But she remained bothered by the fact that they hadn't seemed to treat her request seriously. The family never told her a definitive yes or no, and she ended up parting ways with them a few months after the request.

She has worked for other families since then, and said that simply being seen as a person with needs was also very validating. "If you're making dinner for everyone, make something the nanny can eat too, not just fish sticks and ketchup," she says. "If you're sending them to the bakery, don't give just enough money for the kids to get something, if you can afford that extra five dollars."

Meredith, who nannied in New York City, laughingly told me that some families were so disrespectful that "no amount of money could be enough." I gasped when she told me about a seven-year-old boy who would snap his fingers and tell her to "come" like she was a dog. Another nanny told me that her young charges pulled down her pants as a prank—humiliating enough, but made worse by the fact that the parents seemed too burned out or disconnected to take it seriously or impose any consequences.

Robin, a nanny in Oregon, says that some things that seem innocuous to parents, like asking the nanny to stay for extra time, can come across differently than they might intend. "I would say that 90 percent of requests are just incredibly hard to say no to. In

this job I have now, for instance, the parents just will not stop asking for extra time. So what was one request for an extra Saturday
has turned into nearly daily extra requests," she says. "As the nanny
it very much feels like I either say yes every time, or I should start
looking for other employment."

Boundaries are another repeated theme that I heard from nannies. Families who may unthinkingly say that they want a nanny who
will be a "part of their family" are often wading into dicey territory.

One former nanny, who prefers to remain anonymous, says, "I
am very distrustful of the 'part of the family' line. Parents who said
I was 'like family' were always asking too much of me." When asked
why she thought it was such a common descriptor, she says that the
phrase probably came from the intimacy of the work—nannying generally involves being in someone's home for hours a day, and often
seeing parts of their lives that they may keep hidden from the rest
of the world. But she feels some frustration that parents would not
recognize the power imbalance inherent in their different roles. Just
because the parent in a family feels comfortable venting to a nanny
about their frustrations with their child or their job doesn't mean that
the nanny feels the same level of comfort with the parent. Another
nanny ruefully puts it this way: "Cinderella was part of the family."

One mother I spoke with says that although she considers herself
to have a good relationship with her nanny, she would never say
that her nanny was "part of the family." "Let's be real. If she were
to have a major illness or something, I'm not going to let her live in
my home for free or take in her kids or something like that. That's
what family is." On the other hand, a family friend of ours did just
that—when their nanny was hospitalized, her nanny's similarly aged
kid had a multinight sleepover, at her house, with her own kids, and
she watched them all.

Robin, the Oregon nanny, says that she has considered herself
"part of the family" in some of her employment situations. Before her

current position, she nannied for a family who had asked her care for their children during a family funeral. "I loved this family, for sure, and wanted to help when their beloved grandfather died; and, again, how do you say no to that?" she says. "But while the family I worked for treated me like family during that event, the extended family and invited guests treated me like crap. That was really tough, to be there and mourning with this family I was incredibly close to yet treated by others as if I'm just the caterer." Despite that bad experience, she says that she *did* feel like she had been a part of that family: "They've really been there for me. . . . They helped me get through a really bad relationship, have helped me get jobs, and we still get dinner when I am in town." But she says, "On the nanny side we have to let that happen organically. There are going to be some families that treat you as part of the family to take advantage of you. To some people, 'family' means 'you have to do whatever I say, whenever I say it and can't complain about it.' That is what we need to address. And what parents need to be really cognizant of."

Pay and Benefits

A repeated theme I heard about pay and benefits was that the right question was "What's the most we can do?" rather than "What's the least we can get away with?" Eilis, a Rhode Island commenter on a Facebook messaging group, writes, "Find cuts somewhere else. Make the hard choices for your family; don't take advantage of someone else's. Most nannies I knew had kids at home themselves, not to mention labor laws exist for a reason."

Caitlin, also from the Northeast, agrees. "Does anyone have so much money that they wouldn't miss an extra $1,200 a year [the cost of ten paid vacation days at $15/hour]? Of course not, but it's the right thing to do and cuts can be found elsewhere."

Amy, a mother in Georgia, outlines her arrangement: her nanny works "on the books, legal overtime, two weeks paid vacation, and ten days paid holidays." Her family guaranteed hours (42.5 per week), so even if they were on vacation, their nanny received the same pay. In addition, they covered their nanny's health insurance and carried both unemployment and worker's compensation insurance for her. This all cost her family about $60,000 a year, some of which came out of their savings. However, as she puts it, "I felt strongly about being the kind of employer I would want to work for."

But what about families who are barely getting by themselves? I spoke with a father who is navigating the hard gap between what he would like to pay and what he can afford.

Christopher Zimmerly-Beck
Portland, OR

Christopher Zimmerly-Beck worked on labor rights issues before he became a parent. "I graduated high school right when the Great Recession was starting, and I got a job as a janitor. Through that, I got involved in the union, and became a union organizer," he says. His wife also has a history of working on labor rights issues and currently serves as an administrator for a healthcare workers' union. When they became parents, they were thus more aware than many about the labor rights issues implicated in hiring a nanny. Initially, they assumed they would pay fifteen dollars an hour to their nanny. As Christopher puts it, "That was what's fair." However, after their daughter was born, he realized that "when you're making twenty dollars an hour, paying fifteen an hour just doesn't really work." He described his family as "always broke"—not in an "oh, I wish we could go on vacation" way but in a "we don't have enough money to pay our bills this month" way.

When I first spoke to Christopher, his daughter was two years old. His family had found a nanny to watch her three days a week, and they paid that nanny twelve dollars an hour for the service. Describing their arrangement, he says, "We pay her as much as we can possibly afford, recognize it's less than she deserves, tell her as such, don't make her report the income, and promise that, should our financial outlook change, giving her a raise is the first thing on the agenda." Their nanny, he tells me, can work within their budget because she inherited a house from her own family and thus doesn't have the housing costs that would be typical in an increasingly expensive city. Christopher acknowledged that this was an unusual arrangement and contended that without some kind of help from somewhere it is "genuinely impossible for one family to pay what their childcare worker deserves."

Even though they were paying less than they wanted to pay, childcare costs have been a constant source of stress. Their rent, he says, is pretty cheap for where they live. "But the trade-off is that we're sort of petrified to move—and the place needs a lot of work." On one of the days that I spoke to him, Portland was having a rare snow day; the window in his wife's office wasn't closing properly and snow was blowing inside. "Because childcare is so expensive, trying to move is a massive undertaking. And the cost of childcare impacts the entire standard of living for a family," he says.

I spoke to Christopher a second time in February 2021. His daughter had just turned four. Though they still had a close relationship with their nanny, they had mostly been relying on a part-time preschool program for childcare before the pandemic, which they paid for themselves. That program had shut down in March 2020. When they looked at the math, they determined that it made the most sense for Christopher to quit his job; he currently is pursuing a master's degree while staying home full time with their daughter. When we spoke, the family was approaching the year anniversary of having no childcare whatsoever. "We love our kid, but it's brutal. It's really hard to be home with your kid, balancing work and school, trying to give her the attention that she needs," he says.

In some ways, though, their situation was looking up. A few months before we spoke, Portland had passed an ambitious new initiative that will provide free preschool for all three- and four-year-old children in the city. (The process of getting that initiative passed is extensively covered in chapter 4.) He and his wife had donated money to the effort; Christopher ran his first 5K as a fundraiser for the program. "Talking with our preschool teacher, she's just so thrilled—it's a game changer for people working in early childhood education." (As of this writing, it appears likely that Congress will also pass a federal plan that will both subsidize childcare workers' wages and cap childcare costs for families like Christopher's.)

"Free" Childcare: Families, Friends, and Others

I am eight years older than my brother and eleven years older than my sister, and I frequently babysat for my siblings when I was a teenager. My parents were extremely rigorous about paying me my usual babysitting hourly rate and giving me ample notice of nights when they wanted me to watch them. This is, of course, one of many, many things that made my upbringing more privileged than those of most children in human history. But I've never paid my own parents to watch my daughter. These disparate experiences have made me think about how much family care eludes hard-and-fast rules and about how much is dependent on context and the nature of the relationship.

One thing that seemed clear is that, ideally, you want to start out with a strong, trusting relationship with the family member who is watching your child. It is very rare indeed that a child will heal a troubled relationship, whether romantic or familial. Whatever the nature of the relationship, a conversation about expectations and boundaries—like the conversations that you have with a paid childcare provider—can help set the stage for a more successful situation.

Questions to Talk About When Doing Family Care

- **Money.** Will the family member be paid to watch your child? If they are not directly paid, who will cover expenses for activities or food while they are in charge?
- **Time.** This could be a longer conversation if you're looking for a regular arrangement, or a shorter one if it's a one-time thing—but common courtesy dictates that you share clear expectations around how long you'll be gone and when you'll be back.
- **Household rules and consequences.** This is a tricky one, particularly around grandparents, when the idea that grandparents are "supposed to" spoil grandchildren is so common that you can buy mugs and T-shirts with sayings like "'No' means 'ask Grandma.'" What are the hard-and-fast rules that you want to keep consistent for every caregiver? What are you willing to bend on?

Christina
Suburb in Virginia

Christina, a single mother by choice living in Virginia, became a mother knowing that her own mom would be an important source of childcare for her. Her mother was planning to retire right around the same time that Christina would be giving birth, and her mother was excited and eager to make the shift to "full-time grandmother." I connected with Christina because she had posted to a parenting advice group asking for help figuring out what was reasonable to ask of family. She was particularly concerned about her newly retired mother's predilection for staying up until all hours of the night (often doing what Christina described as "rage-tweeting"). Christina didn't want her mother to be extremely sleep deprived while watching her infant daughter, but also saw that it was problematic to insist that her mother adhere to a particular schedule. She said that it was tough to navigate figuring out her "rules" and expectations, particularly when she is used to her mom being the one who sets the rules.

I asked her what advice she had for someone who is trying to navigate the elaborate dance of family care. She pointed out that, because she is a single parent, she and her mom are navigating what is essentially a coparenting relationship, complete with disagreements about sleep training (her mom doesn't believe in it; Christina views it as a necessity). Some of their fundamental personality differences (Christina favors order; her mother is more comfortable in chaos) are playing out on this new stage. She echoed the sentiment I heard from others that this was only workable because of their strong relationship and open communication.

Christina is far from alone in relying on her mother to provide care. The *New York Times* published an article about the rise of "intensive grandparenting," which it defined as a grandparent "providing regular childcare, often accompanied by housekeeping or other tasks." A grandmother in Pennsylvania, speaking to me anonymously, certainly qualifies as "intensive grandparent"—before the pandemic, she would get three of her grandchildren off to school every weekday morning and watch two of them in the afternoons. She tells me that at school drop-off "it's all grandparents"—in other words, grandparents are filling in the childcare gap left between childcare hours and the parents' work hours, which often are hopelessly out of sync.

Part of the success of her arrangement has been her clarity about what she will and won't agree to do. She finds it more comfortable to watch the children in her own home where she knows how to find everything she needs (some grandparents, she acknowledged, prefer the opposite arrangement and would rather contain all the kid mess and noise in a home that's not theirs). She also grew tired of having all the breakfast preparation fall on her and asked for some help. Now, her son-in-law will prepare some stacks of frozen waffles and bring them over, so she just needs to warm them up. (I told her that, in many families, the grandmother would just continue to make breakfast every morning but grow increasingly resentful about it, and that her way seemed much better.) She's also been very clear with her own children that she and her husband don't want to give up their ability to travel—before the pandemic, they would take twice-yearly trips. Though her children don't pay them for their care, they do, as she puts it, "treat them very nicely at Christmas" and give them getaways to a bed and breakfast.

What makes a successful family care arrangement has many of the same elements as making a successful paid arrangement: showing gratitude and keeping lines of communication open. Along with those basics, many people on both sides of family care arrangements echoed the feeling that it was important to make sure that the grandparent or other family member doesn't give up their whole life and interests in order to provide childcare.

Au Pairs

The childcare "solutions" that the United States offers most families are one of the following: pay more than you can reasonably afford for a daycare or nanny, get a family member to watch your child for free, or do some combination of the two (often with the bonus of a sidelined career for at least one parent because work hours and child-care hours don't match). Given those options, it's not surprising that thousands of families have taken advantage of the au pair program. A common myth is that *au pair* is synonymous with *wealthy families*—but it's actually the lowest-cost childcare solution out there. I heard from several families that they literally could not afford any other option. One Pacific Northwest–based family I spoke with calculated that they could either have a nanny for one day a week or an au pair for five days a week for the same price. The mother in that family was a nurse; au pairs are often used by parents who do shift work and thus have an even harder time lining up their hours with childcare than traditional nine-to-five workers do.

The US's au pair program began in 1986, conceived of as a "cultural exchange" in which young people from Europe, mostly women, would come live with a host family in the United States and help care for their children. (Today, au pairs often come from Central or South America.) They typically live with their families for one year and are expected to take on the role of a "big sister" to their host family. The visa under which au pairs work is only available to people between the ages of eighteen and twenty-six. Since the program falls under the auspices of the State Department, rather than the Department of Labor, protections like minimum wage and overtime laws historically haven't applied to this group of childcare providers. Instead, the fifteen au pair agencies in the United States have agreed upon the going rate: $195.75 per week, for forty-five hours of work, or $4.35/hour, plus room and board.

Rachel Micah-Jones, the director of Centro de los Derechos del Migrante and the chair of the International Labor Recruitment Working Group, has been a vocal advocate for au pairs and a critic of the premise that this extremely low wage is somehow justified because of the "cultural exchange" element. She wrote in an op-ed in the *Baltimore Sun*, "Working as an au pair is as much a cultural exchange as waiting tables is a culinary experience." Micah-Jones has also pointed out that the premise of the program brings up sticky issues about appropriate boundaries. If the au pair is truly "part of your family," Micah-Jones pointed out in her op-ed, can you ground her? Take away her phone?

Though most families are trying to do right by their au pairs, the structure of the program leaves au pairs open to abuse. Some au pairs experience something closer to a stint of indentured servitude than a cultural exchange. An employee of Centro de los Derechos del Migrante sent me screenshots of au pairs in hidden Facebook groups discussing how little protection they received: any time they make a complaint about their families, their agency would tell them to "work it out." The au pairs in the group were aware that the agency had a financial incentive to side with the host families who might be repeat customers, unlike the au pair, whose visa would expire after thirteen months. At the background of every interaction between au pair and agency is both parties' knowledge that, under the provisions of their visa, au pairs are only allowed to stay in the United States if they are working with a host family, and they can be deported if the host family decides not to keep them on.

In 2019 a federal court judge in Massachusetts sided with the au pairs and their advocates and ruled that the program had to comply with the state's minimum wage laws, thus nearly tripling their pay to twelve dollars an hour. Various outlets covered the reaction of stunned and desperate parents whose "work-around" childcare solution had evaporated. Leila Forman, a midwife, and Chris Mulvey, a nurse practitioner, who live in a Boston suburb, told a local Boston news outlet that the program had been a cheaper option than daycare for their two sons. Now that the au pair program wasn't lower cost anymore, they would need to find another option. "But what about everybody else?" Mulvey asked. "When childcare costs are so spectacularly out of control, housing costs are so out of control, and people are getting out of undergrad with hundreds of thousands of debt, I don't see how it's sustainable for society."

Collective Solutions

I heard the same story again and again: parents would find a temporary solution—some combination of reduced work hours, family care, nanny, and daycare all stacked on top of each other like a house of cards—and then see it fall down again when a childcare provider moved away, a family member got sick, or the pandemic upended everything. Childcare workers would land with a family that paid them well and treated them fairly, but then that family's needs would change, and they would end up negotiating all over again with their next family. Both families and childcare providers described themselves to me as "lucky" when things were, however tenuously, working. But a system that requires someone to be "lucky" to have a safe place for their child to be while they work, or to receive fair wages for their work, is not a good one.

Solutions that will address the roots of these problems are bigger than any one family and any one caretaker. For over twenty years, activist and organizer Ai-jen Poo has been a leader in trying to change the way that the United States views care work. The cofounder of both the National Domestic Workers Alliance (NDWA), which focuses primarily on housecleaners and nannies, and Caring Across Generations, which focuses on elder care, Poo has tried to shift our cultural conception of care so that we view it as a collective problem, not an individual one.

The question of whether care is "infrastructure" became widely debated in early 2021, when President Biden's proposed infrastructure plan included $775 billion for care services. Several Republican members of Congress were outspoken about what they saw as the absurd idea that "care" could be infrastructure in the same way that bridges and roads are infrastructure; even the left-leaning website *Politico* called the inclusion of care work in an infrastructure bill "silly" since "no previous politician who put forward a similar caregiving proposal has done so under the guise of infrastructure spending." But the idea of care as infrastructure is not a new idea: Poo discusses the concept in her 2015 book *The Age of Dignity*, and joins a long line of feminist thinkers and scholars who have done so. Poo rejects the idea that more protections for caregivers must come at the expense of the individual family, or that care is just an individual family's burden. "Caregiving," she has said, "is not a problem the market can solve."

As of this writing, it's still unclear whether the Senate is going to pass the Build Back Better package, which includes childcare and pre-K provisions that Elliot Haspel describes in the *Atlantic* as "arguably the greatest victory for American families in several generations." The provisions include large subsidies for childcare centers that will increase workers' wages and allow a sliding pay scale for families. If passed, this bill will mean that the "overwhelming majority of American parents will pay no more than $5,000 a year for child care," Haspel writes. "Millions will pay nothing." This good news comes with some caveats. States would have to accept the federal funding, which could lead to a huge discrepancy in access—lower-income families in red and swing states may well be stuck with our current system if their state does not opt in. Individual localities can opt in, potentially leading to complexities where, for instance, Atlanta has subsidized childcare while other parts of Georgia do not. The bill also has significant limitations: it will expire after six years and can only change the landscape for out-of-home childcare providers, not nannies or au pairs.

The bill is an important step, but there is still substantially more work to be done. Poo and other activists in this space have a vision of Universal Family Care, a social program somewhat like Social Security, paid for by a payroll tax. The program would create a state-by-state insurance fund that families could tap into to meet their care needs. The insurance fund would allow parents to, for instance, take paid leave to bond with a newly born or adopted child; the fund would also help subsidize the cost of a daycare or nanny care when parents ended their leave and wanted to return to work. Such a program sounds almost utopian compared to our current system—but the organizers in this space have already achieved major victories that didn't seem possible a decade ago.

The NDWA's website is a good starting place for any parent interested in the collective solutions to our country's care problem. The
organization has been behind the state-level "domestic workers' bills
of rights" laws passed and helped draft and sponsor a federal bill that
would extend those protections to workers in every state. It has local
organizing efforts in every state, and by simply joining a mailing list,
any parent or caregiver can stay informed about how they can best
use their resources to fight for change, be it signing a petition, voting for a certain measure, or making calls to our elected leaders. Poo
has urged both caregivers and the people who employ them to view
themselves as a voting bloc that needs to elect leaders on both a local
and national level who prioritize these issues.

Working on collective solutions of any kind, particularly for
our country's complicated care problem, takes time and labor, but
it doesn't need to be drudgery. When Poo appeared on the podcast
Forever 35 to talk about her self-care routines, she talked about yoga
and Kiehl's skincare products, but also included her advocacy work
as a self-care practice, adding "winning is the best self-care."

Takeaways

Individual Choices

- **In any childcare situation,** including family care, start with clear
  expectations, clear boundaries, and from the premise that even if
  caring for children can be rewarding, childcare is hard work.
- **If you're hiring a nanny,** begin at Hand in Hand's website to find
  resources about what hourly wage to pay, how much paid time
  off to give, and what benefits to provide. Strive to be the kind of
  employer that you would want to work for: pay a living wage, offer
  paid time off, stick to an agreed-upon schedule, and treat your nanny as a respected professional. Think about how, as Tatiana put it,

your home can be a central expression of your political beliefs. Sign, and live by, the Hand in Hand "Fair Care Pledge": https://domestic employers.org/our-work/fair-care/.

- **If you're using a daycare,** ask about salary and benefits for staff. Factor that information into your decision to add yourself to a waiting list or enroll in a given program.
- **Be dubious of work-arounds.** Any childcare situation that promises low-cost, easy solutions to this problem is probably doing so on the backs of the most vulnerable people. Or, like the au pair program in Massachusetts, it's going to face a lawsuit and get much more expensive.
- **Always ask questions.** Talk to other parents about how they are navigating their childcare choices. Talk to your childcare workers about what they want and need. The American culture of silence around money and childcare issues allows these problems to stay hidden.

Collective Action

- **Find out about local and national organizing efforts** at the National Domestic Workers Alliance: www.domesticworkers .org. If you live in any of the forty-one states that haven't passed a domestic workers' bill of rights, your local chapter's effort to pass that legislation is a good place to start.
- **Sign the petition** and share your personal care story for the fight for universal family care insurance: https://universalfamilycare.org/.
- **Vote for elected officials** who talk about care work, view our current system as a crisis, and offer real solutions.

Further Reading

The Age of Dignity: Preparing for the Elder Boom in a Changing America by Ai-jen Poo (New Press, 2016)

Crawling Behind: America's Child Care Crisis and How to Fix It by Elliot Haspel (Black Rose Books, 2019)

Household Workers Unite: The Untold Story of African American Women Who Built a Movement by Premilla Nadasen (Beacon Press, 2016)

Just Like Family: Inside the Lives of Nannies, the Parents They Work For, and the Children They Love by Tasha Blaine (Mariner Books, 2010)

Maid: Hard Work, Low Pay, and a Mother's Will to Survive by Stephanie Land (Hachette, 2019)

Part of the Family?: Nannies, Housekeepers, Caregivers and the Battle for Domestic Workers' Rights by Sheila Bapat (Ig Publishing, 2014)

Women's Work: A Personal Reckoning with Labour, Motherhood, and Privilege by Megan K. Stack (Doubleday, 2019)

2

SCHOOLS

I WAS AT A CHILD'S FIRST BIRTHDAY PARTY the first time I remember being asked the question. I had my daughter strapped to my chest in an infant carrier and was angling toward the table with the wine on it when a friend came in with her husband, whom I hadn't met.

"This is Sarah, Alice's mom," she said, introducing us, and adding, "the ones who live in Kensington."

"Oh cool, cool," he said, shaking my hand. Then, before the handshake was even complete, he asked, "So how are the schools down there?" He lived in Park Slope, about two miles to the north of me.

The simplest answer to his question was "I don't know." How could I know? At the time, my only child was eleven months old. I'd never been inside any of the school buildings in my neighborhood, much less met any of the teachers or administrators who worked there.

Thinking back on the question (which I've now been asked many times since), I can see that there are two assumptions baked into it: first, that even if I didn't have school-aged child, I could know (via Internet research and public reports, I guess) "how the schools were"; second, that a school's quality is immutable. A school either is "good" or "not good" year after year, and a parent's role is to make sure that she puts her child into the "good" school rather than in a "not-good" one.

I said something about "not really being sure" and something about how "I think they're basically fine" before trailing off and grabbing a plastic cup for the wine.

Now, after having talked with dozens of parents, as well as experts about school choice, I no longer think it's a small-talk question.

There are over thirteen thousand school districts in the United States, each unique. I won't pretend that this chapter will reflect the reality in every district, nor that it will speak to every family's particular considerations when choosing a school for their child. But there are unmistakable patterns that have led to the current situation. In most districts across our country, our public schools are highly segregated by both race and class.

Much of the writing about school segregation uses the term "middle-class family" as a byword for *White family*. I tried to avoid falling into that pattern, and to be specific about both the race and class of the families I spoke with. Black, Latino, and Indigenous parents from every income bracket have additional factors to consider in choosing a school for their child. Regardless of the parent's own race, a parent whose child is perceived by the school to be Black or Brown grapples with issues in schools that are simply not a part of my own experience: for instance, a disciplinary system that views children's normal behaviors as worthy of suspension or expulsion as early as preschool. As much as this is a chapter about the choices parents make around schools, it's also about the decision-making process itself, and about how we can shift the way we talk and think about our public schools to view them for what they are—not just a way to serve our own children, but as an institution necessary for our society to function.

What's at Stake

Ideas about the importance of public education are centuries old. John Adams wrote that government had a responsibility to educate "every rank and class of people, down to the lowest and poorest." Thomas Jefferson urged that the constitution be amended to explicitly direct governmental support of schools. (Though it's not in the US Constitution, every state's constitution includes a guaranteed right to a public education for its citizens.) Yet, as anyone familiar with the history of this country could guess, these progressive ideas about the need to educate the "lowest and poorest" did not include all people—for enslaved persons, it was a crime to learn to read or write.

Public education in the United States is widely credited as starting with Horace Mann's common schools movement in Massachusetts in the mid-1800s. Mann had several ideas about education: that it is crucial to a functioning democracy, that education should be both compulsory and free, and that a good education should be available to every child, no matter his or her background. Mann believed that uneducated citizens would threaten democracy, since a democracy could not survive if its citizens were guided only by "ignorance, selfishness, and passion." One of Horace Mann's most famous quotes: "Doing nothing for others is the undoing of ourselves." Even though this country has never succeeded in fulfilling Mann's ideals, they remain foundational to how many Americans view the purpose of public schools.

There's a bitter irony that some of the schools that bear Horace Mann's names are antithetical to his vision of what schools would be. Horace Mann School, a private school in New York, charges $55,200 a year. The school provides financial aid to only 15 percent of students—meaning that a pre-K–12 education there is out of reach for families who cannot afford to spend nearly $1 million *before* their child's commencement of college. Another namesake school, Horace

Mann Elementary School in Washington, DC, is a public school, but one that looks quite different from the other public schools in the neighborhood, since it primarily serves the wealthiest families in the district. Its PTA raises nearly half a million dollars per year.

It is easy, and tempting, to blame the vast educational inequalities in this country on the existence of private schools. Certainly, they don't help the problem, and some of the wealthiest schools' more obvious excesses—state-of-the-art science labs, ice skating rinks— make them an easy target. Caitlin Flanagan, in a biting *Atlantic* essay, alternately headlined "Private Schools Are Indefensible" and "Private Schools Have Become Truly Obscene," took issue with the idea that a private school could ever be an engine of "equity and even 'inclusivity.'" She concludes, "A $50,000-a-year school can't be anything but a very expensive consumer product for the rich. If these schools really care about equity, all they need to do is get a chain and a padlock and close up shop."

But even if every private school in the country were to do just that, it would only address part of this country's educational inequities. Only 10 percent of US students attend private schools. My interviews and research on the topic have convinced me that the deeper problem is how privileged parents hoard resources within the public school system. The public DC elementary school that bears Mann's name is emblematic of how little resemblance an ostensibly "public school" can have to the "public" around it: only 4 percent of students at the DC Horace Mann school qualify for free and reduced-price lunch. But it's located within a school district where 69 percent of students do.

A 2014 piece published in *Forbes* exemplifies the kind of thinking that has been particularly detrimental to public schools in this country. In the piece, Grant Matthews, a Los Angeles–based attorney, shares that he and his wife have a combined income of $250,000 and could "easily afford private schools." Instead, they opted for public schools since "our society is only as good as its education system."

Yet in the same piece, Matthews describes the careful research that he and his wife did before they even had children about the "best neighborhoods" to move to and the "best schools" to pick, noting that they were looking to separate the desirable schools from the "relative horror shows." The remainder of the piece is laser-focused on his own children's experience in those schools, yet he concludes, "I'd also like to believe that my heavy involvement in these schools helped pave the way for other kids to get a better public-school education, too."

His story is the happy fable that we privileged parents like to tell ourselves—we can move to a certain neighborhood, send our children to a school we've already deemed "good," and still have done something important for society by virtue of not sending them to private school. We have still "paved the way" (how? to where?) and made the school better by our presence.

Private school tuition, even at a relatively less expensive parochial or other religious school is, of course, wildly out of reach for all but the very most economically privileged families. But when families with economic and/or racial privilege maneuver within the public school system (to ensure that their child gets "the best"), it is often both at the expense of other children and to the detriment of public schools as a whole. It's a particularly pernicious pattern among White families.

Changing this destructive pattern, and increasing educational opportunity for all children, shouldn't be viewed purely as an altruistic act. Extensive sociological research supports the notion that all of us benefit, both economically and socially, when we live in a society with a strong education system. Educated people commit fewer crimes, have higher incomes, and vote more often. They pay more taxes, live longer, and have fewer health problems.

But we often fail to take that more expansive view. In his essay "Public Schools for Private Gain: The Declining American Commitment to Serve the Public Good," education professor David Labaree traces how modern families have come to have a narrow view of the purpose of education, focusing on its benefit to their own children but forgetting what it does for our society. As he puts it, "For those families that do enjoy greater wealth, the public benefits of schooling are easy to miss, whereas the private benefits are material, immediate, and personal. . . . It's not that anybody wants to punish other people's children; it's just that they need to take care of their own. But when the public good is forever postponed, the effects are punishing indeed."

As Labaree notes, parents tend to think about their choice of school as both a deeply personal decision and an objective one—that some schools are "good" and others are not, and that they are solely basing their school decisions on the quality of education the school provides. The first step, then, is to understand that, for parents with privilege, it's not just "education quality" that drives parents' school decisions.

The Status Quo: Segregated Schools

It's been about six years since I read the essay that most profoundly shaped how I think about schools: Nikole Hannah-Jones's "Choosing a School for My Daughter in a Segregated City." Near the beginning of the essay, Hannah-Jones, who is Black, reflects upon her own parents' decision to enroll her in a voluntary desegregation program when she was in second grade, which bused her away from her neighborhood school to a majority-White school with significantly more affluent students. She reflects on those years as being difficult socially but "world-expanding," and an integral part of the reason that she was able to eventually become a magazine staff writer. (Vice President Kamala Harris made a similar point in the Democratic primary debates about the role that busing had played in her ability to become a candidate on that debate stage.) In the essay, now that she was a middle-class parent herself, Hannah-Jones grappled with how she saw other middle-class families around her maneuver to opt out of the majority-Black and

Latino, and majority low-income, schools for which she and other families in her neighborhood were zoned. She writes, "I understood that so much of school segregation is structural—a result of decades of housing discrimination, of political calculations and the machinations of policy makers, of simple inertia. But I also believed that it is the choices of individual parents that uphold the system, and I was determined not to do what I'd seen so many others do when their values about integration collided with the reality of where to send their own children to school."

It's odd that it took this essay for me to see what was, in retrospect, an obvious fact: every school I've ever interacted with has been segregated.

In Seattle, where I grew up, I attended both private and public schools, but in all of them, the vast majority of students were White (my Catholic middle school had five hundred students, and only one Black student in the whole school). After college, I taught English in the Bronx. That school had over one thousand students, not even one of whom was White. Yet I don't recall applying the word "segregated" to those schools until I read Hannah-Jones's essay. I believed that the schools reflected the neighborhoods they were in. If I'd really been pressed to explain it, which I never was, I might have said that the schools were a relic of old neighborhood divisions, or that it was really a class issue. I didn't think about any of it as a deliberate choice.

But deliberate choices by White families have led to this status quo, and talking about how parents choose schools is inextricably linked to talking about race. Though racially segregated schools have been outlawed in the United States for over sixty-five years, public schools in the United States today are still segregated. *Brown v. Board of Education* is the landmark 1954 Supreme Court decision that outlawed segregation by law. But the court's 1974 *Milliken v. Bradley* decision explicitly allowed for de facto segregation, in that case allowing the mostly White Detroit suburbs to avoid court-ordered desegregation efforts with city schools.

Today, US schools remain de facto segregated. In 1988 I was two years old; that was also the year that US public schools were the least segregated by race. Since then, in my lifetime, schools have steadily "resegregated"; or to put it more accurately, both individual parents and local, state, and federal government agencies have made choices that have led to a resegregation of our schools. And schools have never been fully integrated; in his essay "The Case for Reparations" Ta-Nehisi Coates writes that there "has never been a point in American history where even half the black children in this country have attended a majority-white school."

In 2019 the UCLA's Civil Rights Project troublingly reported that while White people in the South may have been the most visible segregationists in the 1960s, it's the reliably Democratic states of New York and California that have some of the worst statistics when it comes to school segregation now. In New York 65 percent of Black students attend intensely segregated minority schools, with few or no White students. California is the most segregated for Latino students; 58 percent of Latino students attend intensely segregated schools. The typical Latino student is in a school with only 15 percent White students.

How did it get this way? How does it stay this way? One persistent myth about this issue is that it's only related to residential segregation, and that our intensely segregated school system is simply because parents choose their "neighborhood school," and our neighborhoods reflect past policies like redlining. Yet cities such as San Francisco and Seattle have seen their neighborhoods grow more integrated while their schools have grown more segregated. In 2018 the *Peabody Journal of Education* published a study looking at one hundred of the largest cities in the United States. Between 1990 and 2015, 72 percent of US cities became less racially segregated by neighborhood, but 62 percent of cities saw their schools grow *more* segregated during those years.

Parents don't think they want segregated schools (or at least don't say that they do). Researchers at the Harvard School of Education surveyed 2,500 parents and found that parents across many demographics—Democrat, Republican, White, Black, Latino, and Asian—expressed support for integrated schools. But this professed preference doesn't translate into action; in places where parental choice plays a strong role in determining school assignment, schools tend to become more segregated, not less. One of the findings that was the most uncomfortable for me to read was that, while educated White parents claim to be choosing a school based on a variety of factors, including "economic class, discipline rates, and school resources," those parents were "likely to eschew schools with high numbers of Black students, even controlling for other factors that parents claim influence their decision." In other words, the racial makeup of the school plays a large role in White parents' perception of whether a school is "good." Other research has borne that out; researchers examining data from DC's school lottery found that a middle school parent was 12 percent more likely to choose a school where his child's race made up 20 percent of the study body, compared with a school where his child's race made up only 10 percent of the study body— even if the schools had identical test scores. This effect was the clearest for applicants who were both White and had higher incomes; as the study put it, these parents "had the strongest preferences for their children to remain in-group." For Black and Latino parents, there was little effect. (This study grouped Asian parents, which made up only 1 percent of the parents in the study, with White parents, and those who listed "other" or "biracial" with Black families—a distinction they acknowledged as "arbitrary" and which, as I'll discuss later, reflects the overbroad ways that we tend to talk about this problem.)

The next parent I spoke to is one of the leading voices in confronting these uncomfortable realities and talking particularly about how White families can broaden their vision to see their own individual school choice as a political decision.

Andrew Lefkowits
Denver, CO

Andrew, the father of a fourth grader and a first grader, works as a sound engineer; his wife is a doctor. In the introduction of his podcast, he describes himself as "Andrew, a White dad from Denver." As of this writing, the *Integrated Schools* podcast has released over seventy episodes. He's talked to academics, historians, legal scholars, and regular, everyday parents. The podcast examines all the multifaceted factors of why our schools became so racially and economically segregated, and what we can do to change it.

Andrew grew up in the same Denver neighborhood where he now lives and attended a predominantly Black school (decades later, he could still list off the three other White kids in his grade on one hand). That experience, he says, "definitely shaped me in many ways" and made me "relatively aware of the way race shows up in our lives." But he tells me, "I didn't really think much about schools and education before I had to decide where to send my kids to school." Nikole Hannah-Jones's work—particularly the two-part series "The Problem We All Live With" from the radio program *This American Life*—was his first connection to the problem. When he heard the series on school segregation, he says, "It made sense to me right away. I heard her, and I felt called to do this work."

Park Hill, the Denver neighborhood where Andrew lives, was at the forefront of integration efforts in the 1960s and '70s. The Denver library page about the town's history proudly touts Dr. Martin Luther King Jr.'s visit to one of the neighborhood's first integrated churches in 1964. In 1973 Black and Hispanic families from Park Hill won a Supreme Court victory against the de facto segregation that had been allowed to persist in Denver schools. In the opinion, Justice William Brennan wrote that the Denver school board had "through its actions over a period of years, intentionally created and maintained the segregated character of the core city schools" and ordered the school to desegregate. Andrew's own parents had chosen to raise him in Park Hill in part because they were looking for a diverse neighborhood, and when he was growing up in the '80s, the whole Denver school system had been making strides toward becoming more integrated by both race and class.

But in 1995 the judge overseeing court supervision of Denver's desegregation plan declared that "the vestiges of past discrimination by the defendants [the school board] have been eliminated to the extent practicable" and ended court oversight. Twenty years after that declaration, Andrew was looking at finding a school for his older daughter. When he looked at the demographics for their zoned school, what he saw startled him: the school had only 12 percent of kids who qualified for free and reduced-price lunch, and 18 percent kids of color. He realized, "Wait, that is not what I want for my kids at all." Instead, he and his wife decided to enroll their older daughter (and now their younger) in the school that Andrew himself went to as a child, a school that, to use the Integrated Schools lingo, is "global majority." (The phrase is a nod to the fact that, as the organization puts it, "White people are not the demographic majority of humans on the planet" and refers to a school where White children are not in the majority.)

In Park Hill, despite its history of integration, a familiar pattern had emerged: of the four schools in a mile radius from Andrew's house, one was considered "good" (the one with 18 percent children of color) and oversubscribed, and three were considered "bad" and were underenrolled. The mostly White and oversubscribed school received a lot more money from the district, owing to a practice called "student-based budgeting," in which schools are primarily funded by the number of children they have.

Andrew helped found a group called Park Hill Neighbors for Equity in Education, which he now cochairs. The group is working to make parents aware of how their individual choices contribute to the unequal school system and advocates for redistributing resources more equitably. Part of the group's mission is, Andrew says, "to remind people of [our neighborhood's] history."

In looking to see what else was out there about this topic, Andrew came across the grassroots organization Integrated Schools and met its founder, Courtney Everts Mykytyn.

Courtney, a Los Angeles mother of two, had started Integrated Schools in 2015. She had started blogging about her experience as one of the only White parents in her neighborhood who sent her kids to a global-majority school and wanted to share her experience with other families with racial or economic privilege. She gained a wider audience as, slowly but surely, other families looking for a voice that countered the prevailing narrative about schools found her work and began to share it. She started leading book clubs, and chapters of Integrated Schools began forming in several cities around the country.

When Andrew was in Los Angeles for work, he and Courtney met up to discuss their activism and the challenges of trying to convince parents in their peer group that they could think about school in a broader framework than just trying to "get the best" for their child. "[Courtney] was lamenting the challenge of having conversations with people over and over and over again," Andrew shares. "You get to someone who's just started thinking about this—and you know exactly where the conversation is going to go. You know where you're going to be in forty-five minutes. But I can't just tell you 'here's where we're going to be, can we jump there?' You have to kind of work your way through it. And she was doing that over and over and over again. But it wasn't scalable. And I said, 'It seems like that should be a podcast.'"

Andrew and Courtney joined forces to launch the podcast in October 2018. "We had no idea what we were doing," he said—though as a professional sound engineer, he knew the audio piece. They lined up people to interview (in their first episodes, they mostly just interviewed other parents) and released three episodes in the fall of 2018. Quickly, they were surprised to see that hundreds of people from all around the country were downloading their episodes.

A little over a year after they launched the podcast, Courtney was killed in a traffic accident. She was forty-six; her children were teenagers. At the time of her death, Integrated Schools had grown dramatically, with local chapters in twenty-nine cities, a board of directors made up of five well-known activists and authors, and a parent board. The parent board, which includes Andrew, immediately committed to making sure that the organization would continue despite the loss of Courtney. He's continued putting out podcast episodes, sometimes cohosting with other parents from the Integrated Schools board. In March 2020, when the pandemic brought a whole host of new sticky concerns around schools and equity, he found experts to talk through those new challenges. When I talked to him in November 2020, the podcast had been downloaded nearly two hundred thousand times.

Despite the enormous challenges of the past year, Andrew says that he feels a real sense of urgency, and that his desire to keep getting the message out there makes it hard for him to take breaks from the podcast. He worries about the profound cultural forces that Integrated Schools is up against, particularly the narratives that privileged White families receive at every turn about what "good schools" are like. But his worries are not just about what White and privileged families think.

"I think there's a growing sense—understandably, and deservedly so, particularly among Black educators of 'screw your integration.' What matters is not 'having White kids around,' and we are not interested in waiting around for White people to do this in a way that's not harmful."

The podcast hasn't shied away from dealing with that point of view—one of their earliest episodes featured an interview between Courtney and Chris Stewart, a Black education activist who has been vocal about how integration efforts often perpetuate, as he's written, "the insulting delusion that Black student achievement can only be had in proximity to whiteness." Stewart, and other activists, focus strictly on equality of resources—in other words, as Andrew put it, it revives separate but equal, but says, "Let's get equal right this time."

Andrew speaks delicately about that movement. "I don't think we have earned the right to ask for yet another chance to do this right. I respect and appreciate that viewpoint." But he says, "I don't think the long-term future of our democracy *tolerates* separate but equal. I think Thurgood Marshall is right." (Marshall famously wrote, in a dissenting opinion in a school's case: "Unless our children begin to learn together, there is little hope that our people will ever begin to live together.")

Andrew views the real project of Integrated Schools to be part of what he calls a "third wave" of school desegregation. The first wave was court-ordered desegregation, where Black children were allowed into all-White schools, but Black families were told that there was "no use for your Black schools or your Black teachers." The second wave was magnet schools, intentionally diverse charters, cross-district programs—that still have the idea that "White schools are good schools, and we'll allow just enough [students of color] to feel better about ourselves." Andrew described this as a version of desegregation that still centers White families and tries to "lure and entice White people with goodies so that they can get more stuff, but never ask them to do anything." This second wave of desegregation is the status quo in many cities; it is what Nikole Hannah-Jones calls "carefully curated integration, the kind that allows many White parents to boast that their children's public schools look like the United Nations." This is the place where many cities are stuck: in cities like New York or Los Angeles there are no "all White" schools—that would be nearly impossible in a public school system that's only 15 percent (New York) or 10 percent White (Los Angeles). But that fact doesn't mean that both city's systems aren't extremely segregated. In New York, Hannah-Jones writes, there are two systems: "one set of schools with excellent resources for white kids and *some* black and Latino middle-class kids, a second set of under-resourced schools for the rest of the city's black and Latino kids."

Andrew has a vision for the third wave of desegregation: "The central question . . . 'How do we ask White and/or privileged parents to contribute to democracy?' This is not about getting stuff for your kid. It's about being a participating member of society."

The Integrated Schools website includes various action steps for families who are interested in starting to think about the issue. Integrated Schools encourages families to take a Two Tour Pledge, something families at any stage of their school journey can sign. The pledge reads as follows:

> As a parent who supports the premise that all children learning together is fundamental to the creation of a true multiracial democracy, with the knowledge that the choices I make for my child affect all children, and with the belief that, in making decisions for my child's education, I am also building the world they will live in as an adult, I pledge to join the Integrated Schools movement and commit to . . .
>
> - stepping inside at least two global-majority schools that do not concentrate privilege relative to the district
> - learning more about inequities in the systems of education in my community both past and present
> - begin building authentic relationships with people of color in my community and with other parents committed to integration
> - an ongoing process of self-reflection and learning to know better and do better

Another useful resource from Integrated Schools is the Awkward Conversation Guide, which uses an approach called Affirm, Counter, and Transform (ACT), a framework for conversations about race that was developed by the Center for Social Inclusion. The guide is a flowchart, where the left column shows a statement such as "I'm not willing to gamble with my kids' education" or "That school is rated so low." The middle has an "affirming" statement—something that affirms that you, too, want to give your child a good life, a high-quality education, or to be in a school community where you feel like you "fit in." The next column shares a "counter" statement, complete with supporting links, about how integrated schools actually do support that outcome, and the right column asks a question back to the original asker, which provides the opportunity for "transformational" thinking.

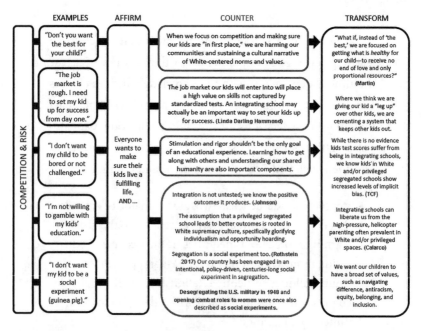

I found the Awkward Conversation Guide helpful, even though I first encountered it in the middle of the pandemic when I was talking to very few parents at the playground. There was something calming about seeing all the arguments against choosing integrated schools in one place, and categorized. Privileged parents tend to think we are making original arguments, saying something that no one has ever thought of about our unique and singular family. In fact, there's mostly only four categories of arguments people use in talking about why they can't choose a certain school: arguments based around school quality, competition and risk (basically, any statement that begins "in today's economy . . ."), social discomfort, and safety. The chart helpfully consolidates decades of sociological, economic, and psychological research to help parents sort out fact from fiction.

Integration Versus Desegregation

Integrated Schools also makes a clear distinction between *desegregation* (having kids of different races within the same school building) and true *integration*. It's an important distinction because the two don't always go hand in hand.

In 2019 sociologist Amanda Lewis and education professor John Diamond spent five years at an unidentified midwestern suburban high school which was, by any demographic measures, a "desegregated" school. It served thirty-five hundred students, 45 percent of whom were White, 45 percent of whom were Black, and 10 percent of whom were Latino, Asian, or "other." It was also a wealthy school overall that did not have large class differentials between Black and White families. The school itself had $18,000 to spend on each student, twice as much as the state average. Despite these advantages, the school's principal was troubled specifically by the Black-White achievement gap that he saw in even this "best case scenario" school, and asked Lewis and Diamond to diagnose the problem. Lewis and Diamond spent years doing interviews of parents, teachers, and students. Their

2015 book *Despite the Best Intentions: How Racial Inequality Thrives in Good Schools* chronicles the ways in which, when it came to everything from school discipline to academic expectations, the Black and White students may as well have been attending different schools. The school was desegregated, but it was not an integrated school.

A particularly interesting aspect of their research concerned the tracking of students between honors and basic tracks. When White students were assigned to attend basic tracks, their parents were more likely to both push back against that designation and to have their requests granted. Lewis and Diamond found that White parents "expressed no hesitation about being entitled to and capable of challenging the decisions of school officials, even against the wishes and recommendations of school personnel." When Black parents attempted to get their children into more advanced classes, they were more likely to encounter resistance and to encounter staff members who "doubted their children's ability to handle these rigorous classes." When this pattern was repeated over and over, the honors classes became a school-within-a-school in which White children were getting the best teachers, a more rigorous curriculum, and the designation of being officially the "smart ones." One senior official at the school bluntly expressed years of pent-up frustration with the system by asking Lewis and Diamond a rhetorical question: "What happened to all the dumb White kids?"

Tracking, or segregation within the same school building, has been a recent focus of legal actions around desegregation. During the Obama administration, the Department of Education's Office of Civil Rights entered into over a dozen "resolution agreements" with school districts to address the segregation inherent in their tracking programs. It's also become a hot-button issue, with right-wing commenters framing any effort to address these disparities as a "war on gifted kids" or a "war on merit."

Tracking isn't the only way that schools can appear, on paper, to be desegregated while having deep divisions within their walls. Dr. King himself noted the problems with a narrow focus on "integration" as a panacea for schools. In a 1967 speech to an auditorium filled with Black educators in Atlanta, Dr. King cautioned that "too many Americans . . . think of integration merely in aesthetic and romantic terms, where you just add a little color to a still predominantly White-controlled power structure. We must see integration in political terms, where there is shared power."

But parents who are accustomed to having power aren't typically good at sharing it. *Nice White Parents*, a blockbuster podcast released in 2020 from *Serial* and the *New York Times*, documents exactly what happens when privileged White families are oblivious to the idea of "sharing" power, even when they are the newcomers to a school. The podcast tells the story of how White families came into a school that served Latino, Black, and Middle Eastern children, pushed aside the parents who were already there, denied them access to the money they raised, and destabilized and disrupted the school.

Megan Hester and Eva Bogaisky
Brooklyn, NY

Megan Hester was no stranger to the behavior highlighted in *Nice White Parents*. She's the mother of two daughters who attend global-majority schools, and she has worked in the education justice movement for more than two decades as a parent organizer, trainer, and researcher. She currently serves as the director of the Education Justice Research and Organizing Collaborative, an organization housed within the NYU Metropolitan Center for Research on Equity and the Transformation of Schools.

In her work, and in her life as a parent, she's seen how White families who enroll their kids in schools that serve lower-income kids of color often come in with a "colonizer attitude" that they're going to "save" the school. The problem is so pervasive that her organization put together a training titled "From Integration to Anti-racism: How We Show Up as White Families in Multi-racial Schools." The purpose of the training, she says, was to help White families reflect upon their internalized racist beliefs "so that we can be productive when we can go into our schools, and build strong relationships, strong community, and not do some of the stuff you hear about in *Nice White Parents*. . . . We don't want parents sending their kids there thinking they're doing something great for the neighborhood, or some kind of charity act."

I talked to Megan with Eva Bogaisky, a parent who had taken Megan's class about four years ago, who is, like Megan, a White parent who sends her children to a global-majority school. Initially, Eva says, when she had moved to her neighborhood, she internalized the belief that "nobody" went to the global-majority school near her, and that it was a place to be avoided. That started to shift when she walked by the school building and heard a little boy ask his father, "Is that going to be my school? It looks like a castle!" She recalls, "He was so excited about it and that made me feel so confused and awful. Part of me really wanted to ignore that feeling, but here he was, looking at this school with so much wonder and openness, while my view was so negative and closed—and if we're going to be perfectly honest, steeped in racism. I realized in that moment that he was right and I was wrong. It really could be a castle."

But after enrolling her children at that school, Eva also had to push back on other White families from the neighborhood viewing that act as one of a "savior." She recalled a neighbor telling her that it was "really great what she was doing for the place" when she casually mentioned where her children went to school, as if the presence of a White family added inherent value to the school. Another parent told Eva, "If you build it, they will come." She continues, "I told my husband, isn't it already built? There are already six hundred children who go there!"

The failure to recognize that these schools have already been "built," and already have value, is the central tension in *Nice White Parents* and a focus of Megan's work. In an interview published on the blog *Everyday Conversations about Race*, she shared some of the questions that families fail to consider when enrolling in a school:

- What has come before us?
- What is the history of this neighborhood?
- What have people been working on?
- What do people want?
- What have the challenges been?
- What have the priorities been?
- What has been achieved in the schools and why?

If we don't ask those questions, Megan points out that "because of the way a person moves through life with privilege—a lot of us tend to expect and assume that what *we* want is what everyone wants."

She also questions the paradigm about what a school "needs" to look like, have, or be to be "good." (I myself don't even have a school-aged child, but I've internalized the pervasive cultural ideas about what children "need": outdoor time, organic gardens, project-based learning, sports.) "Why do we, as White parents, want to give our kids' schools the same things that we can give them in our families?" Megan asks. Of her older daughter, she adds, "I can *never* give her the experiences that she gets at [her school]. We can arrange project-based learning summer camps, or sports, or all those things." She's heard from parents that they couldn't send their child to a certain school because there wasn't enough recess. She pushes back on that: "What you're telling me that despite the fact that your child gets out at 2:20, that the thirty minutes that they might potentially have on

the playground is more important to you than all of these other factors?" Later, in an email, she clarified: "It would be great if my kids
got all the community and relationships and life knowledge and skills
they get at our local school where they're among a small handful of
kids demographically like them, *plus* recess every day and an outdoor
edible garden and overnight camping trips, etc. But because of racism
and inequity and privilege hoarding, that's not a choice American
schools usually offer to us. So given the choice, those experiences just
aren't worth what you have to give up for your kid to get them, and
the lessons your kids inevitably internalize in the process."

At one point in our conversation, I mentioned how she'd found
schools that were "great for her kids," which Megan cautioned as
being oversimplistic. "Everything we define as 'great for our kids' is
connected to privilege and entitlement." She said that her schools are
a mixed bag, with some great experiences, and some not, and that it
may not look like what someone like me would think of when I say the
words "great school." "But," she says, "the *experience* has been great
for my kids and is a thousand times better than it would have been
in one of these selective schools that are super inequitable and embed
in children this mindset that they're better than those who didn't get
in." Megan also doesn't think that the parents who have, as she put it,
"pulled out all the stops" to avoid sending their children to the zoned
school have necessarily chosen an easier road. "As a privileged parent, you get to choose your struggle. One struggle is you get thrown
into making relationships with people of different classes, races, languages, and religious backgrounds, and going outside your comfort
zone. But if you send your child to a more homogenous school, it's
'Now I have to make sure my kid doesn't live in a privileged bubble
and internalize these notions of superiority and entitlement'—that's
another kind of struggle. But is that really the kind of struggle you
want to be engaged in? Do you want all the energy and effort you'll
spend fighting for your child's well-being to be one and the same with

fighting for other kids in your community and for equity? Or do you want it to just further widen the privilege gap?"

She is also clear about the ways that this central decision—to step out of the race for the "best school"—has had ripple effects for the rest of her life. She's spared herself a lot of the agony: "So many things that White parents agonize over . . . I don't have to torture myself over every single thing because the bulk of our lives is aligned around this core decision, which has integrity."

Elisa
Oakland, CA

Elisa (whose name has been changed in this book) is an Oakland parent and described herself in a Facebook post as a "first-generation-college and immigrant mama" looking to "choose the path for my kids that is in alignment with our family values and responsive to their needs/rights." In the conversations about school choice, these are often families whose stories don't get told—much of the sociological research I found about the topic conflated the terms *middle-class family* with *White family*, without speaking to the specific considerations that families like Elisa's face.

Elisa immigrated to the United States from Nicaragua as a child and was the first in her family to attend college, receiving a degree in social welfare and education from UC Berkeley. She went on to get a masters in bilingual, multilingual, and multicultural education, and subsequently has had a long career in the Oakland school system as a teacher, principal, and school head. She is now a community director at a nonprofit that fights for equity in Oakland schools. She and her husband have one college-aged daughter (Elisa's stepdaughter) and three children under the age of ten. Her husband is Black and was raised in Oakland by a single mother—he, too, was the first in his family to go to college. As she puts it, "We're both first-generation college kids who lived in poverty. We're a biracial Black and Brown family. And we talk a lot about what it means to parent when you had mobility because of access to education, and what that means for which values stay intact, which values change."

Her kids, she says, "definitely have more privilege than I did growing up—they have two parents that are educators, two parents that are college educated, we're not living in poverty anymore. But the world still sees my kids as Black and Brown boys, and a Black girl—my daughter's also Latina, but she presents Black. And because of that, there's just a lot to consider. I want my kids to have access to a quality education. . . . But if I was a White, middle-class mom, I would be able to say, because the research shows, 'My kids are probably going to be OK.' And for me, it's more like . . . I *think* they're going to be OK because they have me. . . . But I can't guarantee that. Because, you know, I'm not homeschooling them."

Her family has tried out a host of different options for their children. Her kids started at a Spanish-immersion preschool. Her older son then went to a Catholic school that she described as "where middle-class Black families send their children." Though they loved the environment at the Catholic school, it wasn't affordable for their family long-term; they've also gone to different traditional public schools in the Oakland Unified School District. Two of her three kids are now at a charter public school. Basically, she says, "I've tried all the systems." When I talked to her, all three of her school-aged kids were learning from home because of the pandemic.

An additional challenge for her family has been finding an appropriate school for her older son, who is on the autism spectrum. When he first was diagnosed, Elisa learned that autism is often underdiagnosed in Latino and Black boys because "they're written off as just having behavior issues, rather than a medical need." She and her husband have talked about how "the world is going to already see our children as defiant, and not eager to learn. And then on top of that, our son has great strengths, and also true needs, that have to be supported in loving ways with true partnership between family and teachers."

She hasn't always found that "true partnership," and described the additional labor that she has to do to figure out if she's likely to find it at a given school. "As a mom of Black and Brown children—there's just so much research that has to be done. I look at the racial demographics, the class demographics, the IEP percentages." She can't just look at test scores—she has to look at the specific data that answers the question: How are Black kids doing here? "There are schools that look shinier—*physically*, physically look shinier," she says with a laugh. "And they might have 'shinier' overall outcomes, but those are the places where my children can actually be more marginalized and disenfranchised."

She's experienced that dynamic with her older son. For preschool, her son went to a sought-after Spanish-immersion district school. He hadn't yet been diagnosed as neurodivergent, and he was having a hard time with making the transition from class to class. One day, he came home and reported to Elisa that a teacher had pulled him, that his feet were dragging across the floor so that his "sneakers were squeaking." She went in to talk to the principal about the issue. At that time, Elisa herself was a principal at a different school. But she didn't announce that in the meeting. "I don't move around like that—I don't walk around the world shifting my weight," she says. "And the principal told me, 'Well, maybe this isn't the right environment for him.' And this was another Latina woman. And I couldn't do anything but turn around and walk away."

Which parents "shift their weight around" is the focus of sociological research done by Jessica McCrory Calarco, an associate professor at the University of Indiana. Her book *Negotiating Opportunity: How the Middle Class Secures Advantages in School* focuses on the way both parents and children from different class backgrounds interact

in a school setting. Calarco heard, again and again, from the affluent White families that she talked to, that they want to secure every
"advantage" for their child. But, as Calarco pointed out in an interview
with the *Integrated Schools* podcast, "advantage is a relative term—so
advantage over whom? And advantage relative to what?" In her book,
she details how affluent parents who come from affluent backgrounds
themselves often bend the rules to benefit themselves or their children.

I told Elisa that I couldn't imagine not being tempted to use my
status as a fellow principal to garner some favor. The stakes in that
moment were high—as she puts it, "It was like an emergency, he
didn't have another school." "I have the ability to do that," she says
with a shrug. "But it's not how I was raised."

"Good Schools" for Kids with Challenges

Elisa's story, and the stories I heard from parents of other kids who
are in racial minorities or who aren't neurotypical, made me wonder
if instead of "Is this a good school?" a better question for parents to
ask may be "Who is this school good for?" Many schools serve students from my own daughter's demographic—White, middle class, no
special needs—much better than they serve students who may not fit
that profile. But it's incumbent on me to care about how they serve
all students, not just my own.

JPB Gerald
Queens, NY

JPB Gerald, a Black father, told me that the good-school/bad-school
binary is also different for his family. He is a postdoctoral student
at Hunter College and lives with his wife and his one-year-old son.
He's neurodivergent (ADHD) but was not diagnosed while in school.
Growing up, he went to one of the "shiniest" schools in the whole

country: he spent fourteen years at a private progressive school in Brooklyn, where he shared hallways with both the children of celebrities and students who later became celebrities themselves. (Tuition today is listed at nearly $50,000 a year for elementary school, and more than that for middle and high school.) He describes the school as somewhere that "thought it was better than other private schools because we weren't explicit about our elitism." He was one of very few Black students at the school, and he's both written and spoken about how attending that school led him to internalize the idea that his identity as a Black person was somehow in conflict with his identity as a "smart" person. He also says that it was particularly damaging to experience insidious racism at a school that was, on its surface, such a progressive place.

When he thinks about where he wants to send his own son—a question he's already pondering, even though, when we spoke, his son wasn't even walking yet—he knows that he won't make the same choice that his own parents did. "If he's similar to me in any way, then he's probably going to be pretty good at memorizing things—I'm not saying the word 'smart.' Just, he'll be good at the sort of things that make you good at tests. And he may well be like me, with attention issues and all that. If I put him in a public school and it's boring, then what do I have to do? I have to supplement it. And I could do that—I'm a teacher! But if he goes to a school that's like my school was—I can't really protect him from that."

Morgan and Lyndsay
Atlanta suburb, GA

Morgan and her wife, Lyndsay, a White couple who live in an Atlanta suburb, had a similar experience when trying to find a school for their daughter, Caroline (not her real name), who is also White, and whom they adopted from foster care when she was eleven. Like many children in foster care, their daughter had experienced physical and sexual abuse. She was diagnosed with PTSD because of her abuse history, and oppositional defiant disorder (a conduct disorder where children display argumentative and defiant behavior). She is also on the autism spectrum. She had not attended school at all before her removal from her biological family and was thus very behind academically. As Morgan puts it, "When you start second grade, and you don't even know how to write your name, you're pretty screwed." When she first came to live with them, the couple did what they thought seemed like the right thing—enroll their daughter in what was widely considered in their peer group to be an excellent school.

"When we moved to this area, we were very happy with the very, very good school system." Morgan says. They discovered quickly, however, that "wealthy areas with excellent schools do not have children like Caroline." Their daughter was repeatedly suspended. One particularly bad day, the school called to tell them that they had lost track of her and didn't know where she was. (She was quickly found.) For the whole year, the school had the couple "on speed dial."

Their daughter now attends a middle school that works much better for her and their family. They have special education services, a case manager, and school staff who seem invested in figuring out how to make the school best work for their daughter. But their experience in their daughter's first year of school illustrates the way that a school that may appear to have well-behaved students and excellent academic outcomes might have those outcomes not because they are able to achieve those results for all students, but because they force out the students who can't easily meet those expectations.

Charters and Vouchers

Forty-five states have laws that authorize "charter schools," which is a term for any school that is operated by an independent group rather than by a school district and a local school board. Charters receive public money, but they don't have to follow the same regulations as traditional public schools, nor are their teachers part of a union or subject to the union's rules. Some states, like Nevada and New Mexico, have laws that explicitly forbid for-profit companies from applying to operate charter schools. Others do not.

The first person to popularize the idea of charters was Albert Shanker, a former president of the American Federation of Teachers, one of the two large teachers' unions in the country. In 1988, Shanker gave a speech where he proposed the creation of a "new kind of school" that would encourage innovation and creative solutions to try to reach kids who weren't being well-served by the traditional school system. Crucially, Shanker's vision for these schools included a teaching workforce that would have more power over decision-making but still be part of the union. That part of his vision did not come to fruition; most teachers at charter schools are not union-ized, and the teachers' unions and charter schools have been bitter enemies for nearly thirty years. It's impossible to imagine Randi Weingarten, the current president of the American Federation of Teachers, giving a speech that supported the development of charter schools today.

The first charter school in the country, City Academy, opened in Saint Paul, Minnesota, in 1992, and is still operating today. The three educators behind the school envisioned it as a place that would serve the needs of students aged fifteen to twenty-one who had either already dropped out of school or who were at risk of dropping out. They envisioned a cross between a community center and a school, designed to meet the needs of students whose families were strug-gling with substance abuse or living in poverty. The school was open between 8:00 AM and 8:00 PM, and included support groups, individual counseling, and job skills training.

Who could oppose such a place? A lot of people, it turned out. Both the teachers' union and public school advocates opposed the Minnesota law that authorized charters, mostly on the same grounds that those groups oppose charters today. Teachers' unions opposed the new law on the grounds that a charter school wouldn't have the same kind of accountability for teachers that a public school would. (Today, twenty-nine states automatically exempt charter schools from certain regulations that public schools are required to follow, and thirteen do not require teachers at charters to meet the same certification standards as traditional public school teachers.) Advocates for public schools have also charged that charter schools siphon off funding and force school districts to close traditional public schools to save costs. Charter schools have increasingly become less associated with schools that offer the support groups and counseling services, like City Academy, and more with the schools like those in Success Academy's network of charters, which prioritize sharp-looking uniforms, silent lines, and heaps of homework. Success Academy, and other networks of charter schools, have been accused of leaving behind students who have disabilities, trauma histories, or other challenges that make complying with those expectations difficult, thus concentrating the students with the most resource-intensive needs in traditional public schools. Charter school advocates contend that their students excel because of their school's high expectations for students, and their school's ability to hire the strongest teachers and fire weak ones; opponents say that successful charters hand-select a student body that already has the right aptitude to excel at their parameters.

Charter schools are just one component of the "school choice" movement, which has its early roots in the immediate aftermath of the *Brown* decision (some states used "school choice" to avoid the integration mandates of *Brown*) and has taken many other forms in the intervening decades. One such form is "voucher programs," which allowed low-income families to transfer out of public schools and use the funding that their district would have received in order to pay tuition at a private school. Charter schools, however, have far more traction than vouchers. Voucher programs exist in only sixteen states; charters exist in forty-five.

The 2019 podcast *School Colors* took an in-depth look at charter schools. Mark Winston Griffith, one of the podcast's hosts, said, in the opening of the episode focusing on charters: "Both sides, charter and traditional public school advocates, have claimed the mantle of civil rights, racial justice, and self-determination. Both sides say they're the underdog, and they're the ones under attack."

The episode featured Rafiq Kalam Id-Din II, who founded the Ember Charter School in the Bedford Stuyvesant neighborhood of Brooklyn, an Afrocentric school that focuses on Black culture and heritage. Ember, like the City Academy charter before it, is the kind of school that charter advocates point to when discussing the benefits of charters—schools that are serving a population of kids who have been poorly served by traditional public schools. Ember emphasizes mental health treatment rather than punitive discipline, and they have an innovative model of "teaching firms" in which current teachers make decisions, rather than getting top-down decisions from administrators who are no longer in the classroom.

But features of the charter school model that allow for these types of innovations have, in some states, led to particularly egregious forms of fraud. A story that's played out in many states: charter schools that claim to hold "online classes," and then claim state funding without actually teaching any children—a scheme that I must imagine has gotten infinitely easier to pull off during the pandemic. Charters have also served as vehicles for the families who run them to engage in self-dealing real estate transactions, or simple embezzlement.

Only about 7 percent of public school students in the United States attend charters. But some of the richest and most powerful people in the country are intent on increasing that number. The Walton family, Bill Gates, the Koch brothers, and former education secretary Betsy DeVos are just a few of the billionaires who have poured their dollars into pro-charter organizations. And while they don't exist at all in some states, they're ubiquitous in other cities. New Orleans essentially doesn't have a traditional public school system any longer, and fully converted all its schools to charters after Katrina.

In his 2020 book *Schoolhouse Burning* law school professor Derek W. Black makes an important distinction between what motivates families who are choosing charter schools and what motivates the big-money philanthropy, lobbying organizations, and politicians who support charters. Before 2008, Black writes, public school students "did not have everything they needed, but they typically had more than the prior generation." During the economic recession of 2008, however, states "took out their hatchets and started chopping." Even when the states' budgets recovered, many states did not restore funding but instead kept the funding at levels used during the recession to "redefine their commitment to public education."

Black then suggests that the "choice" of the "school choice" movement is an illusory one, given that public schools have been so starved for resources for well over a decade. Parents who choose charters, Black writes, "have never seen their state fully commit to providing a quality education in their neighborhoods, and have no reason to trust the state ever will . . . , so these parents are not choosing between a decent public school and a charter or voucher." The lobbying firms and private philanthropists, however, are not the same: "The interest of those pulling the political and financial levers behind the scenes to expand charters and vouchers do not align with disadvantaged communities. Their goal, unlike that of minority communities, is not to ensure that each and every child, regardless of wealth, race, or religion, receives an equal and adequate educational opportunity." Instead, for those "pulling the levers" (like the Walton or DeVos families) undermining education is just low-hanging fruit in a vision of the future that includes "less taxes, less government."

It's possible, in other words, to believe both that a school like Ember, or City Academy, should exist, and that the unfettered expansion of charters is not an overall good.

Charter schools are most likely to be a theoretical concern for many of the readers of this chapter: families who have the true "choice" that wealth brings mostly don't choose charters. The whole framing of this chapter, and indeed of this book, is directed toward families who have those *real* choices about where their children go to school, not the official "school choice" programs that attempt to level the playing field for less affluent families. Families who can pay hundreds more dollars each month in rent or mortgage to live inside the district or in the suburb with the "good school" are engaging in "school choice," even if we don't call it that. A 2012 study found that it costs families, on average, $11,000 more each year to afford housing near a high-scoring public school than a low-scoring public school, and that home values in districts with high-scoring schools are $205,000 higher than in low-scoring districts. Even among families who choose public schools and aren't directly paying tuition, money thus plays a powerful role in what choices are available. While in past decades those divisions happened along certain lines (mostly poor families of color in the cities and more affluent White families in the suburbs), those divides are not so clean today: today's divisions are between affluent suburbs and poorer suburbs, and between affluent and poorer parts of cities.

Money

"Resources," or simply money, is at the backdrop of any conversations about schools. Precise school funding structures vary from state to state, but in most places it's a simple formula: roughly 45 percent of a school's funding comes from local money, including property taxes; roughly 45 percent from the state; and less than 10 percent comes from the federal government. This formula has been a perfect recipe for inequality.

In the early 1970s Demetrio Rodriguez, a Mexican American father whose children attended school in a crumbling building, brought a lawsuit against the state of Texas alleging that the district's reliance on property taxes violated the Equal Protection Clause of the US Constitution. The school building where his children attended school was in such disrepair that the third floor had been condemned by the city. His children's school district had a higher tax rate than a neighboring district, but even with that higher rate, the property values were so much lower that taxes only yielded funding which amounted to fifty dollars per student. A nearby district had half the tax rate, yet because its property values were so much higher, it could garner ten times as much, an average of $500 per student per home.

Rodriguez's case eventually reached the Supreme Court, where the court ruled against him, finding that "the Equal Protection Clause does not require absolute equality or precisely equal advantages." (Rodriguez, of course, wasn't seeking "absolute equality"; he was asking for his children not to be forced to attend school in a condemned building.)

San Antonio Independent School District v. Rodriguez isn't nearly as famous a case as *Brown v. Board*. But had it gone a different way, it's hard to imagine that our schools wouldn't look extremely different than they do today.

Stephanie King
Philadelphia, PA

Much of this chapter has been focused on the "softer" harms of segregated schools—the sense of entitlement they breed in certain children, and inferiority in others, and the harm to the greater good of democracy. My conversation with Stephanie King, a writer, mother of two, and education activist in Philadelphia, neatly summarizes the easier-to-quantify harms: when all the wealthy parents go to a particular school, that's where all the money goes. This problem has grown particularly pronounced in the decade-plus since the Great Recession beginning in 2007, during which time many states in this country reduced their funding for public education. The schools where parents can make up the difference are still doing OK, while the schools where they can't are trying to make do with less.

Stephanie is a White parent who enrolled her daughter, and later her son, in a majority-Black, low-income school for kindergarten. She didn't think much about the decision at the time—it was their neighborhood school, and while she knew that other White families in the area were choosing to drive their kids elsewhere, she didn't see anything wrong with their local school.

The ensuing years of her children's education showed her how that "White flight" affected her daughter's school. In her gentrifying neighborhood, more and more White families were moving in, but many of them were sending their kids to a school that was a fifteen-minute drive away. By Stephanie's calculations (which are precise, and supported with publicly available data), there are eighty-eight children, the vast majority of whom are White, who should be at her children's school but whose parents have opted them out. Stephanie's children's school is punished for these parents' decision with a practice that Philadelphia euphemistically calls "leveling"—a cost-saving measure in which teachers from "underenrolled" schools are moved to schools with larger student populations. When her daughter was in first grade, the class started the school year with one teacher only to have that teacher "leveled" in October, leaving her daughter, and the rest of the class, to start over with a new teacher. She knew from various acquaintances that the "White school" was continually adding new kindergarten classes, and she started to talk to journalists and, as she puts it, "goes to yell at the superintendent about school segregation . . . because at a system level they're literally taking stuff from the Black schools and sending it to the White school."

Stephanie laid out clearly for me the differences between the two sets of schools: the Whiter school has a $40,000 annual fund; her children's school does not have an annual fund at all. Her school holds a yearly fundraiser just so that teachers can each have their own ream of paper to make copies.

Privileged families' predilection to all clump together in particular schools delivers a one-two punch to equity: in most states, schools are funded on a per-student basis, even though many of their costs stay fixed. A teacher doesn't get a lower salary because she's teaching twenty-five students rather than thirty-two, but the school has less money for everything else in the per-student funding model. The problem becomes compounded by school's reliance on both their local property taxes and on private fundraising; unsurprisingly, the districts with the highest property values also have the most parents who can write large checks at school fundraisers. This leads to stark differences in what's available at different schools. "You cannot pretend that we are giving all students an equal chance," Stephanie told her local school board, "while [some schools] have a library that looks like something out of Harry Potter, and my school's library looks like boxes of books."

Even though she's fighting hard to close the resource gaps between the schools, she is still happy to have made the decision that she did, even with the shifting teachers and a nonexistent library. "Developing your kids' cultural competence, and showing them that you don't just get to ditch an uncomfortable situation to do better for yourself is also part of their education," she says.

"And my kids have learned that, while all of these other people's kids haven't."

COVID-19 and Pandemic Pods

I wrote much of this chapter during the 2020 school year, when our society's very concept of what "school" is had suddenly shifted: when schools closed, some children transitioned seamlessly to curated "pods" with private teachers. In July 2020 the *Washington Post* and the *New York Times* published op-eds on the same day, each a warning about the equity issues with these pods. The *Washington Post* noted that "pods" had a similar flavor as the "segregation academies" that White families fleeing the public school system in the 1960s South had created; Clara Totenberg Green, an Atlanta learning specialist, made a similar point in the *New York Times*, writing that "whatever parents ultimately decide, they must understand that every choice they make in their child's education, even the seemingly benign, has the potential to perpetuate racial inequities rooted in white supremacy."

In October 2020 *Slate* published a detailed article about parents in Charlottesville, Virginia, trying to navigate the equity issues with pods. Kristin Thomas Sancken, a White Charlottesville mother, told *Slate* that she threw herself into trying to make sure that children who had recently moved to Charlottesville as refugees were included in the pod. She was rebuffed by other families, worried that the refugee families would "compromise pod safety" or who couched their refusal in terms of concern for the refugee family: "Well, what if our pod falls apart and we have to revoke the invitation?" At a progressive elementary school that proudly touted the forty-two languages spoken by its students, almost every student in a pod was affluent and White. The article had the distinct tone that maybe addressing equity issues was just too hard.

A lot of the writing and conversation about pandemic pods took that same defeated tone: Totenberg Green's op-ed states in its concluding paragraph, "Many will read this article and ask what they're supposed to do instead. I don't have the answer. Parents are in an unimaginably hard position." Elizabeth Diehl Newcamp, a host of the *Slate* podcast *Mom and Dad Are Fighting*, made a comment that I found particularly emblematic of how privileged parents think about education: "I don't know that we can handle the schools' social and racial inequalities at the same time as we're going to figure out how the heck are we going to school these children." "Handling social and racial inequality" is, of course, only something that privileged White families have the option to separate out from figuring out how to educate their kids.

Shayla Griffin, a Michigan professor and parent, has written about pandemic pods and education equity in a way that gets beyond handwringing. She is a Black parent of three children under six, and for the past decade she has worked as a social justice educator and consultant in schools across Michigan. She's dealt with crises—her first son was born nearly three months early and spent three months in the NICU. Having come out the other side of that experience—even trying to work during a global pandemic with three children under six at home (one of whom has special needs)—didn't seem to faze her too much. In a blog post on *Medium*, she wrote about the similarities between that crisis and this one: a crisis demands that we use every resource at our disposal, that we don't engage in what she calls "either/or" thinking and instead use "both/and" thinking.

Her insights into how families with class privilege can think about their involvement in public schools has a much broader application than the pandemic. "The biggest social justice risk we face as a result of this pandemic is the destruction of the public education system in the United States. This is the explicit and decades-long goal of Betsy DeVos. . . . If many of the most privileged parents officially opt out of public schools, they will be laying the foundation of destruction that will last long after this pandemic is over." Griffin noted that, for families who care about their public schools, the most important thing isn't for their child to show up to every Zoom class or turn in every assignment but that they remain officially "enrolled." In Michigan, where Griffin lives, there's a "count day" where student attendance is taken, and that determines school funding for the year. So Griffin said if nothing else her son will "be there on count day."

She also suggests that families think about what's necessary versus what's not. "Childcare" may be a necessity; hiring a private teacher to make sure your child doesn't "fall behind" is not.

She didn't have a lot of hope that affluent families could simply make sure to include families of all class backgrounds in their pods as a panacea to avoid perpetuating inequalities. As she succinctly put it, "We are not going to fix hundreds of years of race and class segregation through better pod strategizing." The framework itself, in her view, is something that she just doesn't see most working-class parents being interested in, no matter how many efforts were made to include them. In an interview with Andrew Lefkowits on the *Integrated Schools* podcast, she said, "I don't know any working-class folks who are looking on Facebook for someone to watch their kids. I don't think that's happening. That's a very middle-class phenomenon, that you're going to meet somebody you met on the Internet, and then take your kids to their house and leave them there."

For families with time and resources, that time would be better spent collectively organizing and lobbying our school districts, and local, state, and federal governments for the kinds of supports that would benefit all families. The most useful way you can use your time as a privileged person is "figuring out who in your circles of privilege knows some senators."

Unschooling and Other Nontraditional School Methods

There are families who believe in the importance of public schools but who also have found that those schools simply don't work for their children. Even before COVID-19, approximately two million families homeschooled or "unschooled" their children (precise definitions vary, but unschooling is a category of homeschooling that emphasizes child-directed learning over a traditional curriculum). In the late 1980s White evangelical Christian families made up 90 percent of homeschoolers. The homeschooling population today includes a vast variety of families with differing reasons for opting out of the school system. A rising number of Black and Hispanic families who have the means to do so have been homeschooling their children, often citing a racially biased curriculum or a school system that doled out more punitive discipline to their children as a motivation for moving to that model.

There are also families who have children with needs that can't be met in a traditional classroom. Though under federal law every child has the right to a "free and appropriate" education, many families find themselves in the situation that the next interviewee did—of wanting to send their child to their local public school and coming up against the reality of what their kid needed.

Bridgid Roney
Snohomish, WA

Bridgid is the mother of a six-year-old and a four-year-old who lives on the Tulalip Reservation in Washington State. She and her husband are both White and live on deeded land on the reservation that is owned by her husband's family. Her husband is an electrician; Bridgid has worked as both a professional singer and music teacher, and currently homeschools their sons.

Long before she became a parent, she knew that she didn't like the standard model of education, with its rows of desks and its implicit assumption that "kids don't have anything in their brains until adults tell them what to think." She was intrigued by the Waldorf model (an education model that emphasizes natural learning over traditional curriculum) and sent her older son to a Waldorf co-op school when he was three. When she volunteered in that classroom, though, she figured out "that my kid was *really* different. Seeing him next to all the other kids—I could just tell that, developmentally, he wasn't in a similar spot." The school did a lot of circle time and her son "didn't want to have anything to do with it." While the kids weren't in rows of desks, the Waldorf experience was "another version of 'all the kids sit there quietly and they have to watch this thing.' And he's just a *mover*; he has to move, he has to talk. I was just always embarrassed and trying to control the situation." She describes herself as feeling, "What's wrong with me that my kid can't just sit there and watch this puppet show?"

She was able to get a free evaluation through their local public school system, which confirmed what her intuition had told her. As she puts it, "They don't diagnose a kid that age as being on the spectrum, but he was diagnosed as having a lot of delays." Once he had this diagnosis, he qualified for a public preschool that had a ratio of five kids to three adults; he did well enough in that program that, with the teachers' encouragement, she enrolled him in kindergarten at a school in a county to the north of where they live now.

But traditional kindergarten, with its thirty kids and two teachers, was a "nightmare." She said that the classroom "relied on all the kids being willing to sit at their desks at certain times. The teacher was lovely and very loving, but it was hell. . . . I could tell that [my son] was like, *None of this is natural!*" When she was in the classroom, she noticed him disassociating just to deal with the pressure of being asked to stay in his seat. When he couldn't take it, he would sprint out of the classroom, and sometimes run all the way out the building. One day, just a few months into the school year, his teacher successfully blocked his exit from the classroom, and he started throwing chairs, the first time he'd ever done anything violent. Bridgid realized at that point that she needed to make a change.

She's been unschooling her son for a little over a year. Though Washington state has a few mandates for the subject areas that they need to cover, she's generally able to follow her son's lead to explore what he's interested in. Currently, his passion for Transformers (which were originally manufactured in Japan) has led them to exploring Japanese culture, and he's learning Japanese.

While she feels weird about being in a "White bubble" while living on a reservation, she's sometimes found herself frustrated by the assumption that she's trying to keep him in that bubble, that not sending her child to public school means that she doesn't value the schools—or that this route is somehow the "easier" one for her family. She has a core belief that "everyone should have access to resources and opportunities, and there should be a baseline of support for all families." But she sees a "shadow side" of that line of thinking—that "those resources must be used by everyone, and if you're not doing that it's because you're individualist, only looking out for yourself, and don't want your kids to associate with the common folk." She's quick to acknowledge the privileges—including her own education, which included thirteen years of private school and an arts college— that have made it possible for her to opt out and take on the task of educating her children herself. But she also sees how families with kids who aren't neurotypical, or who have other differences, can be left out of the conversation. In her words, "My heart and soul wants my kid to be going to the local public elementary school. But he just *cannot* hang in a normal classroom." Her younger son is neurotypical, and she thinks will love public school, so she says, "I guess I can assuage my guilt then." (She's also made sure to keep her older son technically enrolled so that her decision to pull him out hasn't affected the funding that the school receives.)

Though she hopes that social movements around increasing school equity can include students who don't thrive in traditional classroom settings as a part of the conversation, she's glad that the racial segregation in public schools is getting more attention and that content like *Nice White Parents* has been so widely listened to and pushed the conversation forward. As she puts it, "This is a great movement for a lot of people, but it's not for me, and it's not for my kids right now. And that's OK. Not everything has to include me or my kids. And true desegregation on every level will mean a decolonized approach to education—more freedom of movement, more critical thinking, more practical skill application, tolerance of different cultures, symbiosis of community—all things that will make school a much better place for neurodiversity."

Takeaways

The idea that our public schools are in crisis has been part of the discourse since before I was born. That perpetual message had led me to overlook the ways that the current moment really *does* represent a fraught moment that will determine the future of public schools for the next generation. In the past decade, many states have dramatically decreased their education budgets. We recently had a secretary of education who, for four years, openly disdained public schools and cheered on their destruction. Finally, the pandemic threw enormous new challenges at an already-struggling system. The next five years will be critical in determining what our public schools look like going forward. It's too early to say, but many education experts suggest that the pandemic may result in large numbers of privileged families abandoning the public school system, even when normal instruction resumes.

Talking to parents for this chapter has forced me to confront many of the fantasies I've had about school. One was that my daughter would—of course!—not attend a school that was segregated by race or class. We lived in Brooklyn; we planned to send her to public school. But from talking to parents and reading the research, I've learned that simply attending public school inside a demographically diverse city does not absolve me from the responsibility to reckon with segregation, privilege, and power. Thinking about those issues doesn't come naturally; the dominant messages I get from my social circles is that my only job is to get my daughter the "best education."

I don't think I can tell you where to send your child to school. But the parents I talked to had a lot of wisdom about how to thoughtfully approach the task of educating our children.

First, in choosing a school . . .

- **Broaden your sources of information.** Eva's story, about feeling like "no one" went to her local school is a common one: we privileged parents get our information from one another. In other words, if Harper's mom tells us that the school down the road isn't good, we're likely to take that opinion as gospel, and repeat it to others, even if we have no firsthand or independent information about the school. One way to get out of that information bubble is to . . .
- **Go on school tours.** For most families in the United States, "choosing a school" happens at least three times—once for their child's elementary school, once for middle school, once for high school. Families tend to be on "tracks" in which groups of children move in prescribed ways through certain schools—attending a certain elementary school means that there may be social pressure to attend a certain middle school. Some of the parents I talked to for this

chapter had come to fully understand their own values around schools after their child was already well through elementary school, or even middle school, and they realized, having attended a so-called desirable school, that perhaps that wasn't consistent with their values. The Two Tour Pledge from Integrated Schools is a place to start, wherever you are in your school journey.

- **Broaden your questions.** As privileged parents, we're generally encouraged to only think about one thing: Is this school the right fit for my child? But a school is not an outfit that you're trying on in a dressing room. It's not a consumer good that we can tailor to our expectations. Strong, adequately funded public schools with the resources to educate every child who comes in their doors are a foundation of our society.

- **Think about segregation.** Segregation is alive and well. It's not just something from the history books. It didn't end in the 1950s with *Brown* or in the '60s with the Little Rock Nine. If you're a White parent choosing a school, think about how race/class plays into your perception of what is and isn't a "good school." Is "tracking" reproducing a de facto segregation within your school building? It's rare for a school to have *no* kids of color anymore, but that doesn't mean that our schools aren't deeply segregated.

Once you've chosen a school . . .

- **Ask questions.** Megan Hester's suggested questions are a crucial starting place before you, say, decide that what the school most needs is a French program and a lavish fundraiser (what the parents in *Nice White Parents* did):

  o What has come before us?
  o What is the history of this neighborhood?
  o What have people been working on?
  o What do people want?
  o What have the challenges been?
  o What have the priorities been?
  o What has been achieved in the schools, and why?

- **Listen.** Before you go to a school board meeting, or march in the streets, or call representatives, or take any other action on "behalf" of disadvantaged families, make sure those families are at the table with you and are asking you to join with them or asking for your help.
- **Remember that your child isn't the only one.** There are certainly situations in which it's appropriate to advocate for your child, or where you need a teacher or school administrator's time and attention. But time is finite. And a common dynamic in schools is for the parents with the most privilege to be the ones who, to use Elisa's phrase, "shift their weight around." Teachers and administrators need to be able to focus attention on all students, not just those who have parents who demand it.
- **Remember that "advantage" is a relative term.** Giving your child "every possible advantage" is such a common way that privileged parents talk about what they want from their child's schools. But the statement has a darker underside, as Jessica McCrory Calarco's work points out. Advantage over whom? Advantage compared to what? Don't we want all children to have "the best education," not just our own?

Caring about schools beyond just how they serve our own kids is often framed as just something that altruistic people do, or as a form of "sacrifice." It's not. We all benefit when we're part of a society with people who can read, write, and think; who can recognize "real news" from "fake news." Who know about our country and world history, and who have had their potential talents realized. In the episode of *This American Life* that inspired Andrew, Nedra Martin, a Black mother says this to parents who wanted to keep her daughter in segregated, low-performing schools: "My child may be the doctor that saves your life one day. My child may be the lawyer that defends your child one day. How dare you."

Further Reading and Listening

"Choosing a School for My Daughter in a Segregated City" by Nikole Hannah-Jones, *New York Times Magazine,* June 9, 2016, https://www.nytimes.com/2016/06/12/magazine/choosing-a-school-for-my-daughter-in-a-segregated-city.html

Cutting School: The Segrenomics of American Education by Noliwe Rooks (New Press, 2017)

Despite the Best Intentions: How Racial Inequality Thrives in Good Schools by Amanda Fields and John Diamond (Oxford University Press, 2015)

The Integrated Schools Podcast, https://integratedschools.org/podcasts/

The Lost Education of Horace Tate: Uncovering the Hidden Heroes Who Fought for Justice in Schools by Vanessa Siddle Walker (New Press, 2020)

Negotiating Opportunities: How the Middle Class Secures Advantages in School by Jessica McCrory Calarco (Oxford University Press, 2018)

Nice White Parents by the *New York Times,* https://www.nytimes.com/2020/07/23/podcasts/nice-white-parents-serial.html

The Problem We All Live With, https://www.thisamericanlife.org/562/the-problem-we-all-live-with-part-one

School Colors, Brooklyn Deep, https://www.schoolcolorspodcast.com/

Schoolhouse Burning: Public Education and the Assault on American Democracy by Derek Black (PublicAffairs, 2020)

3

COLLEGE

———

I MET KENDRA (a pseudonym—I don't actually remember her real name) when she had just turned eighteen. Sitting across from me at my office in the Children's Law Center, she rattled off some quick details of her life story: she had been removed from her parents as a young child because of their drug use and neglect, placed into foster care, and then adopted by a woman who had some serious mental health issues.

Nothing about her story was unusual among the clients I saw, except for one bizarre, startling detail that stands out in my memory. She wasn't living in the adoptive home anymore, but her adoptive parent continued to get a subsidy check for her care. When she'd asked for some of that money, the woman had instead mailed her an envelope filled with Monopoly money.

The other reason I remember her is the conversation that we had about colleges. Kendra wanted to apply to college. She had graduated from high school (which less than a third of children from the foster care system do) and saw college as an important next step to, as she put it, "be somebody." So after we talked through her legal options to get some non-Monopoly money, the conversation turned to college.

"So I've heard that Berkeley College is really good," she said.

"You want to go to California?" I asked.

She looked confused. "No, no, it's in New York."

A quick Google search showed me that she meant a for-profit college that had been sued for deceptive lending practices. I turned my computer around to show her the results (a headline reading NEW YORK CITY SUES FOR-PROFIT COLLEGE) and her eyes grew wide. "OK, so what about DeVry?" I had never also heard of it. Another search told me that it, too, had been sued by the FTC.

This isn't a story about how I "saved" Kendra. I represented her in court for a case that lasted a few months, and then never saw her again. In fact, I don't even know the ending to her story: I have no idea whether she ultimately enrolled in a for-profit school, or any college at all. But I remained struck by the fact that the word *college* meant a completely different set of schools to Kendra than it did to me.

I come from a college-going family; many of my relatives have masters or doctorates as well. My late grandfather was the provost at Stanford and the president at Harvey Mudd, one of the five colleges in the Claremont college consortium. Higher education has played a major role in all our lives. It was where many of my relatives met their spouses and made lasting friendships. I didn't meet my husband at Whitman College, but I did make most of the friends whom I am closest to today at college, friends I have moved with and traveled with, whom I gladly flew thousands of miles (and then drove hundreds more) to see at our ten-year college reunion.

And, though it's very far off, I will confess that it's not easy for me to imagine a future for my own daughter that doesn't include college. It's such a large part of my own life trajectory, and that of everyone around me.

At the same time, I have come to think the way that privileged families think and talk about college is toxic, and antithetical to every value that I hope my own family holds.

I'm certainly not alone in the observation of how absurd the college admission culture has become. After news of the Varsity Blues scandal broke, there was a flurry of think pieces about what had led these wealthy and (in some cases) famous people to engage in such brazen and silly schemes in pursuit of a fat envelope from the "right" school. In one of those pieces, Jim Jump, a dean at a private high school, wrote that the "the ultimate suburban legend" was at the root of the scandal—"the belief that parental status, and perhaps parenting success, is determined by the prestige of the college attended by your child."

There's no shortage of books and articles telling parents to stop buying into that particular "suburban legend," both for their own good and their child's good. Julie Lythcott-Haims, a former dean at Stanford, has been vocal about negative effect that this obsessive focus on selective colleges has had on both children and parents. In her hometown of Palo Alto, teens have a suicide rate that's many times the national average, a fact that she and other experts attribute at least in part to the pressure-cooker environment around college admissions. As she writes in her book *How to Raise an Adult*, "We love our kids fiercely and want only the very best for them. Yet, having succumbed to . . . a college admissions arms race, and perhaps our own needy ego, our sense of what is 'best' for our kids is completely out of whack." As she sees it, overinvestment in the college admissions race can lead parents to take "real chances" with their child's mental health, which of course can have outcomes for kids far more devastating than the failure to get into a particular college.

Admission to a school like Stanford—extremely selective, extremely expensive—is the "end goal" of snowplow parenting (or what Lythcott-Haims calls overinvolved parenting). In the conclusion of her book she offers various solutions for parents to break out of the narrow mindset they have about colleges and suggests that parents start dropping the names of out-of-the-box colleges into conversations: "Tell your friends, I'd just love it if my daughter would consider Carleton or Whitman or our strong City College." Though I like the book, I found that passage eyeroll inducing, partially because I'm a Whitman alum. If an extremely White, extremely affluent school like Whitman is someone's idea of an out-of-the-box choice, their worldview is narrow indeed. Along the same lines, it's a miniscule group of students for whom the main thing standing between them and Carleton College is their failure to "consider" it—the school has an acceptance rate of under 20 percent and a price tag of nearly $60,000 a year. She does raise the possibility of community college at a later point in the chapter: "If your kid is . . . starting off at a good community college, and your sister's kid is at a very well-known college, you've got to learn to say 'so what?' in your head (really believing it helps)."

But the "calm down" message only takes you so far. Two of the parents who crossed legal and ethical lines in their college admissions search tried to subscribe to that message themselves. Felicity Huffman sold mugs with phrases like "Good Enough Mom" on her blog. Another Varsity Blues parent, Jane Buckingham (who paid $50,000 to have a professional test-taker take the ACT on her son's behalf), wrote a social media post about how she tried to "take joy in who my kids ARE and not who I want them to be." Melissa Korn and Jennifer Levitz uncovered these ironic posts in their deep dive of the scandal, *Unacceptable: Privilege, Deceit & the Making of the College Admissions Scandal*, and note wryly that "Huffman and Buckingham would not follow that advice to chill out."

The parents I interviewed emphatically endorsed the idea of chilling out, and of approaching college admissions with a mindset of abundance, rather than scarcity. But it's helpful, if frustrating, to learn about what really goes on in college admissions, and to see the many ways in which gaining admission has very little to do with merit.

The Real Purpose of College

George Washington didn't go to college. Neither did Abraham Lincoln, or six other presidents; four others attended some college but never graduated. College just wasn't very common throughout most of US history: at the turn of the last century, only about 5 percent of men ages eighteen to twenty-one attended college at all. Those who did were almost exclusively wealthy, White, and Christian.

The 1940s brought a major shift in how the country viewed both the purpose of higher education and who its beneficiaries could be. The 1944 GI Bill, which helped returning veterans pay for college, led to "grizzled, battle-hardened soldiers" coming into schools and often outperforming the wealthier students who had normally been in college classrooms, which, as one professor put it, "altered faculty and administrators' expectations about who could succeed in college"—and, in turn, "the myth of who were appropriate college students began to shift." Black servicemembers, however, were disproportionately less able to claim the benefit, and were encouraged by the state officials to attend vocational or trade schools rather than academic institutions. Their options for attending college at all were also simply more limited: many colleges, particularly in the South, refused admission to all Black students at the time that the GI Bill was passed.

Three years after the GI Bill had been passed, then-president Harry Truman commissioned a task force on higher education in 1947. (Truman himself, whose family couldn't afford the price of college, was one of the presidents who didn't have a four-year degree.) That task force's six-part report, released in 1947, was widely read at the time, and has echoes of how the Founding Fathers talked about the need for public education in the lower grades. Unsurprisingly, it makes no mention of the GI Bill's discriminatory implementation. One notable section of the report reads:

> Equal opportunity for all persons, to the maximum of their individual abilities and without regard to economic status, race, creed, color, sex, national origin, or ancestry is a major goal of American democracy. Only an informed, thoughtful, tolerant people can develop and maintain a free society.

In the years after the GI Bill, college increasingly became (and remains) *the* way for students who didn't come from intergenerational wealth to gain access to a middle-class life. In his book on college and economic mobility, *The Inequality Machine: How College Divides Us*, Paul Tough summarized the trend: "In prewar America, it may have taken pluck and elbow grease to rise above your station; in postwar America, it usually took a college degree." But a college degree "is no longer just a tool for upward mobility; it has also become a shield against downward mobility." Adults who have a high school diploma but not a college degree are three times more likely to live in poverty than college graduates. It is also a shield in a crisis—in the early months of the pandemic, the unemployment rate for adults who graduated high school but didn't have a college degree was double the unemployment rate for those with a college degree.

There are, of course, exceptions. Several Silicon Valley founders have become billionaires without a college degree; some plumbers, electricians, and other skilled laborers make a better living than many college graduates. Millions of people support themselves and their families without a college degree, and the many jobs that don't require a four-year degree are important for society to function. If our country were to make another real investment in post–high school options, vocational programs should receive more funding, support, and attention than they currently do. But families with privilege tend to talk out of both sides of their mouth on this issue: on the one hand, decrying the "stigma" of trade schools and of blue-collar professions, yet never seriously considering anything other than a four-year college and white-collar work for their own children. Columnist David Leonhardt summarized the pattern in a 2015 *New York Times* article: "There are few surer ways to elicit murmurs of agreement than to claim that 'college isn't for everyone.' On both the political left and right, experts have taken to arguing that higher education is overrated (at least when it comes to other people's children)."

You don't have to think that college is necessarily for "everyone" to think that it plays an important role in US democracy and social mobility. There are many equity issues concerning the private and public bachelor-degree-granting institutions that privileged parents typically mean when we talk about "college"—in whom they admit and deny, and in what happens to students from different class backgrounds once they're inside those colleges' doors. But zooming back, there is a bigger equity issue in the world of higher education: the divide between for-profits and community colleges and the rest of higher education.

What Does "College" Mean?

When privileged families talk about "college" they may be talking about public or private schools, liberal arts colleges or research universities. But they almost certainly *aren't* talking about for-profit schools, nor community colleges. I've had hundreds of conversations about college with privileged people and can say, anecdotally but with some degree of certainty, those institutions don't even figure into our conception of what a college is.

It's no great mystery why. Privileged people generally don't go to those schools. There are nearly a thousand community colleges in the United States, which typically offer both associate degrees and vocational training. A 2019 op-ed on the website MarketWatch encapsulated the way these schools are often discussed in privileged circles. The op-ed bemoaned the many ways that rich families gamed the college admissions system, including, but not limited to, the Varsity Blues parents' antics. In the piece's conclusion, the author wished that as punishment, those parents' kids would be "dinged everywhere but their local community college" and opined that such an outcome would be "exactly what the parents deserve." In other words, community college is a punishment, and a just comeuppance, only slightly less humiliating than a stint in prison.

Two of the major signifiers that privileged families use to determine if a college is "good" are price and exclusivity. There's a pervasive belief that an expensive school means that you're paying for quality; likewise, the fewer students admitted to a school, the "better" the students are who get in. By both metrics, community colleges aren't good schools at all. They aren't nearly as expensive as traditional colleges—tuition costs around $3,500 a year, versus around $10,000 a year for public four-year institutions (an average that jumps to nearly $40,000 when considering only private, nonprofit colleges— the Harvards, Williamses, and Pomonas of the world). With a few exceptions, community colleges admit any student who has a GED or a high school diploma.

And yet, by other metrics, these schools do an excellent job of educating their students. I talked to several community college attendees from around the country for this chapter, who transferred to finish their degree at a four-year program after completing two years at community college. Some of them are now parents themselves. In a parenting group discussing college costs, one parent wrote, "I wish there were less of a stigma around community colleges for the first year or two. A lot of kids, and parents too, seem to think of them as a downgrade. I think of them as a great place to earn those core class credits at a less expensive price—making sure the credits will transfer, but they almost always will for core classes." First Lady Jill Biden, herself a community college professor, has called community colleges "America's best kept secret." But they aren't just a "secret" from families who can easily afford other options. They're also often a secret from students, like my client Kendra, who want to pursue higher education but have few financial resources and few adults who understand how to navigate the higher education in their lives. Instead of going to community colleges, those students are often taken in by for-profit recruiters.

In the past twenty years, for-profit colleges have become an extremely lucrative industry, mostly by convincing students like Kendra to enroll in their institutions and pay for their education with federally backed student loans. Kendra's hardships were extreme, but she was in many ways a typical for-profit college student: Black women with few financial resources are overrepresented in for-profit college enrollment. Kendra and "at-risk students" like her receive pervasive messages throughout their life that "staying in school" is the ticket to success, and that education leads to good jobs. She had taken that advice seriously and was doing what she thought would help her get ahead, but she didn't have the framework to understand the different types of institutions, nor connections with anybody who would steer her away from a for-profit school.

Tressie McMillan Cottom's 2017 book *Lower Ed: The Troubling Rise of For-Profit Colleges in the New Economy* is a definitive account of how for-profit colleges have capitalized on the "stay in school" message and convinced students that enrolling at a for-profit college is a strong investment in their future. Elite colleges, McMillan Cottom writes, "legitimize the education gospel," while for-profit colleges "absorb all manner of vulnerable groups, who believe in it: single mothers, downsized workers, veterans, people of color, and people transitioning from welfare to work." For-profit colleges, however, have repeatedly been found to leave the students who attend them worse off than they were before: their job placement data has often been found to be fraudulent, and their aggressive marketing departments encourage students to take out more loans than they have any hope of paying back. Caitlin Zaloom, an NYU professor who wrote a book about college debt, put it starkly: for-profit schools "too often tether [students] to the disadvantage that they came from." For-profit schools charge an average of $466 more per credit than community colleges. But community colleges generally don't have much in the way of an advertising budget, and thus remain "secret" despite being a lower-cost and better option for the group of prospective college students that for-profits prey upon.

Every year thousands of students from lower-income families enroll at "elite" schools, and in recent years, those elite schools proudly tout the percentage of first-generation college students in their admitted classes (22 percent at Princeton, 20 percent at Harvard, for the class of 2025). How schools fail to serve these students once they attend those schools is itself the subject of a recent book, Anthony Jack's *The Privileged Poor: How Elite Colleges Are Failing Disadvantaged Students*. Despite what schools put out in their PR copy, money, power, and privilege play a larger role than most families realize in who gets admitted to what we think of as the "best" schools.

Rankings and Hierarchies

The idea that there can be only one "best" college in the country is inherently ludicrous. Nonetheless, since 1983, *U.S. News & World Report* has profited from parents' and students' desire for a clear hierarchy, and each year the edition that includes their ranked list of colleges is a bestseller. (The list completely ignores for-profits and community colleges.) Most colleges despise it; only 3 percent of admissions officers agreed that the list actually reflected college quality. But, for many families, this list is crucially important. (In Paul Tough's book, he profiled one student at an affluent Maryland high school whose father took the *U.S. News* rankings of "most selective colleges," drew a line at number thirty, and told her not to bother applying to anything below that line.)

The *U.S. News* ranking is widely criticized by those inside higher education for rewarding perverse behavior that has nothing to do with a college's actual "quality." For example, colleges get a bump in their ratings when they have a lower acceptance rate. This incentivizes colleges to heavily advertise to students to induce them to apply—only to increase the number of applicants they'll reject, thus increasing their "selectivity."

The competition over rankings has also played a devastating role in how colleges allocate their scholarship money, and whether the money goes to the students who need it the most. Liz Willen explained to me how that's happened, and how families can figure out if the college they're looking at is committed to serving students outside the top income brackets.

Liz Willen
Brooklyn, NY

Liz Willen is the editor in chief of the nonprofit news site the Hechinger Report, which covers equity issues in both K–12 and higher education. She's been an education reporter for many decades, and her own two children are recent college graduates.

Inequality, she tells me, looks different in the college space than in K–12 education. "I would never consider private school for my kid K–12. Ever, ever, ever," she said. "But I thought very differently about the application process for college. I did not feel that the only option was for them to go to public schools, because the choices are different, the populations are different, the issues are different. . . . But here's the problem—there's only a few schools that can afford to be need blind [to admit students regardless of their ability to pay]. And what you have is a lot of colleges just giving lip service to this. There are definitely some schools that do better at it, and who make more of an effort than others, and the best way I've found to quantify this is to look at the Pell grants."

Pell grants are a form of need-based financial aid that are primarily given to low-income students. Though it's not a perfect measure—Paul Tough notes that, because of a complex eligibility formula, "some families making more than $80,000 receive Pell grants, and some earning less than $30,000 do not." But a school's Pell grant percentage will at least give some picture of how many students at given colleges are outside the very top income bracket. Many colleges list the percentage of Pell recipients on their website; *U.S. News & World Report* also publishes the information, broken down by type of school. There's a vast spread. Among liberal arts colleges, the percentage of Pell recipients at a given school ranges from over 90 percent down to only 10.

While colleges like to boast about their generous financial aid packages, those same colleges are often spending the bulk of their financial aid dollars on wealthy students. In *Indebted: How Families Make College Work at Any Cost*, Caitlin Zaloom traces the pattern: since the *U.S. News* ranking system rewards colleges for admitting students with high GPAs and test scores, colleges and universities "give preference for admission to students from middle-class and upper-class families whose grades and test scores reflect their class advantages. . . . Instead of increasing resources for low-income students, merit aid curtails them." A school that charges $70,0000 of tuition and fees each year will make a gamble by giving a $30,000 "merit aid" scholarship to a high-scoring student whose family *could* pay the full sticker price. They are betting that the "discount" will induce the student to choose their school, bringing both their high test scores and $40,000 in tuition with them. Merit aid students, Zaloom writes, "bring in a double financial benefit for the colleges and universities: not only do they pay more in tuition, they cost less in financial aid."

Liz has seen this practice in action. She's seen the children of millionaires receive large merit scholarships, a practice that bothered her. In one instance, she said, after learning that a student from an extremely wealthy family got a $30,000 scholarship, she says, "I just felt like screaming at the admissions people, 'This was not necessary! He was going to go there anyways!'"

In her reporting, she's also seen what happens to low-income students when so much of many college's financial aid budgets goes to students without financial need. She spent a year following six low-income Black and Latino students at a Boston charter school while they navigated college admissions. She tells me, "In the end, most of their choices were really disappointing because even the schools that gave them what they considered really generous scholarships of $30,000 to $40,000—it simply wasn't enough." (Those numbers used to be the amount of a "full ride"—today, they're often less than half of tuition at a private school.)

In addition to looking at the percentage of Pell grant students, another resource for parents is the website TuitionTracker.org, a data compilation put out by the Hechinger Report, that tells families both the "sticker price" of a school and how much students in different income brackets can actually expect to pay. (Unlike the U.S. News & World Report, it includes for-profit schools and community colleges.) It's a valuable resource for families to figure out their own likely cost, but also to help determine whether a schools' rhetoric about their commitment to economic and racial diversity is backed up by their numbers.

After I talked to Liz, I looked at the Tuition Tracker data for Dartmouth College, a school that had come up in our conversation. The site showed that the "sticker price" is a whopping $80,327 a year;

55 percent of students actually paid that sum. For students who don't pay full price, Tuition Tracker shows the projected "net price" for students from families at various income levels. That "net price" reveals that Dartmouth, like many other colleges, spends much of its financial aid budget on its higher-income students. For instance, the Tracker shows that a family making an annual income of between $0 and $30,000 would need to pay approximately $18,042 a year to attend Dartmouth, only $2,000 less per year than a family making more than twice as much—a family making between $75,000 and $110,000 would have a projected price of $21,186. The "sticker price" of over eighty grand a year isn't affordable for either of those families, of course. But the site shows that the school's financial aid reduces the price for these very differently situated families to the same number—roughly $20,000 a year. That's a huge outlay of money for anyone, but it's more in the realm of possibility for a family making close to, or just over, six figures, who may have been able to start a 529 account, than it is for a family in the bottom quintile of income earners, who almost certainly has not been able to save. The issue, in other words, isn't that the students in the higher bracket don't need aid but that the lowest income students need much more than they are likely to get.

The demographic information on Tuition Tracker also reflects whether colleges are, as Liz put it, "fulfilling their promise to low-income and minority students." The tracker includes the racial demographics of a school and the graduation rate broken down by student race. "When we were looking at schools for my kids, in an instant I could look at it and say, 'Wow, this school is way too White, or wow, this school is way too filled with wealthy kids, or this school does way too little. . . . And it definitely hit me about three schools [which her sons considered] that were very much in that category: Oberlin, Skidmore, and Kenyon. Three excellent liberal arts schools which were very, very White."

She cautions that it will take more to achieve equity in college education than for schools to simply admit (and offer aid to) low-income students. "The other story that's often ignored is not just what kind of a job colleges do to get them in the door, but how the students do once they get there. How comfortable do they feel? Do they have groups for first-gen students? Do they offer things in different languages?" One of the six students Liz followed from the Boston charter school, Daniel Inoa, is a Dominican first-generation college student who got one of the rare full rides to Dartmouth. He's on track to graduate on time; Liz expects to attend his graduation next year. But during his time at college, he's repeatedly been excluded and made to feel out of place, including being told that by a fellow student at a party that he "looked suspicious." As she put it, "He's struggled a lot as a minority student at a very White town, in a very wealthy school that's very big on taking the children of alumni." (More than one-fifth of Dartmouth students come just from families in the top 1 percent of earners; the overwhelming majority of students there come from families in the top 20 percent of income earners.)

Liz anticipates that these equity issues are going to get worse before they get better, since the pandemic has sent shockwaves through the higher education system and left all but the wealthiest schools slashing budgets and, in some cases, shuttering altogether. For those that remain, Liz says, "The full-pay students are absolutely going to get in so much easier. They're going to be favored—colleges are not going to want to admit it, but it's going to be the case."

Her message to all parents, regardless of whether they're interested in the broader equity issues in higher education, is to disentangle themselves and their own egos from the process. During her older son's application process, the *Washington Post* published Liz's top ten don'ts list for parents, which included this advice: "DO NOT think of college admissions decisions as a reflection or referendum on your parenting skills or how you raised your child." Even with her extensive expertise about colleges, admissions, and education in general, she reflects on the fact that "all of the things I thought about as a parent were almost irrelevant, it was really about who they were, and what they wanted to do." Both of her sons attended music conservatory schools that didn't even look at their SAT scores—for her own children, the process came down to how well they performed at an audition. She added, "I spent a lot of time and effort helping both of them, and they both found their own way without me. There was nothing they needed from me at all."

In a piece she wrote shortly after the Varsity Blues scandal, she noted that the United States "can't produce more college graduates without getting more low-income students to and through college." So just because her own two sons didn't need much help doesn't mean that Liz's expertise on college matters has gone to waste. She's seen it as part of her own mission to use that knowledge to help kids whose parents might not be college educated, or who don't have access to the college counseling that's standard at wealthier schools. "I use all this expertise and help kids on the side," she said. "I've probably helped about forty kids over the last few years with their essays and their applications."

A New Ranking System: Mobility Report Cards

The Hechinger Report's Tuition Tracker is one resource for families looking to see how colleges are actually spending their money. You can also look at a college's "mobility report card."

The mobility report cards are the result of an extensive research project by a team of economists, headed by Raj Chetty, John Friedman, and Nathaniel Hendren, who used millions of anonymized tax records to track both where students from different income brackets attended college and how much money those students made in the decades after they graduated from college. The researchers were then able to produce a list of colleges with a high proportion of students who come from families in the bottom fifth of the income distribution but who, a few years after graduating and entering the workforce, rise to the top three-fifths.

The list of the ten colleges with the highest "mobility rate" doesn't look much like the *U.S. News* "top college" list; it's mostly made up of public universities in New York and California, two states that historically have invested in what a *New York Times* article called their "working-class colleges." But these are the school that are fulfilling one of the original purposes of higher education in this country.

The study also revealed that the colleges that do make the "best" list on the *U.S. News* list are mostly perpetuating the already-existing advantages of their students. These schools do very little to provide economic mobility, in part because they admit so few students who aren't already at the top of the income distribution. Thirty-eight highly selective schools, including five of the eight Ivy League schools, have more students who come from families in *just* the top 1 percent (from families with incomes over $630,000 a year) than the entire bottom 60 percent. At a few highly selective liberal arts schools, nearly one-quarter of the student body came from families in the top 1 percent alone. These schools often do give very generous aid to the students whom they admit from lower-income brackets; they just admit so few of them as to be statistically insignificant.

Just as students from affluent families are often unaware of the for-profit and community college systems, lower-income families often aren't aware of options outside those two systems. Two professors, Caroline Hoxby and Christopher Avery, have extensively studied the application behaviors of students from different income brackets. Students from the top two income brackets tend to apply to a wide variety of schools, including schools that are extremely competitive. However, they found that "the vast majority of high-achieving students who are low-income do not apply to *any* selective college or university." Changing that pattern has been part of the mission of the College Advising Corps.

Nicole Hurd
Raleigh, NC

In 2004, when Nicole was working as a dean at the University of Virginia, she was invited to a meeting with the Jack Kent Cooke Foundation, a philanthropic organization that focuses on college access and scholarships for high-achieving, low-income students. She went into the meeting prepared to talk about all the reasons that the foundation should help fund UVA students in their postgraduate work. During the meeting, though, she saw some numbers that changed the course of her life.

"Coming from an administrator and academic background, I am moved by data," she says. More than fifteen years later, she still remembers the numbers that she saw in that meeting: 79 percent of high school seniors in Virginia were graduating on time, but only 53 percent were attending college. The ratio of school counselors to students in the state was one counselor to every 369 students. "My children were not old enough at the time for me to fully comprehend that ratio at the high school level, but my immediate reaction was *This is unacceptable*," she says. It seemed that looking at those numbers, in her capacity as both an educator and a parent, they told a story of "an incredible waste of talent and potential." Walking out of the meeting, she was already thinking about how she might be able to move those numbers in a different direction.

Later that week, after sharing her idea with a few colleagues, she sent an email to the foundation outlining her proposal: a college advising program that would place recent college graduates, particularly those who themselves were first-generation, low-income, and students of color, into underserved high schools to serve as college advisers and help the students a few years behind them through the application process. "Who better than somebody who looks like the students, talks like the students, comes from the same community, to say those four words that every student needs to hear—the words 'I believe in you'—to help them get to higher education," she says.

The program started with fourteen advisers in Virginia. After a successful first year, the foundation decided to invest $10 million to take the program to scale. At the time, she was still working as an administrator and teaching; she also had two kids under the age of five. "It wasn't the calmest time in my life," she says with a laugh. A big career transition hadn't been something she'd expected. "I thought I'd be at UVA forever, I was very pleased with my job. My husband was happy. We had two young kids." But after she got that phone call, she went back to her husband and said, "I've never been involved in anything more important. I've never been involved in something more meaningful. And I want to go with this." She left her administrator role. In its early days, the organization was incubated by the University of North Carolina at Chapel Hill. It became a freestanding nonprofit in 2013. Today, the program has 803 advisers with 31 university chapters; 55 percent of the advisers are first-generation college graduates, 66 percent are people of color, and 69 percent were Pell-eligible students in college. They are, as Nicole describes, "a living embodiment of the Michelle Obama quote about when you walk through the door of opportunity, your job is to pull the next person through and not let the door close."

Though her own children are not direct beneficiaries of the program, she sees the work as connected to her parenting values. "One of the things that's always motivated me from the beginning of this was thinking about my kids, and thinking about what kind of institutions I want them in, and what kind of world I want them to be part of. I've always thought about doing this work as a way to ensure they grow up in a more just, more inclusive, more diverse world that holds more people up."

When I spoke with Nicole, her daughter was a college freshman, her son a high school senior. Seeing them navigate their own college application process, particularly during the pandemic, made her even more passionate about addressing the formidable obstacles that prevent kids from getting to college. "I was here when [my son] took his AP tests in his bedroom . . . , but he has a bedroom to take his AP tests. And I thought about all the students that we've encouraged to *aim high, take an AP test*, who were forced, because of the pandemic, to take their AP tests in a closet or a bathroom."

She also saw how, even for her own kids, who have college-educated parents and what she described as "an incredible support system around them" that the process was stressful and exhausting. "I still saw the stress. I still saw the tears. I still saw that the insecurity that we all have when we're putting ourselves out that way. . . . It was a vivid reminder of how important our advisers are and how we need to support student and families at this critical time."

She sees problems on both sides of the college divide. First-generation families get the messages that student loan debt is out of control and that maybe college isn't for them. "I always worry that when we tell the story of student loan debt in this country, we don't explain where that debt is sitting. The reality is that college, if you make an informed choice, is the best investment you can make"— unless you are, as Nicole puts it, "snapped up by a bad actor" from the for-profit industry, which is overwhelmingly responsible for the number of students with high debt that they have no way to pay for.

On the other side of the income scale, she sees how students from the highest income families receive incredible pressure to attend certain institutions. "There's a lot of pressure in certain segments of our society that if you don't go to school X, you are failing. That's not true. It's just not true. A matter of fact, I love the fact that we're living at a point in time where, you know, President Biden went to the University of Delaware and Vice-President Harris went to Howard, an HBCU. These are great institutions, and they are not just those 'top five schools' that dominate the rankings."

She encourages parents from every background to change their mindset when thinking about colleges, from scarcity to abundance. "We have an incredibly diverse, powerful higher education system in this country. And its diversity is part of its strength. Look at it from the vantage point of abundance: There is a college for you. There is an opportunity for you. And if you don't get into your dream college the first time, you can go someplace else and then transfer if you really think that's the place for you. But the reality is that you've got to look at this space from the perspective of abundance. Otherwise, it can be a toxic process. And we don't want anybody to go through that."

She has several ideas for parents who are troubled by the equity issues in higher education, whether they have college-aged kids or not. She shared Liz Willen's thoughts about the important role that parents can have in sharing their knowledge beyond their own family. The founding principle of the College Advising Corps was the idea that, for the advisers in the program, "You've just built a muscle by applying to and succeeding in college, now you can help somebody else apply to college." Nicole elaborates, "So I would say to parents, 'Are you and your student using the muscle that you developed for you to get through this process—in service of others, how might you pay it forward to somebody else?'"

She also thinks that college-educated parents can be part of ensuring that their own alma maters take this issue seriously. If you give to your college, she says, "You can actually designate money for scholarships for first-generation, low-income, and underrepresented students. Or if they have a College Advising Corps chapter, if they have a bridge program, a pipeline program, a talent identification program—give to those things. Make it a priority that your alma mater has a strategy to build pipelines of talent and opportunity."

Finally, alumni need to hold their institutions to account for how they serve all their students. "Hold your university to account if this is something you care about. Look at graduation rates, see what priorities are funded, and use your voice. Ensuring we have diversity, equity, and inclusion in higher education is a shared responsibility— administration, faculty, alumni—we all need to address these critical issues of access and opportunity together."

Colleges and Wealth

A depressing reality of the current admissions landscape is the number of colleges and universities that do get away with what Nicole referred to as a "Hallmark card" approach to expanding access to underserved students—splashing pictures carefully curated to highlight "diversity" and touting its need-blind admission policies, all while giving the wealthiest students the easiest path to admission. The problems with equity in higher education won't be fixed by simply encouraging more low-income students to apply. The schools have to let them in. And two books, written fifteen years apart, tell the same story: students from donor families, student athletes, and legacy students take up a huge percentage of any admitted class at highly selective colleges.

Daniel Golden's 2005 book *The Price of Admission: How America's Ruling Class Buys Its Way into Elite Colleges—and Who Gets Left Outside the Gates* includes a reference to a study that found that, at a certain unnamed Ivy League college, only 40 percent of slots for the freshman class were open to students who didn't have a "nonacademic preference." A "nonacademic preference" might include being a recruited athlete, a "development case" (the euphemistic term for students whose parents have donated millions to the school), a legacy (the child or grandchild of an alumni), a child of a celebrity, or the child of a faculty member. Even worse, candidates admitted for one of the five aforementioned reasons can actually take away several slots. As Golden writes, colleges and universities will resort to underhanded strategies of "admitting a subpar candidate for institutional reasons and then defusing potential criticism . . . by taking every other higher-ranking applicant from the same school." Golden discovered that a well-connected student secured admission to Princeton not only for himself (whose grades and scores were far below other admitted applicants) but for every other student who applied to Princeton at his private high school. In other words, in its effort to dodge claims of unfairness from parents at a particular high school, the school tilted the already-competitive admissions numbers even more against students outside that particular student's elite bubble.

Though *The Price of Admission* was published over fifteen years ago, Jeffrey Selingo's 2020 book *Who Gets In and Why: A Year Inside College Admissions* suggests that little has changed with the admissions landscape. One notable chapter looks at the role that sports play in who gets into highly competitive liberal arts schools. For instance, Amherst College, a small, selective liberal arts school, reserves 157 of its 490 admissions slots for athletes—nearly a third of every admitted class. Amherst isn't a school that anyone would immediately associate with sports. It doesn't have a giant stadium or sold-out homecoming games. But relative to its size, it has a greater percentage of student athletes than Ohio State. The sports for which Amherst and schools like it recruit—water polo, squash, sailing, crew, skiing—are, as both Golden and Selingo note, almost exclusively played by wealthy, White students.

Another revelation in Selingo's book (covered in Paul Tough's work as well) is that families who can pay full or close-to-full tuition price have a much easier road to admission than families who need financial aid. In the past decade, selective colleges have begun employ "quants" from consulting firms who engage in complex statistical analyses in order to "optimize" a college's incoming class. "Optimizing" a class, in this context, means doling out *just* enough financial aid to maximize tuition revenue. As Selingo puts it, this practice is "a far cry from the origins of financial aid in the 1960s, when it was intended to help poor and middle-income students afford college." Nowadays, he writes, "College leaders talk about pricing strategies like airline executives and retailers do." One unusually candid admissions officer at DePaul University told Paul Tough that this computer algorithm leads them to admit "students we'd like to turn down" if those students have the ability to pay full price. And of course, the flipside of that practice is that low-income students may get shut out from college altogether, particularly if their grades and test scores aren't at the very top of the pile.

The algorithm, and the skewed distribution of financial aid, also hurts middle-class families. In *Indebted: How Families Make College Work at Any Cost*, Caitlin Zaloom defines "middle class" as families in which "the parents make too much money or have too much wealth for their children to qualify for major federal higher education grants" (such as the Pell grant) but who "earn too little or possess insufficient wealth to pay full fare at most colleges"—a definition that may apply to many readers of this book. If a child from a middle-class family beats the long odds in the admissions game and gets into a selective school, their parents are often encouraged to take on crushing levels of debt to allow their child to attend their "dream school." Though these families may receive some financial aid, they're often shocked by the dollar amount that colleges calculate is "affordable" for them to pay each year. This is the optimization algorithm at work again—colleges are making the gamble that, once a family is invested in their child attending a particular school, the parents (or the children themselves) will "make it work," even if that means that either the student or their parents will have student loan payments for decades. Colleges are excellent at marketing to both students and parents, and at convincing eighteen-year-olds that their entire futures and their very sense of self should hinge on attending a particular school.

Legacy Admission

Of course, students aren't the only ones who get enamored with certain colleges. If you're a parent reading this book, you likely went to college and may feel a strong connection to the school you attended. That feeling, shared by many parents, makes the issue of "legacy admissions" particularly fraught. Parents who loved their college may dream of sending their child to attend the same school. And the "legacy preference" that many private institutions give to the children of alumni can smooth the path toward making that dream a reality.

The size of the legacy bump came under particular scrutiny in the past five years in connection with a case that wasn't overtly challenging legacy admission at all—*Students for Fair Admissions v. Harvard.* ("Students for Fair Admissions" evokes a grassroots organization of concerned students, but the case was brought by Edward Blum, a wealthy legal strategist with a lifelong goal of ending the practice of affirmative action in college admissions. He has no connection to Harvard whatsoever and has bankrolled many other cases with the same goal.) The trial made public some previously hidden information about the role of legacy in Harvard's admission process, including the fact that legacies are admitted to Harvard at nearly five times the rate of other applicants. Many commenters noted that if the court found that Harvard's affirmative action policies, which gave preference to students from minority backgrounds, were unconstitutional, it would be particularly egregious to leave in place legacy admission, which some have called "affirmative action for the rich" or "affirmative action for Whites."

In May 2021 Colorado became the first state in the country to outlaw legacy admissions for its public universities, a move that many saw as mostly symbolic, since legacy admission mostly aren't used at public colleges to begin with. At many private universities, however, particularly at those with extremely competitive admissions practices, legacies remain in use, and remain a fraught topic.

Ashton Lattimore
Bryn Mawr, PA

Ashton is the editor-in-chief of Prism, a nonprofit news organization whose mission statement is to "center the people, places, and issues currently underreported by national media." She lives with her husband and two young sons. I reached out to talk to her about legacy admissions after reading a nuanced op-ed that she wrote about the subject for the *Washington Post*.

She received both an undergraduate degree and a law degree from Harvard. On the one hand, she loved her experience at the school and would love for her sons to go there too. Harvard and other elite colleges, she told me, can be particularly powerful for Black students like herself. These colleges, she says, "are places where when you walk in the door, they tell you how special you are, how you're meant to rule the world, and here are all the ways you're going to do it. Now, for John C. Wigglesworth XIV, he probably doesn't need to hear that—because he's from generations and generations of families who have already been on top of every part of society, the banks, the courts, the governments." But Ashton says that for her, "a Black girl from a middle-class family in New Jersey, . . . to have that institutional imbuing of privilege, and a sense of entitlement that's not bred into us by society—it can be dangerous in the wrong hands—but there can also be a great deal of value."

She wrote in her article that, because of the ways that her Harvard education benefited her, and because of admission acceptance rates that "seem to be inching ever nearer to zero percent," it's tempting to wish that Harvard would hang onto its legacy admission practices. As she puts it, "For underrepresented Black, Latino and Native American alumni, the prospect of our children finally being able to lay claim to the legacy advantage after hundreds of years of being shut out feels hard-won and precious. . . . It's been only a few decades since we were welcomed into predominantly white colleges and universities in any significant numbers; we've had only a generation or two to begin building our own legacies."

But she doesn't think that legacy is overall a good thing, nor does she want Harvard to continue the practice, even if it has the potential to benefit her own children. As she relates, "I continue to think that broadly speaking, it's not a social good—and I continue to hold that with the fact that I really liked Harvard, I really liked that I got to go, and I'd really like it if my children got to go—but I can hold those two things at the same time."

At the time she wrote the op-ed, she says, she had assumed that *Students for Fair Admissions v. Harvard* would reach the Supreme Court and that the conservative majority would rule against affirmative action, thus leading to a natural end for the legacy preference as well. But shortly after we spoke, the court of appeals sided with Harvard and upheld their use of racial preference in admissions. It's unclear as of this writing whether the Supreme Court will hear the case; in June 2021 the court asked the US solicitor general to file a brief expressing the views of the US Justice Department, since the case has potential national significance.

Legacy, and affirmative action policies, thus remain in an unclear limbo. (Harvard could, of course, on its own volition, get rid of its legacy preference without any further court rulings, a move that many of its alumni are pushing for.)

Ashton concluded her article with this statement, which leaves any parent with something to think about: "Much more than I want my son to walk an easier path to the Ivy League, I want a higher-education system that welcomes new and diverse families. Instead of him gaining an advantage on a college application, I'd rather see him inherit a fairer world."

Takeaways

There are parents who read about the gamesmanship behind admissions decisions and decide to play to win, who urge their kids to pursue competitive squash at an early age, or if they have the money, try to become a "development case" themselves. (Daniel Golden, the journalist who wrote *The Price of Admission*, described being besieged by parents after the book's publication who saw his work as a "how-to" guide and begged him to name the size of donation they'd need to make to get their child into an Ivy League school.)

There are also those who say, *Enough!* Who, for their own peace of mind, their child's mental health, and their financial well-being want to find another way to approach college admissions.

It's not easy to opt out of college admissions mania, and I know that as a parent of a four-year-old I don't even fully appreciate the extent of the pressure. But Jeffrey Selingo's book has good news for parents who want to opt out of the panic over the "ever-shrinking club of elite colleges." There are, he writes, "plenty of seats available at U.S. campuses for the two million high school graduates each year who plan to go to college." Nicole Hurd of College Advising Corps echoed the same idea when she talked about approaching college admissions with a mindset of abundance rather than scarcity earlier in this chapter.

A few changes in recent years have given small nods to equity problems in higher education. In 2019 the College Board launched the Environmental Context Dashboard, colloquially known as the "adversity index," which allows admissions officers to view information about a student's neighborhood and high school when viewing his SAT or ACT scores. This would allow an admission officer to, as the board put it, "view a student's academic accomplishment in the context of where they live and learn." I first heard about the adversity index from at a panel on college admissions sponsored by Yale. A speaker on the panel who ran an expensive test prep company said that after the announcement of the index came out, his phone was "ringing off the hook" from families worried that their child came from a "low-adversity family." But he assured the assembled parents it wasn't worth worrying about; it wasn't like colleges were going to stop admitting privileged kids. (The College Board quickly scrapped a plan that would assign every student a single "adversity score" after facing a "storm of criticism from parents and educators," presumably parents and educators invested in the admission prospects of "low-adversity" kids.)

But the adversity index, and other solutions like it, is based upon the faulty idea that colleges are desperate to admit low-income students, if only they could find appropriately qualified applicants. One innovative program that is challenging that framework is an initiative started by the National Education Equity Lab, which enrolled hundreds of low-income students in a few select classes at top universities. The students, who came from all around the country and were low-income students of color, attended the classes virtually and had to complete college-level coursework to pass. Out of the group, 86 percent passed their courses, thus proving that they were, in fact, capable of doing the work that the colleges (Harvard, Yale, and Cornell, among others) required. Leslie Cornfeld, the founder and CEO of the organization, pointedly told the *New York Times* that she hoped the program would encourage colleges to pursue high-achieving students from low-income backgrounds "with the same enthusiasm and success with which they identify top athletes." But, of course, the colleges must take her up on that challenge. And behind the secretive admission curtain, the reality is still that, at most colleges, full-pay students with middling grades and test scores face a much easier path toward acceptance than higher-scoring but lower-income students.

Many of the problems outlined will require legislative action. In 2019 Representative Pramila Jayapal and Senator Sherrod Brown introduced the Students Not Profits Act, which would deal a major legislative blow to the predatory practices of for-profit colleges, who rely upon economically disadvantaged students' ability to get federally backed student loans to finance their educations. State legislation likewise has an important role to play. Just after the 2008 financial crisis, states slashed not only their funding for K–12 schools but also funding for their state colleges. One report found that overall state funding for both two- and four-year colleges was $6.6 billion less in 2018 than it had been in 2008, a decrease that's partially responsible for the rapid increase in the tuition that public colleges were charging during that time. Families who are dealing with the fallout from these policies tend to focus on trying to scrape together the tuition for their own kid; calling representatives about restoring state funding is low on their list. Staying informed about proposed legislation on both the state and federal level, and urging lawmakers to pass it, is one important part of the solution.

But the equity issues at private, selective colleges—the ways that financial aid is used not to open doors for students who need it but as a "discount" to get wealthier students in the door, or the role that legacy admissions and sports play in giving further advantages to the already advantaged—won't be solved by legislation. Change must come instead from both administrators and trustees of individual institutions, and from a cultural shift in which we all demand that colleges do more than replicate the existing advantages of the students that are admitted.

The problem, like all deep-rooted social problems, is a bigger one than any one family can solve. But for parents who are troubled by the status quo, here are some proposed steps:

- **Work locally to address the gap in college counseling.** Jerry Lucido, the executive director of the Center for Enrollment Research, Policy, and Practice at the University of Southern California suggested in an email that a place for parents who are troubled by these gaps in higher education to start is "to demand that their local middle and high school counseling offices include a concerted program of college guidance." College Advising Corps, Nicole Hurd's program, is in seventeen states and working on expanding to others; it also has an online program to provide individual counseling to students who have high grade point averages and test scores and come from families that make less than $80,000 a year. College counseling, whether it comes from an online counselor or an in-school one, can help first-generation students overcome the admission hurdles that students with built-in parent support can get over with ease. Counseling can also help steer students away from for-profit recruiters—these recruiters rely on being a prospective student's only source of information about college.

- **Share your knowledge with students who need it.** I don't know as much about college admission as Liz Willen does (few people do). But I know generally how to put together a college application, how to write an essay, and how to fill out a FAFSA. I can follow Liz's lead and lend that knowledge to help college-bound students navigate the college admissions labyrinth. The parents with the most knowledge about colleges are often concentrated in high schools where students have no shortage of adults who can guide them, and many privileged parents have no one in their immediate circles who need their help. Consider the following places to look for opportunities to provide that help:

  o College Track, www.collegetrack.org

  o College Essay Guy has a program called Matchlighters that connects students with someone to help with their essay: https://www.collegeessayguy.com/matchlighters

  o Go Ladder Up, https://www.goladderup.org/get-involved/tap -volunteering/ (a good choice particularly for parents with an accounting or financial background who can help fill out a FAFSA)

o UPchieve, https://upchieve.org/volunteer

- **Change the conversation.** Tuition Tracker and the mobility report card have given me a different framework for evaluating colleges and the ability to look beyond the platitude that nearly every school spouts about valuing "diversity" or being "need blind." It inevitably affects the culture of an institution when nearly every student comes from a family of extreme means. I loved my experience at Whitman, but I'm not very excited about my own daughter going there after having seen the depressing picture that those two websites have shown me of the institution. It was a wealthy, White school when I attended, and has become dramatically more so. It gives some of the least financial aid to needy students among its peer institutions.

- **Hold your alma mater accountable.** Institutions are extraordinarily sensitive to pressure from groups of their alumni (particularly if those alumni donate money). In the spring and summer of 2020, many alumni groups from private colleges wrote open letters to administrations that detailed the colleges' history of marginalizing, underserving, and discriminating against Black students. Some of these letters garnered hundreds of signatures; nearly all received extensive responses from the colleges. If colleges thought their prospective donors were paying attention to their financial aid numbers, to their commitment to antiracism work beyond facile "diversity" initiatives, they would change. Colleges also justify their use of legacy admissions by saying that alumni won't donate to the school without that. If alumni banded together and demanded that colleges stop the use of legacy admissions, the practice could be gone in a few years.

- **Give to the programs that will make a difference.** Universities and colleges almost always push alumni to donate to an "unrestricted" fund—but most have specific programs that benefit low-income, first-generation students. Give to those if you're in the position to.

Further Reading

Indebted: How Families Make College Work at Any Cost by Caitlin Zaloom (Princeton University Press, 2019)

The Inequality Machine: How College Divides Us by Paul Tough (Houghton Mifflin Harcourt, 2019)

Lower Ed: The Troubling Rise of For-Profit Colleges in the New Economy by Tressie McMillan Cottom (New Press, 2017)

The Price of Admission: How America's Ruling Class Buys Its Way into Elite Colleges—and Who Gets Left Outside the Gates by Daniel Golden (Broadway Books, 2006)

The Price You Pay for College: An Entirely New Road Map for the Biggest Financial Decision Your Family Will Ever Make by Ron Lieber (Harper, 2021)

Who Gets In and Why: A Year Inside College Admissions by Jeffrey Selingo (Scribner, 2020)

4

ACTIVISM, MUTUAL AID, AND GRASSROOTS ORGANIZING

NEFERTITI AUSTIN, a writer and teacher in L.A., writes in the opening pages of her memoir *Motherhood So White* about her many privileges: stamps on her passport from three continents, a law degree, standing hair and massage appointments. But none of that had prepared her for the reality of parenting her Black son, a child she'd adopted out of the foster care system. In the opening scene of the book, she decides to take her then-five-year-old son to a protest after Trayvon Martin's death, even though doing so will disrupt his bedtime routine. She writes, "Trayvon's murder spoke to all aspects of my identity: Black woman, single Black mother, historian, sister, cousin, coworker, friend, lover. I could not ignore what was happening to Black boys all around me, or rationalize the violence away to convince myself that [my son] would be spared. . . . I was part of a club whose sole membership requirements was being the mother of a Black boy, and feeling the weight of that keenly for the first time."

Four years after Trayvon Martin's death, Martin's own mother, Sybrina Fulton, gave a speech at the Democratic National Convention that evoked a similar idea. She described herself as "an unwilling participant in this movement," saying "I would not have signed up for this. . . . I didn't want this spotlight. But will I do everything I can to focus some of that light on a path out of this darkness."

Fulton, and other mothers who lost their children to gun violence (often at the hands of police), have formed the advocacy group Mothers of the Movement; many of them have run for office. Some mothers had a long history of local organizing, but others didn't. Lucy McBath (whose seventeen-year-old son Jordan Davis was shot to death by a man angry about his "loud music") had worked as flight attendant for her whole career but felt called to a different kind of work after her son's murder. She has since become a spokesperson for gun control; in 2018 she ran for and won a seat in Congress.

As I read and thought about social movements and activists, both present and past, I came to think that one way to define privilege is that you are never forced into activism. Activism, organizing work, and grassroots movements are about disrupting the status quo. If the status quo serves you, it's the easiest thing in the world to get busy with the exhausting day-to-day responsibilities of parenting, and to put that kind of work at the bottom of the list.

In the place of the harder work of organizing, it can be extremely tempting to do things that feel like activism but really don't accomplish any change. Andrew Lefkowits, the podcast host of the *Integrated Schools* podcast, says that he frequently sees parents who want to see improvement in the school system but don't put in the time to make that happen. "So it happens on social media now," Andrew comments, "it's nasty, and it's personal, and I don't think it's productive. Our democracy muscles are weak. We don't know how to build community power and actually advocate to change things for the better. So we think that writing something nasty or shouting at a school board member in three-minute increments is how to get things done." A prevailing attitude he sees today is that our only role as citizens is just to yell at the people in charge or to "point out how dumb they are for not getting it right."

That kind of "speaking out" feels good, and I do my fair share of it on Twitter. But it's not the same as actually getting something done.

Activism and Privilege

But an easy trap for people with privilege to fall into is tipping over from excitement and dedication into a savior mentality. In his book *No More Heroes: Grassroots Challenges to the Savior Mentality*, Jordan Flaherty traced the damage that the savior mentality has done in various social movements around the world. The savior mentality means "that you want to help others but are not open to guidance from those you want to help. Saviors fundamentally believe they are better than the people they are rescuing. Saviors want to support the struggle of communities that are not their own but believe they must remain in charge. The savior always wants to lead, never to follow. When the people they want to rescue tell them they are not helping, they think those people are mistaken. It is almost taken as evidence that they need *more* help."

The rapid disintegration of the Wall of Moms group in Portland, Oregon, during the summer of 2020 offered an example of how the savior mentality can derail a well-intentioned movement.

In July 2020 federal law enforcement officers responded to nightly racial justice protests in Portland by snatching protestors off the streets in unmarked vans. A Portland parent, Bev Barnum, had put out a call in a Facebook group for mothers to shield the protestors from these guerilla arrests and other violent tactics by the police. In her original post, she wrote, "I want us to look like moms. Because who wants to shoot a mom?"

What it means to "look like a mom" was at the background of everything that happened next. Because of course Black women, Latina women, Indigenous women, disabled women, teenagers, and poor women can all *be* moms—but in this society, "looking like a mom" means "being middle class, middle aged, and White." And the presence of hundreds of women who fit that precise demographic profile at the Portland protests almost immediately garnered national and international attention from the press.

But Black activists who had been doing work for years became disturbed and frustrated when they were invited to join the "leadership" of Wall of Moms while not being included in substantive conversations. The final straw came when Barnum filed papers to make Wall of Moms an official nonprofit without telling other members of the leadership team. Barnum was fired; the group renamed itself Moms United for Black Lives, and women who had already been leaders in the movement took over the leadership role of that organization too. Numerous news outlets published lengthy pieces on what had gone wrong. Keisha N. Blain, a history professor who has written extensively about present and past social movements, told the news website *Vox* that it's not uncommon for White activists to receive greater attention for their work, particularly in Black spaces. The *Vox* article stated that "in Chicago, for example, Black moms formed Mothers/Men Against Senseless Killings in 2015 . . . but have not received the national attention in five years that Wall of Moms did in 10 days." Portland's own deeply divided history was at the backdrop: in the mid-1800s Oregon became the only state in the union to ever explicitly forbid Black people from living in its borders. The city is 77 percent White; the *Atlantic* called it "the Whitest city in America."

In one of the Wall of Moms postmortems, which ran in the magazine *Portland Monthly*, the Portland Black Lives Matter activist

Rachelle Dixon talked about the root problem, and offered a helpful reminder for those who are newer to activism: "As a new organizer, you need to understand that there are things you don't know, and the reason why you want Black leadership is to show you where the minefields are. Because they are out there, and you already stepped on them. And it's not like your voice isn't valuable, but it's that you came in on a conversation *400 years* into the conversation."

Some of Megan Hester's list of questions to ask when joining a school community are also helpful if you're thinking about joining any kind of movement for social change: What has come before us? What have people been working on? What have the challenges been? What have the priorities been?

Activism and Aid Work with Kids

Kids are often disturbed by the injustices of the world. They can see things that adults take as inevitable parts of the status quo (for example, that there are unhoused people living on our city streets) for what they really are—pressing problems that need to be addressed. Local media love to feature stories of children who start their own nonprofits or charities. These stories often follow a similar pattern: a child learns about a social ill in the world (homelessness, illness, deforestation). They want to stop it. They (obviously with parental support and help) launch a new nonprofit; in stories featured by the media, usually they've also raised a large amount of money in a short period of time for a given cause.

And then . . . it's unclear what the next chapter of the story is. Often, those efforts don't have much staying power. Of the ten charities highlighted in a 2013 Buzzfeed article, "10 Incredible Charities Started by Kids," six of the ten were no longer operable, with dead links and no trace of their work beyond that article. One of the few that still remained had been founded by Craig Kielburger when he was twelve; he was still running the charity in his thirties. Yet even he wrote a blog post in *Medium* titled "Don't Start a Charity." He writes, "The problem is that too many people assume they can run a charity, without considering all that it requires in terms of expertise, resources and personnel. Few people believe they could wake up tomorrow and start a highly specialized multi-million-dollar company, but they don't apply that same thinking to starting a nonprofit." In short, if you have a kid who is interested in social justice issues, rarely is it best to channel that passion in such a way that gets media attention or a line on a resume.

Several of the parents I talked to for this chapter mentioned that instead of charity work, their family has become involved in local mutual aid groups. The model has been around for decades but got renewed attention at the beginning of the pandemic. Mutual aid looks different in different parts of the country, but it's essentially a neighborhood group that lives by the idea that everyone in each community has both things to offer and things that they may need. It emphasizes consensus-based decision-making and the dignity and self-determination of the people who need the aid, rather than a model in which self-appointed experts from the outside tell people what they need.

In a book on the practice, *Mutual Aid: Building Solidarity During This Crisis (and the Next)*, Dean Spade, a law professor and trans rights activist, writes about the difference between traditional "charity" and "mutual aid." Deep involvement in mutual aid work, he writes, shouldn't feel like something we are just trying to fit in around the rest of our lives: "Activism and mutual aid shouldn't feel like volunteering or like a hobby—it should feel like living in alignment with our hopes for the world and with our passions. It should enliven us."

Many neighborhoods have preexisting mutual aid groups; in my own neighborhood, it mostly happens through a Facebook group where people can post both requests for help and offers to help with basic tasks: picking up groceries, delivering prescription medicine, or just doing one-on-one Zoom check-ins with people living in isolation. I've found it easier to fold into my life than the way I used to do formal "volunteer" work, which usually involved setting aside hours and going to specific places, often nowhere near my neighborhood. My daughter is too young to really get the idea yet, but having the occasional extra errand be just a part of our regular life will, I hope, teach her about the obligation to help others more than a long lecture ever could.

Tiffany Koyama Lane
Portland, OR

Tiffany Koyama Lane, a third-grade teacher in Portland with two young sons, talked with me about the central role activism and mutual aid work plays in her family's life. "I was doing this work before quarantine, and before George Floyd's murder, but something was cracked open in me and was ignited even more after that," she shares. "It feels like that's such a huge part of my family's values, and what we are a part of, and what we do. And I've shared that with my partner: I want our kids to see that this is what we *do* as a family. We go to marches; we are going to spend our time helping people who are unhoused. This is not an, 'Oh, we're just going to volunteer here or there.' . . . This is part of our family's identity. It's how we spend our time and our resources." She stays connected to the people doing the work, looking for opportunities to work in a behind-the-scenes capacity with various groups serving the city's most marginalized populations.

For parents who have similar visions for their own families, Tiffany suggests that they visit the website Teaching Tolerance as a place to start. Teaching Tolerance started in 1991 as a project of the Southern Poverty Law Center and provides a wealth of resources aimed at helping to "educate children and youth to be active participants in a diverse democracy." Its Social Justice Standards helpfully breaks the large, unwieldy topic of "social justice" into four categories (identity, diversity, justice, and action) and describes what children should be able to actually *do* at various ages. "I don't think there's a thing like 'every kid needs to understand what structural racism is at this point,'" Tiffany says. But she uses the standards in figuring out what conversations to have with her own young sons. At the moment, her own family is focused a lot on the "identity" standards, working toward meeting objectives such as "students will develop language and historical and cultural knowledge that affirm and accurately describe their membership in multiple identity groups" and "students will recognize that people's multiple identities interact and create unique and complex individuals." Tiffany identifies as both White and Asian; her sons are, in her words, "White passing, but they know they're a quarter Asian." The groundwork she had done with the identity standards helped her explain to her older son why, while it was great for him to show up and be loud at protests, it was also important to let Black protestors hold the megaphones and lead chants at the marches.

Even in a city like Portland, famous for its progressive politics (and heavily featured in this chapter), Tiffany sees a lot of resistance among her parent peers to some of the harder work. "It's fascinating watching what people are willing to give up, when they're actually asked to have some skin in the game," she says. "It's really tricky. 'This is what I believe on a bigger level,' can quickly turn to, 'Whoa, you're talking about taking *my* kid's spot,' or 'You're taking that out of *my* pocket?'" She particularly sees that attitude among her White peers, who aren't harmed by the status quo. "I'm pretty shocked at the people I'm close with, who maybe come to some marches . . . , but I can tell, they don't actually see this as their work to do. They'll opt in when they want to. I'm trying to understand that," she says. "I wouldn't want it to be the only reason when everyone is engaged in this work, but I really believe in the idea that 'I'm not free until everyone is free.'"

Grassroots Organizing

The first chapters of this book have focused mostly on individual choices—how your family, individually, treats their childcare provider or chooses a school. These choices matter. But individual choices don't themselves transform an unfair system. In a truly equitable system, Tracy, the Indiana parent choosing between two daycares, wouldn't have had to *decide* not to send her son to the daycare paying seven dollars an hour to its employees; all daycares would pay their staff a living wage. Many European countries have childcare systems that both pay reasonable wages to their staff (still not wages that reflect the difficulty of the job, in my view) and cap a parent's contribution to that childcare at a small percentage of their total wages. Even Tracy's "cheap" option for daycare is dramatically more expensive than childcare would ever cost in countries with subsidized systems. Likewise, in a school system that wasn't rooted in segregationist policies, or reliant on inequitable funding mechanisms like property taxes, the choices of individual parents wouldn't play such a crucial role in determining whether a given school has the resources to educate the children who come through its door.

I spoke with some parents who have created systemic change in their local childcare systems and schools. I wanted to hear from them about what it took to get that done, how they overcame obstacles, and how they stayed motivated during the long path to victory.

Measure 26-214 (Universal Childcare) Portland, OR

The people who are most directly affected by our country's childcare crisis fall into two groups: they are either parents of young kids or childcare workers themselves. Neither of those groups are known for their free time or their disposable income. And any kind of collective action effort takes both time and money.

Tracy, the parent in the childcare section who chose the more expensive of two daycares, succinctly explained why collective action in this space is so hard. Her workplace gave a credit to be used toward childcare, but the amount hadn't changed in decades; it covered less than half the cost of even the cheapest daycares in town. She saw the problem and wanted to make a case for both increasing the amount of the credit and having it reflect inflation. But, she says, "It's such a short part of your life. You feel passionately about it, but you're so exhausted." By the time she felt like she had the energy to bring her case for increasing the tax credit to the higher-ups at her work, she was no longer using it.

In the fall of 2020 organizers in Portland, Oregon, many of whom are parents, achieved an important victory: they succeeded in getting a ballot measure passed that will guarantee universal preschool for all three- and four-year-old children in the county. The measure also guarantees wages starting at eighteen dollars per hour for childcare workers. They achieved this feat despite the measure involving raising taxes, despite a lawsuit that halted their ability to gather signatures, and despite much of their final organizing being done during a pandemic.

I talked to two parents who were involve in the effort, Lydia Kiesling, a novelist and essayist, and Tiffany Koyama Lane. Each of them has two children who, at the time of their organizing, were both under the age of six.

The process of securing universal preschool had taken years of behind-the-scenes work, which started shortly after the 2016 election. (Lydia wrote, in an essay about the process in the *Cut*, "It seemed like America had started wars with less effort than it would take to deploy this one regional preschool program.") Two distinct groups had worked on the project—groups that, to an outsider, would seem to have identical missions: Universal Preschool NOW! and Preschool for All. But the groups were initially split on an important point:

Should the program provide universal *access* to preschool (meaning that parents with the means to pay for preschool would pay out-of-pocket for their own costs)? Or should it be a truly *universal* preschool program, where families wouldn't have to pay tuition, and the costs of running the program would be funded by taxpayers? Preschool for All had developed a vision of a rollout that focused on racial equity, and which had been formulated with a lot of input from communities of color and other groups that were normally marginalized from policy discussions. But its vision of the program did not include paid preschool for all Portland families.

Lydia and other members of the Universal Preschool NOW! group believed that the program needed to be truly universal. She had moved to Portland from San Francisco, partially due to the crushingly high cost of childcare in San Francisco. At one point her family was paying over $3,000 a month for care for their two daughters. Lydia had seen firsthand how the small efforts that San Francisco had made toward solving its childcare crisis, which focused on universal "access," had never gotten enough funding and left huge gaps in coverage. The gaps affected both lower-income families who often didn't know about the program, and families who didn't meet the strict income cutoffs but also couldn't just absorb the extraordinarily high price of daycare or preschool.

For a time, the two groups divided, and Universal Preschool NOW!, the group pushing for a fully universal program, moved forward with getting their initiative on the ballot. Then, the group faced two separate lawsuits, one from the Portland Business Alliance that challenged the constitutionality of the measure, and one from a private preschool that challenged the way the program was described on the ballot. (A few people I spoke with speculated that the suit was motivated by the association's dislike of the new tax that would pay for the program, a marginal income tax on the top 8 percent of earners in the city.) The legal challenges were ultimately unsuccessful, but it cost the group five months of the allotted time to gather the necessary signatures to get the measure on the ballot before the deadline.

By the time the group got the go-ahead to gather the signatures, it was May 2020 and the COVID-19 pandemic had made many common organizing tactics impossible. Given that many people didn't want to leave their homes or be near strangers, the path to getting the measure on the ballot was daunting: the group had less than five weeks to gather 22,636 signatures. They briefly considered trying to get special dispensation to lower the signature requirement owing to the extraordinary circumstances of the pandemic, but they abandoned that plan. Lydia recalled that it was a moment where they just had to throw themselves into the project. She remembered one parent saying, "We should just do this! We can do this; people want this, let's just try to get the signatures."

What happened next proved that parent right—people *did* see the value of the program, and they were willing to sign. "I was stuck at home with my kids and put a bench in my driveway and would ask people to sign," Lydia tells me. She got three hundred signatures by just doing "mom chats"—going to the park, or what she described as "sitting in the driveway accosting people."

Tiffany describes the process of fighting for the initiative as a partnership, in which she and her partner, Tim, each chose the role that played to their strengths. Tim is a stay-at-home parent to their sons; before the pandemic, he had gone to meetings about the project. "For him, going to a meeting in the evening felt like a treat," she says. Her own role was to gather signatures, something that came naturally to her: "This is something I can totally do—I can talk to people, convince people, have conversations."

The five weeks during which Tiffany was gathering signatures intersected with the end of her school year, and the family had even less childcare than they usually do. She credited her supportive partnership as an important part of her ability to gather signatures. While she sometimes brought her sons with her, she would also go out alone, after her workday, and talk about the program to anyone willing to listen.

Several hundred other parents and organizers around the city had done the same work, and after just five short weeks, the group ended up turning in nearly ten thousand more signatures than they needed.

At that point, the Preschool for All group joined forces with the Universal Preschool NOW! group and they worked together to campaign for the initiative's passage. The measure presented to voters included elements that had been championed by the Preschool for All group (a rollout focused on racial equity, and a ban on expulsions from preschool, which have a disproportionate impact on Black boys) and elements from the Universal Preschool NOW! group's vision (a truly universal program that included high wages for teachers). Members from both groups made calls and educated the public via local Facebook groups. In the November 2020 election, it passed with wide margins. The *New York Times* writer Claire Cain Miller called it "one of the most progressive universal preschool policies in the nation." (It's hard to imagine that it's not *the* most—it doesn't have much competition.)

Lydia and Tiffany are both thrilled with the victory but realistic about what comes next. Portland, like most cities in the country, is so far behind on creating necessary care infrastructure that even a plan that's widely touted for being "ambitious" is going to be a long road. "I fought so hard for this thing, and now we got it. . . . But it will take ten years; there's going to be unintended consequences, and sorrow. If the rollout is cumbersome, or if there's too many hoops to jump through, people will initially feel betrayed," Lydia observes. "And I really hate that, but there are just no preschools. There were only spots for 43 percent of kids *before* the pandemic."

I also asked both Tiffany and Lydia how they'd found the motivation to put so much time into something that neither of them will benefit from. By the time the program is fully operational, their children will be teenagers, long past the age when they'll need a childcare program. Lydia said her motivation came partially from knowing that she was a part of creating something that "would have changed my life and helped me so much." When doing phone banking work, Tiffany said the fact that she wouldn't be a direct beneficiary of the program was actually a selling point in getting people to take seriously her pitch that the program would provide indirect benefits to everyone in the community.

Lydia also pointed out that many of the people who were most central to the program's success weren't parents themselves; they were just people who shared a vision of the future that included better access to necessary services for people who need it. And she was also quick to credit the work of the lead organizers for running the process so well. No meeting ever lasted longer than it needed to; every meeting was fun (even over Zoom); and the strong sense of community and shared purpose made even some of the tasks that feel like drudgery feel less taxing. "We joked that it was like a multilevel marketing scheme," Tiffany reflects. "Where each parent got another five parents, and it just spread from there."

Equality in School Funding
Evanston, IL

Around the same time that organizers in Portland were laying the early groundwork for the universal pre-K program, two parents in Evanston, Illinois, started their own ambitious project to change the way schools in their district were funded.

The two parents had only been acquaintances when they had started the project. They lived in different neighborhoods and their children attended different schools. Suni Kartha has a high schooler and a fifth grader; Biz Lindsay-Ryan has a sixth grader and twins in fifth grade. Suni is an attorney and was a school board member at the time we spoke, and Biz works as a racial equity consultant and currently serves on the school board as well, though she wasn't a school board member when they began their project. Four years ago, when their younger children were in first grade, they sat down for their first meeting at a Potbelly Sandwich Shop to begin the process of solving the seemingly intractable problem of inequities in PTA funding.

During the first few years of their children's educations, both Biz and Suni assumed that the schools that their own children attended had roughly the same resources as the other schools in the district. Biz's school had a very small PTA budget; she described herself as "one of a limited number of families who could donate $100 or more to school projects." However, she says, "I didn't know that my kids had less. I assumed that was just how schools worked, and that what we had was what everybody else had." At Suni's school, which had predominantly wealthier families, fundraising looked very different. When Suni's oldest child was in elementary school, the school spent $75,000 (a combination of funds that the school's PTA had in reserve and money raised through a fundraising effort) to install an athletic court and a track. That amount, according to Biz, would have been her school's entire budget for almost three years. Yet because parents were typically siloed within their own school communities, the resource discrepancies often went unnoticed, or at least unacknowledged.

Suni started to realize the extent of the district's issues when she served as PTA president at her school and worked on a referendum that was seeking to right a past wrong. In 1967 the only elementary school in a predominantly Black ward of the town had been closed in the name of desegregation; the neighborhood had been without an elementary school ever since. "That wound has never been dealt with in this community," Suni says. Her work on the referendum, in her words, "shocked me out of my 'liberal bubble' sense of what Evanston was. I realized that there's a whole subset of families that experience the schools a very different way. And those families were predominantly Black and Latino."

After her experience working on the referendum, Suni ran for the school board on a platform of increasing equity in the district. Being on the school board allowed her to fully see the way that PTA fundraising made a stark difference in what activities, facilities, and opportunities different schools could offer. When playground equipment became broken or damaged at some schools, for instance, it would be replaced by PTAs in short order; other schools wouldn't be able to make replacements and would just do with less. When Suni started asking around to see if anyone else saw this is as a problem, she heard from various administrators something along the lines of, "Yeah, this is a problem, we've tried to address it, but it goes nowhere." She was "just naïve enough, optimistic enough to think, *We should be able to do something about this—we are an educated, resourced, knowledgeable community.*" She also learned from talking to older members of the community, whose children were now adults, that they remembered the problem from when their own children were in school. That fact strengthened her sense even further that something needed to change. She thought, "*This is the worst kept secret. This is not a new problem. . . . We just have to be willing to sit down, talk to each other, and share information,* and once we do that and have a bunch of different perspectives . . . I felt confident that if we could get to that point, that people would feel like, 'Yeah, we can and should do something.'" She learned that Biz, who at that time was working as a racial equity consultant for the district, was also interested in the issue. When they sat down to talk about it, they didn't know that they were embarking on an all-consuming project that would also turn into a close friendship. "There's no one in my life I see more than Suni, and that includes some of my family members," Biz says.

As a school board member, Suni could have sought to mandate, as a matter of board policy, that all schools in the district use a new funding structure. But her research made her wary of that option; it had gone badly elsewhere. In 2011 the Santa Monica–Malibu Unified School District had passed a policy barring parents from making donations to their individual schools and centralizing funding. That decision had led to what *Slate* described as a "parent revolt" among the Malibu parents. Nine years later, as of this writing, the two districts are in the midst of what the *Los Angeles Times* called a "stormy, high-profile divorce."

Biz and Suni both agreed that what they really needed was buy-in from the people in power at every school. To get that buy-in, they saw another fork in the road. "We knew we could stack the deck," Biz recalls, by choosing representatives from each school who would support the plan. But if they did that, they anticipated meeting resistance later. Instead, they went with a second option: "Make it as hard as possible to get off the ground but then have the buy-in we needed."

After more than three years of meeting resistance from parents in their peer groups, both Biz and Suni have deep insight into resistance to funding equity—both its root causes and how it manifests. Suni reflects on the typical mindset that she saw: "Every parent wants to believe that they're doing the best thing for their child. Society has trained us that there's a certain way to advocate for our children and that it's 'we've got to make sure we get as much as we can.' And if everyone else is doing that too, everyone else will be OK. The other kids aren't my concern—it's just my kid, and I just have to make sure that they're in the best position with all the best things." But she says, "When you're doing equity work, and asking people to broaden that lens, it's always going to be touchy because you're talking about kids, a parent's most precious thing. But also, 'You're telling me I've been a bad parent because I've been doing this? That doesn't make sense with what I've been told all along.'"

And in Evanston, Biz adds, "saying you've been a bad liberal is a dirty word." What they were asking of people often ran up against "the idea of themselves, and the narrative that folks believe about their own allyship."

Of course, their detractors didn't generally come forward and say that their discomfort with the plan stemmed from the way that the plan challenged their perceptions of themselves. Nor did they openly say that they didn't want to share their money with less-resourced schools. "As is common in equity work," Biz says, "nobody is coming forward and saying, 'This is a bad idea and we don't want to share our money.' It was more like, 'This is not the right time because of this, or that'—and we spent a lot of time responding to things that weren't *the* thing." Not all resistance was bad, though. People who opposed the plan, Suni says, would often "raise really valid concerns and questions that maybe we hadn't thought through, which made us stronger."

Keeping equity at the forefront was nonnegotiable, but they were committed to being receptive to ideas on how things could be done and flexible on interventions and final outcomes to ensure there was collective problem solving. As Suni puts it, "A lot of our work at the beginning was saying, 'There are no judgments here. No one has been doing anything wrong. We've all been doing what we thought we needed to be doing.'" At one of their first meetings, they did what they called some "low-stakes sharing" in which they went around the room and asked representatives from each school whether they had various "extras" (for example, a science fair, or a garden). A clear pattern emerged. Certain schools had every extra, while other schools had none. Showing the extent of the discrepancies, and using an approach that emphasized collaboration rather than blame eventually got them the buy-in they needed.

They also had to navigate working with families who agreed that there was a problem but who wanted to solve it in a way that felt paternalistic or ineffective. Some parents floated the idea of assigning the school with lower-income families in the district a "sister school," a school with wealthier families who would teach them to fundraise. Biz and Suni pushed back on that: "This is not about 'not knowing how to fundraise.' This is about the donor capacity in your school." Next came the idea that the lower-resource school should have to give "deliverables" and account for how they were spending the money. "We had to push back on that too, and say, 'Look, we trust PTAs,'" says Biz. "Just as we don't micromanage how you spend your money, we're not going to micromanage lower-resource schools."

They first got buy-in to a model of more incremental redistribution, in which a percentage of the fundraising at higher-resource schools was redistributed to lower resource schools. But their vision was bigger: they believed that Evanston could be a trailblazing school district that would have "one fund," a system in which all PTA fundraising across the sixteen district schools would go into a pot and then be distributed equitably. In May 2020 they were able to capitalize on the disruptive nature of the pandemic in order to make an important step toward that vision. The pandemic highlighted the problems with tying fundraising dollars to particular schools: families at several higher-resourced schools were able to rapidly raise funds for pandemic relief but often had lower numbers of families in the school that actually needed support. Meanwhile, Biz says, "The middle school with the most need had the least capacity to raise it."

By combining their resources, the district was able to quickly raise $500,000. Another parent volunteer, who works as an accountant, helped with crunching the numbers to figure out how much each school should receive. Then, individual school principals and social workers were put in charge of getting that money out, in the form of gift cards, to the families who most needed it. The exercise involved "supreme trust"; Suni's school, which put $47,000 into the fund, only got $8,000 back. But the ability to swiftly respond to a crisis and help families across the district, regardless of what school they were in, was overall a "big win." In December 2020 the stakeholders voted to move for the next three years to move to a "one-fund" model, a move that Biz and Suni hope will become permanent.

Though they've achieved more than they thought they would in four short years, they also talked about the ongoing work that was still ahead of them. They're working with a group to develop a racial equity impact assessment tool; one fear is that the schools who used to have the largest PTA fundraising budgets will cut programs for lower-income families of color once their budgets aren't as big, while keeping the programs that primarily benefit wealthier, White families. They are looking for ways to ensure that the program doesn't end up hurting the very communities that have borne the brunt of the district's problems for so long. "Some of this work is reparations work," Biz acknowledges. "It is White supremacy that has broken these systems, has benefited these decisions, and I believe that the labor really is White people's responsibility."

Beyond the Big Wins

In both Portland and Evanston, the parents behind the projects had achieved a difficult task: getting people with the most to buy into the idea that they should give up some of what they had for the greater good. And though their work is ongoing—Portland still has to actually implement the initiative, and Evanston is working on the racial equity impact assessment—both groups of parents achieved a clear victory.

But I also wanted to talk to parents who are doing work that doesn't have a clear "end" or where they don't expect to see a clear victory. Who are finding a way to live out their values in day-to-day life, even when life gets in the way.

Jess and Dan
Campton, NH

Jess and Dan are parents to two boys under five; Dan owns a telecommunications company and Jess works as a science teacher. They live on what they call a "farmlet" in New Hampshire where they grow vegetables and raise chickens. Both grew up in farming families. "I think we want to pass on those values to our kids, of having that self-sustainability—having that ability to know your food and where it came from, growing your own food, caring about the environment," Dan remarks.

When their older son was six months old, Jess quit her job with the plan that she would farm full time and have the kids at home. A few years into that plan, she was offered a part-time job teaching science to youth who have been adjudicated delinquent by the juvenile justice system. "Now it's full time, and my youngest is in daycare full time, my oldest is at school; and I'm really invested in where I work, and there's such a high need," she says. "As soon as I started working more than fifteen hours a week, I realized how much time we spent making food, cleaning up from making all that food. I realized, 'No wonder everybody gets things disposable.'" But they remain committed to keeping their farm and to growing at least a significant portion of their own food. They estimate that they grow 90 percent of the vegetables their family eats and about a quarter of their protein. As their lives have shifted, they've had continual conversations about, as Jess put it, "how to be the parents we want to be within the constraints of our situation, whether it was financial, geographical, time. . . . We want to grow more of our own food, but it just may not be realistic at the moment. It came down to, 'Let's revisit what our core values are, then look at the things that we do.'"

Talking to Dan and Jess reminded me of advice from the parenting writer Bruce Feiler, who wrote the book *The Secrets of Happy*

Families. One of the "secrets" he proposed was to have a family mission statement, essentially a list of core values. The purpose of the list isn't that you perfectly adhere to those values all the time, but that you remind yourself what your family is about and what you're striving for. A family mission statement can help parents articulate values beyond the vague idea of raising "good people."

Being in continuous communication about their values has made it easier for them to correct when things do get off track. "We got into a rut with purchasing things online," Jess says. "Amazon is just so easy. It's like Facebook, and it sucks you in, and we thought, *What are we doing . . . ? We have all these boxes, where did this even start? We hate that company!*"

Figuring out where to push themselves, and what's nonnegotiable (no Amazon, for instance) has been an ongoing process. "We can't do all the things," Jess says. "There's this drive, at least in myself, to want to do all the things, and it's completely overwhelming, especially as a project completer. Because none of them really can be completed, and none of them are really 'achievable'—there's a lot of days that I wish we were far more politically involved. But with running the farm, managing little kids, and trying to take care of myself . . . mentally, I just don't have enough to give. So trying to think about where we can make effect, in the little ways . . . , as soon as we had some flexibility financially, we've donated to groups that are doing that legwork because we can't allocate a lot of time."

For families who want to lessen their environmental impact (and have that be a part of their own family's mission), they have some advice. "The number one thing you can do to have an environmental impact is your food," Dan says. "Buying local food, not buying mono-crop things, like grain, corn, and soy. Corn and soy are destroying the environment. Trying to grow the food ourselves, buy it from a local farm, has the greatest environmental impact. Grow any amount of food that you can. Have three chickens. Have a potted strawberry plant or a tomato plant on your porch. Any amount of food you can grow will teach your kids where food can come from, will reduce your environmental impact, and get you outside." And buying less, consuming less, is a big part of the work; recycling isn't as helpful as reducing your consumption to begin with. As Dan puts it, "Reduce, and *then* reuse, and then recycle."

We talked about the existential threat that climate change poses to future generations, but Dan and Jess don't believe that you need to have frightening conversations with young kids about the rising sea levels in order to inspire the next generation of activists. "It's more about teaching them to have a love for the earth," Dan says. "And then it will just be natural for them to have an awareness of how climate change is affecting it as they grow older."

Changing Things from the Inside

I struggled with how to write about foster care in this book. I knew I didn't want to ignore it: despite there being millions of families who have had their lives intersect with the US foster care system, it's usually ignored in mainstream parenting books. Our society has a conflicted relationship with people who care for children who are not biologically their own. On the one hand, they are subjected to insulting questions, treated as somehow very "different" than "traditional families." We also put them on a pedestal. They are saints or angels, not like the rest of us.

When foster care is written about, it's often written in such a way that perpetuates some of the most harmful kind of "savior" narrative. The United States has a long history of separating families of color, removing the children of enslaved people or of Indigenous families and sending them to boarding schools, or to White families to be adopted, often while touting a message that this trauma was actually in the child's interests. That horrific history has gained new attention with the recovery of unmarked graves of Indigenous children at residential schools in both Canada and the United States. Much about modern foster care echoes those past systems: families of color are significantly more likely to have their children removed than White families, and often the reason that parents have their children removed is essentially a criminalization of poverty.

Hayley, the foster parent I spoke to, is in the midst of doing the hardest kind of activism: trying to change a system while still being a part of it.

Hayley DeRoche
Henrico, VA

Hayley is a librarian and writer who lives with her husband, seven-year-old biological daughter, and four-year-old foster son.

After having their daughter through IVF, Hayley and her husband started looking for ways to grow their family without going through the expensive, emotionally exhausting process of IVF again. Growing up in an evangelical church community, Hayley had known a lot of foster parents; becoming a foster parent was presented in that community as "what you do if you want to make a difference." "I came to foster care the way most people come to foster care—that this would be a way for us to adopt, and to do it ethically," she says. "That's what I thought when I got involved. So I understand why people think that, because I was that person."

But during her training to become a foster parent, she heard the message that, except in very limited circumstances, foster care was about trying to reunify children with either their biological parents or other relatives. Hayley and her family took that directive seriously. When her foster son was placed with them at seven months old, they saw their role as being a safe space where he could stay while the system pursued its ultimate goal of reunifying him with his biological family.

Yet Hayley saw that the system itself didn't seem to take that mandate particularly seriously. When her foster son's aunt expressed interest in taking custody but couldn't do it without getting some help with expenses, Hayley reached out to their caseworker to ask if the aunt knew that she could qualify for daycare assistance. The social worker told her that the aunt wasn't eligible for any of the funding or support that Hayley herself received. She wondered, at that point, "Isn't the whole point to keep this family together? And if it is, then why are you making these blockades to the help?"

She also started seeking out and speaking to former foster youth, not just foster parents. What she heard complicated the picture more for her. "It's unfortunate—because if more people listened to former foster youth, then people like me wouldn't be saying these [savior narratives] because people would be listening to them. The narratives that are coming from former foster youth are generally not what people want to hear—and just generally, we don't want to hear that the person who was 'saved' isn't happy about it." It took, as she puts it, "a lot of reading on my part to become a little more radicalized, and to say, 'This system isn't doing what it's supposed to be doing at all.'"

Even though she's come to that realization, she's still serving as a foster parent. "What's difficult about becoming a foster parent, is that you can't walk away from it. In a grand sense, you're very frustrated, but what you do with that information impacts a very specific child. I don't think that the system is helpful, but at the same time, now I'm in the soup. What I'm trying to do with my advocacy is to try to have more people see what the system really is."

She's tried to help prospective parents understand that, with some limited exceptions usually involving children whose parental rights have already been terminated, you shouldn't go into foster care thinking that you'll be adopting a child without a home. "It's really not about that. It's about making sure that this child's home *stays* this child's home."

In October 2020 she published an essay titled "It's Time to Abolish Foster Care" in which she connected the removals of children at the border done by Immigration and Customs Enforcement (ICE) to the foster care system. "ICE pulling children from their mothers' arms is a logical extension of the way America treats the most vulnerable on its soil," she wrote. "No amount of Good Guy Social Workers or Good Gal Foster Moms . . . or single tweaks to the system can fix this." In place of the current system, she proposes family-based treatment care for parents who are suffering from addiction issues, as well as a renewed focus on kinship care.

Another part of Hayley's activism has been to bring attention to the ways that privilege allows foster parents to engage in behavior that wouldn't be tolerated by families with less privilege. For instance, the self-help and parenting writer Rachel Hollis has written about her own family's foster-to-adoption journey and the hardships she faced through it. Hollis writes that she got through with "vodka as my copilot." "And it's like, OK, as a foster parent, you can say that, because you're a wealthy White woman," Hayley says. "You know that saying *hee hee, vodka is my copilot* is not going to get your children taken away because of addiction."

Hayley also writes and speaks publicly about how offers of help are often given to those who need it the least. She's been bombarded by offers of free babysitting, free presents, and other help, which often comes from organized efforts in nearby church communities. But she says, "I really wish this offer of help did not come to me, because I don't need it. I'm paid as a foster parent. And this child has *more presents.* . . . I'm just the last person who should be offered help." She sees the deep needs that families have who are trying to keep their children out of foster care, and the families who desperately need reunification support. "I don't see the same help being bombarded at people who actually need it."

The family is waiting on appeals of the termination of parental rights petition to find out if their foster son is going to be eligible for adoption—despite her strong belief that his family should have a chance to raise him, it ultimately isn't up to her. She has written about how, even though it would be devastating not to adopt him, she can still hope for a different outcome: "Of course, I love my foster son—but I can be angry that the system is doing his parent a deep injustice."

In doing other activism work with her family, she's conscious of how they show up in spaces as a multiracial family: her foster son is Black, and the rest of her family is White. "Over the spring, there were a lot of Black Lives Matter protests, and I went, but I did not bring him. I think there's an easy thing that happens for White women who have Black children, and you can go to something, and feel like having a Black child gives you a kind of pass. . . . And I try not to bring him around in situations where the implicit message is going to be 'That lady saved that little Black child.'"

To teach her own children about volunteering and activism work, she tries to avoid an approach that she saw growing up where children were used as "sign-bearers." She tries to take a gentler approach: "I tell my children, 'We're bringing this stuff to mutual aid. We're going to go to this march.' I try to let them observe and be interested in it and ask questions."

The Darker Side of Activism

Privileged parents are often a force to be reckoned with. They are well-connected, vocal, accustomed to getting their way, and comfortable with pulling whatever strings they need to in order to make things happen. These are all excellent qualities when they're used in service of a necessary cause.

But there are also darker sides to the ways that parents can be activists. In 2019 in Oakland, a group of activist parents shut down consecutive school board meetings and got arrested over the school board's decision to merge two schools: one "hill school" of affluent families, and one a "flatlands" school, a mostly Black school where 90 percent of students qualified for free and reduced-price lunch. The meetings became so intense that one parent suffered a torn ACL and had to use crutches after being pushed to the floor by police. The hill school, which was beloved by the parents who sent their kids there, was slated for closure, which they vehemently opposed. Elisa (the Oakland parent interviewed in the schools chapter) still has a sense of amazement in her voice when she talks about what had happened: "The hill parents fought *really hard*—they brought out lawyers, they started their own organizations! And what was most interesting to me was that they were basically using words, and fights, and causes of Black and Brown families . . . in reverse."

The school that the hill parents were advocating for, Elisa told me, was fairly racially diverse, but very wealthy, with little economic diversity. The school that the district had proposed merging them with was both majority Black and majority low income. She sent me some writing that she'd done during one of the contentious school board meetings about the topic, which she'd turned into a poem called "Gentrified Justice." The poem depicted a disturbing scene: affluent, mostly White families, shutting down a meeting by singing protest songs that had been used by the civil rights movement, such as "We Shall Not Be Moved." The parents, Elisa told me, claimed to be "speaking on behalf of both schools" when they talked about the problems with the merger. But the flatlands parents were also there and were speaking for themselves. What they were saying was "We need resources now and are willing to merge with whoever wants to merge with us." Nevertheless, the affluent parents, Elisa notes, "really believe that it's about protecting disenfranchised Black and Brown children—I have to think they believe that, because I don't want to imagine a world where people do that in a manipulative way."

JPB Gerald, the Queens father and Hunter fellow, coined the phrase "altruistic shield" to describe our own resistance to the idea that we're anything other than "good people" who are pursuing justice. He defines it as a "psychological mechanism that allows us to outright deny or otherwise defend ourselves from anticipated or in-the-moment accusations of racism because of what we consider to be the altruistic nature of our work." He came up with the term specifically after seeing how White teachers respond to accusations of racism. The way to put down the "shield" is to provide space for the people affected by issues to speak, and to actually listen.

The first time in my own parenting journey that I encountered this kind "activism" was when my daughter's childcare was shut down. During the pandemic, we had enrolled our three-year-old in an outdoor-only preschool that operated inside Prospect Park, the largest park in Brooklyn. Since the program only covered a few hours and required a lot of expensive gear, it wasn't surprising that the parents I saw at pick-up/drop-off were, like myself, people with the kinds of jobs where we could work from home, making the kind of money where you can afford a 3T North Face rainsuit that will only fit your child for a season.

What I didn't realize was that, despite having been open for years, the program had never gotten a permit to run a childcare facility in the park. The city's regulations for childcare didn't easily apply to a program that only operated inside a park without having any physical building, and the program hadn't sought special dispensation. No one had noticed for years. But when an inspector from the body that licenses childcare facilities showed up, the program was instructed to cease operations until they'd gotten the proper permits.

Within hours of the shutdown, the hundred-plus who had children in the program had organized an email chain. One parent wrote that she was a former city hall staffer. One noted that he was "in close communication with our local City Councilmember." Another parent chimed in with the councilmember's personal email and encouraged the group to "cc" the personal email as well. One parent floated a plan to call the New York City mayor himself on a radio show.

I thought a lot about whether I would have jumped aboard the "activism" train if I hadn't been in the midst of writing this book and thinking critically about the issues. I'm not sure what the answer is. With the interviews and research for this book fresh in my mind, I was able to take a step back and see a bigger picture. The implicit assumption behind all those emails and calls was that, in the middle of a pandemic and with hundreds of thousands of children receiving no education at all, the top priority of various city officials should be finding a special work-around for a program that served some of the most privileged children in the city.

Takeaways

As stretched thin as all parents are, we often find new reserves of time and energy to throw into advocacy for our own kids. The hard work comes in finding that same amount of time and energy for "other people's kids."

All the activists I spoke with had overcome that hurdle. None of them were fighting for things that directly benefited themselves, their child, or their child's school. Their commitment came from different places. As Lydia puts it, the knowledge that the childcare system she was advocating for would have changed her life was a major motivator. Suni and Biz were motivated by the prospect of righting a long injustice in their community, and in making their community more fully reflect the values that it said it held. Both Tiffany and Jess mentioned the idea of making their commitment to improving their community a central, defining value of their family, one that they return to again and again.

No one family can give time and energy to every cause, or can, as Jess put it, "solve all the problems at once." But defining activism, political involvement, and protest as a core part of not just what your family *does* but who your family *is* can help keep it at the forefront, even when life gets in the way. Below are some ideas:

- **Write a family mission statement.** Think through your values—and make sure to do something every week, or at least every month, that brings you in line with those values.
- **Beware of saviorism.** If you're advocating for a marginalized group, or "using your voice" on their behalf, ask, Has the group asked you to help speak for them? Are members from that group in the room with you? If not, that's a problem. And *definitely* don't claim to be advocating for marginalized groups while pushing for a solution that benefits your own family—that's an extra layer of toxicity.
- **Be willing to do the unglamorous stuff.** Real change happens behind the scenes. Providing childcare, meals, or other help to people who are doing the public-facing work is a necessary part of any movement. By the time most people learned about either of the large projects profiled in the chapter, hundreds of hours had gone into each project. Invisible work is needed to move the ball.
- **Change doesn't happen alone.** No one person can do all the work needed to make systemic change. Every parent I spoke with had both close partners in the work, and dozens (or in some case, hundreds) of people also involved. Big problems require big groups of people to solve them.
- **For more information on starting or joining a mutual aid group:** Mutual Aid Toolkit, https://mutualaiddisasterrelief.org/wp-content/uploads/2020/04/NO-LOGOS-Mutual-Aid-101_-Toolkit.pdf
- **For more information about starting your own PTA equity project:** https://ptaequityproject.com/about
- **For more information about getting an initiative on your own local ballot like the Portland parents:** The National Conference of State Legislatures has information broken down by state for the process at https://www.ncsl.org/research/elections-and-campaigns/initiative-and-referendum-processes.aspx.

Further Reading

Mutual Aid, Building Solidarity During This Crisis (and the Next) by Dean Spade (Verso, 2020)

No More Heroes: Grassroots Challenges to the Savior Mentality by Jordan Flaherty (AK Press, 2016)

Our Time Is Now: Power, Purpose, and the Fight for a Fair America by Stacey Abrams (Henry Holt, 2020)

The Purpose of Power: How We Come Together When We Fall Apart by Alicia Garza (Random House, 2020)

Road Map for Revolutionaries by Elisa Camahort Page, Carolyn Gerin, and Jamia Wilson (Clarkson Potter, 2018)

The Secrets of Happy Families by Bruce Feiler (William Morrow, 2013)

5

MONEY, WEALTH, AND LEGACY

ORIGINALLY, I THOUGHT THIS CHAPTER would be about "teaching your kids about giving." Whenever the subject of kids and charitable giving came up on a parenting forum or listserv, parents were always quick to bring up the "three jars" system popularized by the *New York Times* Money writer Ron Lieber and covered extensively in his book *The Opposite of Spoiled: Raising Kids Who Are Grounded, Generous, and Smart About Money*. The system suggests dividing a kid's allowance into (fittingly) three different jars: a jar for spending, a jar for saving, and a jar for charitable giving.

I did a few interviews with parents who used and liked Lieber's system. The stories about what happened with the "giving" jar usually involved a small child dumping out a pile of bills at the front desk of a children's museum or an animal shelter with a proud smile. These were fun interviews to do. Unfortunately, they made for deadly dull reading.

I also began to think differently about the purpose of this chapter after reading sociologist Rachel Sherman's book *Uneasy Street:*

The Anxiety of Affluence. Sherman interviewed fifty very affluent US-based parents, who had a median net worth of $3.25 million. She was interested in the question of how they think about themselves, their parenting choices, and their wealth. Almost universally, she found that they had a concept of themselves as "legitimately privileged." In the United States, "legitimate privilege" comes from being "ordinary, down-to-earth, hardworking, and prudent." She found a pervasive belief among her interviewees that it was OK for some people to have much more than others, as long as those with the most "inhabit the privilege appropriately." As parents, Sherman found that her subjects were deeply invested in raising children who weren't "entitled." But, Sherman writes, as parents, her subjects often embodied a contradiction: "They want their children to see themselves as 'normal' (and therefore just like everyone else) but also to appreciate their advantages (which made them different from others). . . . They instill and reproduce ideas about how to occupy privilege legitimately without giving it up."

Sherman's ideas still felt applicable to parents falling anywhere in the top income brackets, and they made me rethink the project of this chapter, and, in some ways, of the whole book. I didn't have much interest in writing a book that just told privileged people (myself included) that it was fine to hold onto all our privileges, just so long as we did so while being "good people."

At the same time, I didn't want to write a chapter that was scolding or that ignored the financial realities that people face, particularly given the unexpected hardships and job losses that people have faced during the pandemic. The journalist Anne Helen Petersen has coined the term "the hollow middle class" to talk about Americans with decent incomes whose lives are nevertheless financially precarious because of student loan debt, medical debt, credit card debt, and the costs of childcare and housing. It's a group that grows wider each year, as wages stay stagnant while the costs of the typical trappings of middle-class life continue to rise.

The interviews I ended up including in this chapter were with people who were grappling with the bigger questions about wealth, inequality, and fairness. They thought about both what they'd inherited from their own parents and what kind of legacy they hope to leave behind. Two of the people who I spoke to for this chapter are extremely wealthy; the rest are not. But all of them are thinking deeply about the line between "charitable giving" and "justice." The chapter is really about what adults do with money, and what messages they pass on, more than what kids do, or don't do, with their allowance.

Speaking Transparently with Kids About Money

Several parents I spoke to about money and kids struggled with the idea of how to convey their financial circumstances to their kids. Kids often aren't particularly good at nuance. One parent told me, "I try to not say, 'We can't afford it.' Because usually it's not true. We *can* afford the sneakers, or the sheet of stickers, or whatever it is. But then we have to have a longer conversation about why we're not getting it." The next parents are a financially privileged family who have taken an unusual approach to their kids and money: radical transparency.

Sarah Andrews and Aniket Hirebet
Pittsburgh, PA

Sarah is a lawyer at a corporate firm who lives with her nine- and eleven-year-old sons from her previous marriage and her fiancé. I spoke with her and her fiancé, Aniket, who is a project manager for global IT projects.

Both grew up in families that didn't talk very much about money. "I wasn't raised particularly financially literate," Aniket observes. "I grew up in India, in an upper-middle-class family. I knew the basics—like, I knew my dad worked and got paid a salary, and that was what allowed us to have the lifestyle we had."

"And I didn't even know that," Sarah says with a laugh. Her own parents, she said, had been raised in families that faced money struggles, and she speculated that once they were secure themselves "they didn't have to burden their children with the knowledge of harder things."

The two had vastly different experiences with money as young adults. Aniket moved to the United States for college at age eighteen. "As an immigrant, I wasn't eligible for any kind of financial aid, nor for any social safety net–type stuff. So I spent several years living in really a very acute state of poverty. It was a matter of literally counting every dollar. Many days I had one meal, some I had none." He was quick to say that this situation was different from those who are living that way without a clear plan to get out—he was able to view it as a temporary sacrifice that would culminate in a degree and a well-paying job. But, he continues, "Some anxiety stays with you."

Meanwhile, Sarah adds, "It never occurred to me in a million years as a really privileged White girl that anybody I went to college with was hungry." She took out loans for a bachelor's, a master's, and then a law degree without a clear understanding of how interest worked, or how she would pay them back. "I was so, so lost being launched into the world as a young adult—I racked up so much money in debt just living how I thought I should get to live."

Sarah's decision to be transparent with their sons about money also came about from the circumstances of her separation from their father. Their father, with whom she shares custody, makes a significantly lower income than she and Aniket do, and the boys were old enough to notice that fact. For a time, they were in litigation over child support issues. "You normally wouldn't talk to a nine- and eleven-year-old about those adult tensions if you can help it. But we felt that the best thing [we] could do to [address] their anxieties was to be forthright," Sarah says. She acknowledges that of course being forthright is a lot easier to do in a household where she can honestly tell her children that they *don't* have to worry about money.

Conversations about income and prices have become a part of their everyday life: "We tell them what things cost: the car they drive in, the cost of the Airbnb we just stayed in, the mortgage payment. They always look at the receipt with us when we eat at a restaurant and help us calculate the tip." During the interview, she called her younger son over to see if he could correctly identify her salary (he didn't know the number, though he was in the right ballpark and correctly identified that Aniket made a higher salary than she did). They told me the numbers of both their salaries without hesitation.

These conversations about money are also connected to conversations about privilege. She's talked with them about redlining and how it influenced her own family's ability to accumulate wealth. Sarah says, "We have told them that they're in the top percentages of people in the world in terms of resources. We're not Jeff Bezos rich . . . , but we're really rich compared to almost everyone on the planet." The day after the 2016 election, they recall telling them, "You will be White, educated, economically privileged men . . . , and you will have a duty to counter what's about to happen in our society."

The fact of their sons' many privileges doesn't mean that they don't have a lot of fears about their future. "We're very cognizant of the fact that it could also just all be smoke and mirrors—just because we're well off doesn't mean our children are going to be," Aniket notes. "We don't know what the state of the economy, or the state of the planet, is going to be." But rather than channel their fears into trying to hoard every possible advantage for their sons, they've taken a different approach. "We have actually told them that they should think about careers based on how useful they would be even if society were to change drastically," Sarah adds, which is a "dirty thing to talk to your kids about." But when thinking about climate change and other forces for societal unrest, she feels like she has to. "I feel anxiety—I think the world might make it through for me to have a comfortable life. But I'm not sure about my kids—or my grandkids, if I have any, can do that."

Rachel Henderson
Menomonie, WI

Rachel lives in rural Wisconsin, about an hour-and-a-half from the Minneapolis–Saint Paul area with her husband, and two sons, ages eight and five. Her primary job is running a mixed fruit orchard that sells to local farmer's markets; her husband works for a renewable energy development company. She responded to a call I'd put out on Twitter looking for families who made under six figures and who made giving a big part of their lives.

Giving, she says, wasn't always something that she felt like she could do. "I grew up in a lower-middle class family. We weren't hungry, we weren't in danger of losing our home . . . , but we didn't have extras. So I grew up in this very 'saving' mindset, of, if you have money, you save it, because you might need it to buy groceries, or you might need it because you're suddenly going to have to replace your shoes, or whatever." As a younger adult, she says, "I was kind of stingy with the idea of donations—$25 there, $50 there—if I donated $100, it felt like a really big thing to do. It's taken me a long time to get out of that mindset, to realize that we have the privilege. . . . That even if a year from now, my husband lost his job, we could find another one, because we have these college degrees, because we have this privilege. I don't have to hoard my resources for my future, when someone else needs them now."

She also thinks about her children's privileges when thinking about what they'll need in the future. "I'm raising two future White men. . . . They'll probably be able to support themselves in their adulthood and not need an estate or a trust fund or anything like that—not that we have enough money to make a trust fund where they'll never have to work anyways."

One thing her family has been successful at, which in my experience is very hard to do, is to avoid "income creep"—the phenomenon where, whenever your income goes up, you find new expenses to match it. When her husband got a pay raise and bonus this year that put them over the six-figure mark, they've increased their giving. When they didn't need the income from the second stimulus check, they gave it away. They mostly give locally or to nonprofits that they have a connection to. Recently, they've given to local food pantry, which has been overwhelmed with demand, and their small-town theater, which lost all its revenue during the shutdown.

Her sons are too young to have much of an understanding of the issue yet, though she's thought about the message she wants them to hear. She wants them to see themselves as living in an atmosphere of mutual exchange, and mutual benefit, rather than, as she puts it, "me as a wealthy person giving, because I'm so generous." "We have some good friends who struggle financially, but their kids are teenagers, so they give us a *ton* of stuff, like hand-me-down clothes. They repair things for us. And they would never want to take money from me, so I try to do things like pay them to take care of our chickens. What I hope is that our kids see us in kind of a mutual-aid relationship with a lot of our community, rather than a benefactor relationship."

The Limits of Philanthropy

Trying to avoid the "benefactor" mindset was something I heard repeatedly from the parents who I spoke to. A certain segment of socially conscious people have always been mistrustful of that word. But mostly, our modern culture venerates those who "give back."

So it was startling to learn that, in the not-too-distant past, wealthy people who wanted to set up charitable foundations, and to act as "benefactors" of the public, were viewed with deep suspicion. At the turn of the century, Congress fought hard to regulate such "generosity," believing that it was antithetical to democratic ideals. The history and debate surrounding two of the most famous foundations provides some interesting complexities in how to think about wealth.

Modern-day foundations were invented by two very wealthy men at the turn of the last century: Andrew Carnegie and John D. Rockefeller. Carnegie and Rockefeller had both made staggering amounts of wealth through building companies that would come to hold monopolies on products that were a necessity for the Industrial Age: steel (Carnegie) and oil (Rockefeller). They also ran their companies ruthlessly. In his extensive history, *Philanthropy: From Aristotle to Zuckerberg*, British journalist Paul Vallely details some of their tactics. Carnegie, he writes, operated his factories "non-stop, with two twelve-hour shifts every day of the year except the Fourth of July"; he demanded a twenty-four-hour shift every two weeks. Later in his career, he attempted to set a "sliding scale" for the steel worker's wages, where, if the price of steel went down, so too would the worker's wages; when workers staged a strike in response, his business summoned a militia to quell the uprising and install new workers, who signed a "no strike" clause in their contracts. Likewise, in the oil industry, Vallely writes, Rockefeller "drove out rival firms through cut-throat competition, arranging secret deals and fixing prices."

Because of the ways they acquired their wealth, both men attracted their share of impassioned critics when they sought to start foundations to give some of that wealth away. Rockefeller opened a floodgate of criticism when he asked Congress to pass a bill authorizing the incorporation of his foundation. Theodore Roosevelt, who had been president when Rockefeller gained most of his wealth, quipped that "no amount of charities in spending such fortunes can compensate in any way for the misconduct in acquiring them." Reverend John Haynes Holmes, a minister who would later become the president of the ACLU, testified at one hearing that Rockefeller's proposed foundation "must be repugnant to the whole idea of democratic society."

Of course, as readers likely know, these criticisms did not stop Rockefeller from starting a foundation that still exists today (having failed to get the federal government to authorize its creation, he succeeded in persuading New York state legislators to do so). Most modern-day foundations are modeled after Rockefeller's. Many of them have accomplished incredible feats: the Bill and Melinda Gates Foundation, for instance, has indubitably saved millions of lives, primarily through its vaccine programs in Africa. But foundations like Gateses' are necessarily in tension with democratic ideals. The World Health Organization (WHO), for instance, is supposed to be accountable to its member governments alone. But the Gates Foundation supplies 12 percent of its budget. Lawrence Gostin, a director of the WHO Collaborating Center on National and Global Health Law, has expressed alarm about the influence wielded by Gates, particularly when Trump announced that the US government would be pulling out of the WHO in the summer of 2020, thus making Gates its largest single funder (a situation that did not actually come to pass). When the WHO was formed, Gostin said, it "would have been unimaginable" to think that the majority of its funding could come from a single donor, and that "a single rich philanthropist" could, essentially, "set the global health agenda."

Anand Giridharadas's 2018 *Winners Take All: The Elite Charade of Changing the World* offered a wide-ranging critique of how the "winners," in a system that distributes wealth in a wildly unequal manner, use philanthropy as a way to boost their own images while not actually pushing for real change. They are, instead, often "taking on the problems that people like them have been instrumental in creating or sustaining." Unsurprisingly, as Giridharadas demonstrates through multiple examples throughout his book, the solutions they offer are always ones that leave their own advantages intact. A modern movement of philanthropists have begun to identify themselves as "social justice philanthropists" (inviting the question of what, exactly, traditional philanthropy is doing *other* than advancing social justice). Social justice philanthropy is both focused on including the purported beneficiaries of philanthropic projects as decision makers (something traditional philanthropy rarely does), and is more transparent about where its money is coming from; traditional philanthropy dollars are often invested with companies that have a large hand in creating the very problems the charitable arm of the organization is tasked with solving.

What does any of that have to do with the average parent, who has some amount of economic privilege but not Rockefeller-Gates-Carnegie wealth? Who just wants to teach their child about giving? So much of what we think charitable giving looks like comes from the foundation model of those older philanthropists, just on a smaller scale—it centers the giver. The only relevant question is, Where do you want to give? It's up to the giver to decide how much to share. And the intended beneficiary of the giving is rarely included as a partner to decide how the money would be best spent.

Some grow weary of these critiques—after all, if people are giving away their money, does it really matter *how*? Edgar Villanueva, a prominent social justice philanthropist, wrote a book tackling exactly that question, titled *Decolonizing Wealth: Indigenous Wisdom to Heal Divides and Restore Balance*. In the comments section of a published interview with Villanueva, one commenter wrote, "Now we are finding ways to criticize people who give away their money . . . Only in America!"

But charity and philanthropy are systems in this country, like the school system, or childcare system, or higher education system.

The fact that we think about giving away money as an unadulterated good is a perception that benefits the people who give away money, while changing nothing about the underlying power structure that makes some people philanthropists, and some people have to rely on the whims of that philanthropy to do crucial work or otherwise meet their communities' needs.

Taxes

One of the most common critiques of traditional philanthropy is that it's a technique used by the richest to avoid taxes. Though technically charitable giving by anyone, at any income level, is tax deductible, it only makes sense for a person to itemize their charitable giving if they're a top-income earner (rather than to just take a standard deduction). In this way, charitable giving by the top-income earners is subsidized by the federal government while charitable giving by those with less is not. And of course, family foundations are nonprofits that pay no tax. Family foundations are required, by law, to give away 5 percent of their wealth annually—but 95 percent of it is allowed to sit there and grow, tax free.

Of course, it's not like the rich are going to lobby for higher taxes, right? Except a few of them actually do.

Stephen Prince
St. Simons Island, GA

Stephen Prince doesn't have much in common with most of the parents in this book: his children are adults in their thirties and early forties; he is also a grandfather. Most his friends are Republicans, and he described himself as a staunchly devoted capitalist. All of that makes him an outlier among the interview subjects of this book, though not in the country at large. But he's unusual in every circle in one way:

he's a multimillionaire who has devoted enormous amounts of time and money to the project of increasing his own tax burden.

Stephen started the printing business that would eventually make him very wealthy in the late 1980s; in the early 2000s, when every retail outlet and restaurant began to offer branded plastic gift cards, his business was there to fill that new demand. "It's allowed us to become part of the 1 percent in this country, and that's not a thing I take lightly," he says. "I feel a high degree of responsibility to society for providing me the chance to be so successful and want to pay it back to the United States, and to all of humanity."

Stephen is approaching seventy; in his lifetime, the marginal tax rate for the highest income earners has plummeted from being in the 90 percent range (for some very top earners) down to less than 40 percent today. "In 1973 we started changing the tax laws substantively, and allowing wealthy people to shelter significant amounts of our income—I just thought, *We're creating a mess here*," he says. He is quick to say that, just like most people, he doesn't like to pay taxes. But his own dislike of parting with money doesn't hold any weight, in his view. Taxes are simply a necessity to a functioning society. He waives away suggestions that charitable giving or philanthropy are a substitute for taxpayer-funded service. In a blog post, he wrote, "The rich don't feed and house the less fortunate; educate the masses (people who can't afford the private schools that we send our kids to); they don't build roads and other infrastructure that society needs to grow and prosper . . . Government does and always has performed these tasks. It's silly to think the rich ever will."

He originally thought about starting his own group of high net-worth people—he would throw in $1 million, find ninety-nine other people to do the same, and with their resources combined they would lobby for higher taxes. But a friend suggested he look into a new group that had already been formed—Patriotic Millionaires. Patriotic Millionaires has three foundational principles: first, that all citizens should enjoy political power equal to that enjoyed by millionaires; second, all citizens who work full time should be able to afford their basic needs; third, taxes from millionaires, billionaires, and corporations should make up a greater proportion of federal tax receipts. That mission comported with Stephen's own beliefs, and he started donating, attending rallies and events, and lobbying in Washington.

The group's lobbying efforts in Washington are met with a mixed reaction. "They know who we are. . . . Republicans, obviously, think we're crazy. We usually get a very good response from Democrats. Nancy Pelosi thinks we're great. I think Chuck Schumer looks at us a little askance, and maybe thinks we're a little crazy too."

He's been asked many times why he doesn't simply "write a bigger check"—that is, increase his own taxes voluntarily. He has a two-part answer to that question. "I want to fix the problem, and the problem is not caused singlehandedly by Stephen Prince having amassed a lot of money. Now, if you were God, and you came to me and said, 'I want you to write a check for every penny you have, thus robbing your children of their inheritance, but I will fix the structural problems in this country,' . . . I'd do it. America matters more to me than leaving my children a boatload of money. They know I feel that way. . . . If some sort of miraculous thing comes along and I think I can save this country, I'm going to spend a boatload of money on it."

He also *does* pay more taxes than many of his neighbors, simply by not exploiting every loophole available to him. He lives on one of the four wealthy island townships in Georgia that are just a few miles from Brunswick, the poorest township in the state. The homes on the islands are worth millions, and thus have high property taxes, which theoretically should benefit the local schools, including those in Brunswick. But many island residents of those townships claim an exemption under the Homestead Act that allows them to simply opt out of the education component of their property taxes. "To me, that is the most absurd, selfish thing, anyone could ever do," Stephen said.

"Education is foundational to any society—but they send all their kids to private school anyways, so they don't care about the local schools. They're robbing these local schools of tens of millions of dollars. They just don't see the problem; they think it's a good thing to do, to rob the kids that don't have the money for it. They so miss the responsibility of all of us to pay for all of it, not just what you want to pay for." Against his attorney's advice, he didn't check the box that would allow him to claim that exemption.

But counting on individuals like Stephen to voluntarily part with their money isn't the solution, nor, as he pointed out, does he believe that he can singlehandedly fix the problem. He plans to devote time, energy, and money to solving what he views as the underlying issues—to keeping the estate tax in place, raising taxes for the wealthy. He doesn't view this as exactly altruistic; he thinks that future generations, including his own granddaughter, will suffer if this problem isn't fixed.

"We can't continue what we're doing—we're piling up too much money in too few pockets. I have no desire to stop America from being a country where you can make a lot of money, . . . but I believe that success in a capitalist society comes with a burden, and a responsibility, for taking care of society at large."

Inheritance

If our country has a conflicted relationship with wealth generally, there is one category of wealthy people who are universally disdained: trust fund babies. The children of the wealthy, who inherited their money rather than worked for it, are the subject of endless negative stereotypes. In part because of those stereotypes, and in part because of the aforementioned cultural silence around money, people who have inherited wealth often keep that fact to themselves.

In the 1990s two women with large trust funds, Tracy Hewat and Lynne Gerber, wanted to start a group that would bring together those with access to wealth who wanted to align their social justice values with their philanthropy. The group's original name was Comfort Zone, and it started out as a space for its members to talk about the tensions inherent in being a young person who both cared about social justice and had access to wealth. The organization transformed over the years, moving from being a place where wealthy inheritors could simply "talk" about wealth toward its current incarnation: an organization that pushes its members to give away both the wealth and their decision-making power over it. Their name changed as well, from Comfort Zone to Resource Generation.

The main membership is for people ages eighteen to thirty-five; the group also has an alumni program for people ages thirty-five and up. When the group has been covered by the media, it's frequently covered with a great deal of skepticism, with a tone conveying "wacky, idealistic rich kids give away all their money before they've learned to get serious and grow up."

The current mission of the organization is to "do voluntary redistribution in service of involuntary redistribution"—in other words, to give away money in a way that shifts the balance of power so that underrepresented communities can push for the policy changes that will lead to "involuntary" redistribution down the line.

I talked to a member of Resource Generation about inheritance, privilege, wealth, and redistribution.

Karen Pittelman
Brooklyn, NY

Karen Pittelman is a writer and singer living in Brooklyn who previously served as a program coordinator at Resource Generation. She wrote two books while at Resource Generation: *Classified: How to Stop Hiding Your Privilege and Use it for Social Change* and *Creating Change Through Family Philanthropy*.

Growing up, she says, she had no idea the extent of her family's resources; they weren't conspicuous consumers, and since she attended private school in New York City, she was surrounded by wealth. That experience is common, by her observation. "Most of the people that I know, who I've organized and worked with who come from a background of class privilege, their experience is similar to mine—you're not supposed to talk about money."

In her early twenties she learned that she had a $3.5 million trust fund. She knew that she wanted that trust fund to be dissolved and redistributed. But that request caused "a lot of tension and conflict in the beginning." "For my family, it felt really hard, because it felt like I was rejecting them. And when I was younger it was hard for me to figure out how to deal with that." Her family felt like "this money is for you, to take care of you, and what's most important to us is to take care of you and have everything you need. And I wanted to walk a line of saying, 'Thank you and I appreciate that,' *but* . . . I wasn't trying to be cool, or a rebel. I just felt like, where do you draw that line between who is family, who is kin, who are you responsible to, and who are you not responsible to? It just didn't feel true to me to draw that line just at our family, and just our blood relations."

She understands why her family felt so anxious and how parting with money can be particularly difficult for families who have lived through trauma. "My family is Jewish, and they came here fleeing the pogroms in Russia—my great-grandfather, who started the company with my grandfather that made us all this money, had to flee. And he got some of his family out, but not all of them." That has led to a mentality through the generations, Karen said, that "building wealth will keep us safe."

She was quick to say that she doesn't think they're *wrong* about that mentality, exactly. "I don't think it serves the cause to minimize the risk—which is why people have held onto any money and any power they could get. Who gets out when they're closing the borders? Who can afford a passport, or bribe someone. . . . I'm not trying to pretend that that's not true. But it's also like are you going to plan your life out—is that where your values come from? Fear, and that your only purpose is to protect your immediate family? I'm not sure we can talk anybody into redistributing wealth and power by minimizing that fear—but at the end, it's about, Is this the world you want for your kids?"

She turned over her trust fund to activists in the Boston area, who in turn spent down the principal in grants to organizations helping women and girls who lived in poverty. At the time, she says, she heard two refrains both from her family and other people in her life. The first was concern for her theoretical future children: "Nobody said, 'If you have kids.' It was just, 'You're a woman; *you're going* to have kids.'" In addition to deep concern about her imagined future children, both her family and others who knew about her plan were worried for a future version of herself, asking, "What if you change your mind? How do you know that you're doing it right?" Now forty-five years old, she has not had children; she also hasn't changed her mind. She also said that some of the worry about "changing your mind" comes from a "a really inflated idea of our own significance as wealthy people"—the idea that you might be doing giving "wrong" or that there's some perfect way to give that will solve the world's problems. "None of us have enough money to 'fix it,'" she says. She rejects the idea that she sees among wealthy people that anything short of totally fixing a problem means that the giving itself wasn't worth it.

She had initially approached giving away her trust fund as a one-time big project, something to essentially get out of the way so that she could better move on with the rest of her life. For a time, her family stopped giving her what she calls distributions from the family business; they've since started again. When we spoke in November 2020, she'd given away $20 million, an amount that she characterized as a "wild and ridiculous" amount of money to have had access to. She's given much of it to the Trans Justice Funding Project. But she no longer thinks of giving as something that she can just be done with. "It's something I'm going to be dealing with the rest of my life." And even if she did manage to give away every cent, she says, her family's wealth is in her health, her teeth, her paid-for Ivy League education— privilege isn't something that you can ever completely "give away."

I asked her about how to decide what you can afford to give. "On the one hand," she says "you've got to take care of your kids—I don't think there's any good political philosophy that says you don't provide for your children—and the whole question of how much is enough is something that everybody grapples with, and that you should grapple with. But there's a difference between doing responsible budgeting— making sure you have enough for emergencies, and making sure you can care for the people who you're responsible for—[and] a feeling of fear and lack of security; there's no amount of money that will ever make that go away."

To figure out how much to give, she uses the model of tithing, a concept in many religions, in which you commit to giving away a certain percentage of your income. Karen's set a lifetime goal for herself of 90 percent of all her assets. "I can tithe myself at a very high rate, because I have all this money coming in," she said. "But by just doing a 5 to 10 percent of tithe, no matter who you are, you're saying, 'This is my commitment to a different kind of world.' And if you have access to more, you should be tithing yourself at a higher rate. But if you're not ready to do that, then tithe yourself at 5 to 10 percent." Figuring out the actual amount of your tithe, she claims, also has the added benefit that it "forces you to acknowledge the material fact of those resources." The subject of her first book, *Classified*, was the difficulty of simply acknowledging what we actually have: "All of us who have values that don't line up with our privilege—we're hiding stuff under our bed."

But whom do you tithe *to*? A lot of the charitable giving in the United States is directed toward two institutions: the religious institutions where people worship and their alma mater. Both of those are institutions that people have a stake in. Some of those institutions do a wonderful job of distributing funds in a way that has a positive impact on the lives of people living in poverty, but plenty don't. The neediest people are often the ones left out as recipients of charitable giving. But even when they are recipients, they don't usually have control over the money itself. A crucial part of Resource Generation's mission is to think about giving away not just money but power. When Karen dissolved her trust fund, she didn't decide who got its proceeds; a board of women who had experienced poverty themselves oversaw grant making.

For parents with the resources to do any level of giving, Karen suggested that much of the traditional advice that's family-centered or child-centered perpetuates problematic power dynamics. The traditional story of family giving, she says, is "we have this money, so *we* decide together where it goes, and that brings us closer as a family" and that giving means that "we don't even have to feel bad about having more than other people, because look at how benevolent we are. . . . People get taught very young that we're rich because we *deserve* to be rich—because your grandfather was an amazing busi- nessman, and he was very smart and made good choices, and through all his hard work and his smarts, he built this wealth and he handed it down to us. You have more because you deserve more. But if you're not going to say that, you're going to say, 'We have more than other people, but it's not fair.'"

I asked her about some of the common things that people are encouraged to say to kids about how money or material wealth don't matter, and won't bring true happiness. The takeaway from her own life of giving wasn't that comfortable fiction that *You don't need to hold onto anything—money doesn't matter.* "Of course, it matters!" she insists. "We've set up a society where money is maybe the thing that matters the most—but only a few people have it."

Giving, with kids or not, isn't about making yourself feel like a great person. "If you're trying to look for a quick fix to make guilt go away, it won't work. To stay connected to the struggle for wealth and power, you have to stay connected to the grief. And be in it for the long haul. Be resilient enough to hold the truth of injustice, instead of wanting to run away. Because if you're in a position to give, you're also in a position to use your resources and privilege to run away."

Reparations and the Racial Wealth Gap

As Karen says, only a few people *do* have money—and overwhelmingly, they are White. It's not that everyone who is White is wealthy, of course, but wealth is disproportionately held by White families. Law professor Dorothy A. Brown's 2021 book, *The Whiteness of Wealth: How the Tax System Impoverishes Black Americans—and How We Can Fix It*, is filled with jaw-dropping statistics that bear that out. The median wealth of White households is $171,000, of Latino households is $20,600, and of Black households is $17,100. White families are equally likely to have zero or negative wealth as they are to be millionaires; Black and Latino families are twenty times and fourteen times more likely, respectively, to have zero or negative net worth than to be millionaires.

Wealth is different from income. Income is how much you make every year, but wealth is your net worth—a number you get by adding up your assets and investments and subtracting your debt. I have never had a particularly high income. In my career I've been a teacher, a public interest lawyer, and, lowest paying of all, a freelance writer. But those career choices haven't changed the fact that I have wealth—not because of anything I did, or didn't do, but because of the family that I had the good fortune to be born into.

And wealth, not income, is what really matters in determining your ability to live a life without major stressors or catastrophes, to live anything approximating "the good life" or a vision of the American dream. As Nikole Hannah-Jones wrote in her essay on reparations in *New York Times Magazine*, "Wealth, not income, is the means to security in America. Wealth . . . is what enables you to buy homes in safer neighborhoods with better amenities and better-funded schools. It is what enables you to send your children to college without saddling them with tens of thousands of dollars of debt and what provides you money to put a down payment on a house. It is what prevents family emergencies or unexpected job losses from turning into catastrophes that leave you homeless and destitute. It is what ensures what every parent wants—that your children will have fewer struggles than you did. Wealth is security and peace of mind."

Heather McGhee, who wrote *The Sum of Us: What Racism Costs Everyone and How We Can Prosper Together*, made a similar point in an interview on *Fresh Air*. The word *wealth*, she said, can connote "diamonds and yachts . . . but we're really talking about a little bit of home equity, the fact that you grew up in a house that your parents owned, even if it was not a very expensive house, the fact that your aunt or uncle may have had some GM stock or a CD that they gave you, you know, when you turn eighteen." McGhee points out that this kind of intergenerational wealth stemmed in large part from public policies that, from the New Deal through the Civil Rights Movement, were often explicit about benefiting only White people.

White families have had a "head start" of hundreds of years. They have accumulated wealth through theft of land (from the original inhabitants of this country) and labor (through chattel slavery). And repeatedly, the government has enacted policies that explicitly help White families amass wealth while leaving out families of color—Brown's book is a careful examination of how the tax code was written in a way that advantages White Americans, and continues to do so today.

The concept that this gap should be addressed through reparations isn't a new idea. The first case of reparations predates the end of slavery by decades; in 1783 a formerly enslaved woman, Belinda Sutton, successfully petitioned the Commonwealth of Massachusetts for reparations from the estate of the family who had enslaved her. The most famous, and first widespread attempt at reparations to formerly enslaved people was the "forty acres and a mule" promised after the Civil War (an order that was swiftly reversed when Andrew Jackson came into office).

In 1989 Michigan congressman John Conyers introduced HR 40, the Commission to Study and Develop Reparation Proposals for African-Americans Act. If passed, as its name suggests, the bill would create a commission tasked with determining whether "any form of compensation to the descendants of African slaves is warranted." In April 2021, thirty-two years after the bill was first introduced, the House of Representatives' Judiciary Committee voted to bring the bill to the House floor; it has not yet been voted on in the House as of this writing, and its proponents acknowledge that it faces long odds in passing the Senate.

Reparations are a controversial and messy idea. Questions about who would pay, and how much, and to whom abound. But as Ta-Nehisi Coates has pointed out in his celebrated essay "The Case for Reparations," if the *practicalities* of reparations were the only sticking point, passing HR 40 would be the solution—the commission would be tasked with finding answers to those questions. It would not actually authorize payment.

But not everyone is waiting for wide-scale, national reparations to do their own work. The next interviewees have begun to grapple with and take actions to address their own family history and their legacy on their own.

Lotte Lieb Dula and Briayna Cuffie
Denver, CO, and Annapolis, MD

Lotte Lieb Dula is a retired financial strategist who lives in the Denver area. Three years ago, shortly after she had retired, she decided that she was going to use some of her newfound time to learn more about her family's history. "We've had these storage lockers filled with family records," she says. "And I thought to myself, *Oh, how fun. I get to find out more about my ancestors—these fabulous people!* You know where I'm going with this."

In one of the boxes, she had found a small ledger book that listed the names of forty-four people her family had enslaved. She also found a relic from her family's more recent past: a 1907 yearbook from her grandmother's college that listed her as member of the KKK "social club."

Before making that discovery, Lotte says, racial justice work had not been at the forefront of her mind. "I was your typical White person who identified as a liberal but didn't really walk my philosophy. I had never read a racial justice book. And yet, I thought I was a model antiracist, though I had not done the tiniest bit of work. So I know really well what it is to live in a White bubble, being completely unaware of the impact my life had on BIPOC folk. Part of my journey of trying to unwind harm has been talking publicly about the process of learning to see the confines of my White bubble, and making the decision to step outside, and look at my own history and the history of our country through a different lens."

Through a conversation with a local activist, Lotte learned of the group Coming to the Table, a national group whose stated mission is to provide "resources, leadership, and a supportive environment for all who wish to acknowledge and heal wounds from racism that is rooted in the United States' history of slavery." Many members, like Lotte, had ancestors who owned enslaved people. At Coming to the Table's national gathering that year she met Briayna.

Briayna Cuffie, a Black woman in her twenties I interviewed with Lotte, is a county council staff member, activist, and racial equity consultant. Unlike Lotte, she grew up deeply aware of some aspects of her family's history. Her grandmother's mother had worked as a sharecropper, a history she learned about from her family: "My mother and my elders told me, 'Here's what happened between slavery and Jim Crow that won't be in your history books.'" She knew that members of her family had been enslaved. But how she'd ended up involved with Coming to the Table was much more happenstance than Lotte's journey to the group. She recalled her mom coming home and telling her that a local church was having a "group of White people talking about slavery." Briayna had given her mother a ride to the group, planning to turn right around and go home. But once there, she decided to save herself a trip and stay, and thus learned about Coming to the Table's work.

The national gathering where she met Lotte wasn't her first choice for a weekend activity. "I have a weekend to myself, and I don't really want to spend it driving to the depths of Virginia," she recalls. She'd planned to leave after making a brief appearance but stayed an extra half day to attend a group session on the topic of reparations.

At the session, Briayna brought up the ways that the racial wealth gap had affected her personally. Every member of her family, including herself, worked multiple jobs; she had worked two or three jobs since the time she was fourteen. Yet she almost hadn't graduated from college because she ran out of money her senior year; only a GoFundMe had enabled her to finish her degree. She graduated with six figures of student loan debt, which hangs over her head and hinders her ability to do a lot of the work that she would like to do. While attending the session on reparations at the conference, she felt some frustration hearing the theoretical conversations about future scholarships as a means to reparations, which ignored the reality of people like her: "I have six figures' worth of debt, and I'm making literal pennies doing the work you say you all value," Briayna said.

"During the session, I had raised the possibility of creating a website for White families to learn about and engage in the reparations movement, but no one seemed interested in partnering with me," Lotte says. "I was so disappointed; I left the session feeling a little defeated."

However, Briayna approached Lotte after the session about the ideas behind what would eventually become their website,

Reparations4slavery.com. Briayna also challenged Lotte about the scholarship ideas she had mentioned during the session. A few weeks later, Lotte wrote her an email. Briayna remembers pulling her mom over and saying, "Mom, read this email, and tell me if it says what I think it says. And my mom said, 'Who is this woman? Give her all of your information except for your Social Security number.'" Lotte had offered to pay off Briayna's student loans. She's been making payments now for about three years.

"Every year I pay off some. . . . It's not a huge amount, but we're getting it done. It's going to get done," Lotte says. And Lotte has another vision—to both pay off the student loans and help Briayna build long-term wealth so that by the time Briayna's forty years old she will have the same median wealth as a White woman her age. "Now, that's a bold idea. Of course, there are flaws with it, because it's my idea, not her idea . . ."

Briayna adds, "Yeah, my goal is just to be at zero. I'm fine with just not having student loans. But Lotte's like, 'No, this is the game plan.'" She laughs. Lotte continues, "Part of the thing, with White people, is that we're so used to controlling resources, and part of repair is giving up that control. I'm not good at that yet, but I'm working on it!"

Lotte also brought Briayna on as a consultant to help her build the website. "My goal," Lotte shares, "was to create a site that would allow you to research your ancestry, repatriate your documents of slaveholding, and form a relationship of repair based on your own history."

Both Lotte and Briayna have a deep fascination with genealogy and ancestry. But their ability to learn about their families' pasts differs sharply: Lotte has documented over a thousand ancestors on her family tree on Ancestry.com; she has traced her lineage back to her tenth great-grandfather. Briayna can get back about 150 years before running into what genealogists call the brick wall of 1870—before that year, enslaved people weren't recorded in the US census by name, which makes tracing her family lineage an extremely difficult task.

The more detailed records kept by slaveholding families are often the only way around that wall, which is part of why Lotte wants to encourage families to repatriate slaveholding documents if they make a discovery like she did in a family basement or garage.

Part of creating her own relationship of repair has, for Lotte, involved looking at the role her family played in various institutions. "My family's footprint in this country really revolved around three areas, one of them being civil service in government. They did a lot of harm, certainly upholding if not drafting laws establishing slavery in several states. And I decided that if I'm going to unwind the harm my family did, why not do it directly? Briayna's not only doing all this work in social change, but she's also working in international relations, and has this political science background—I just thought, '*Hell yeah* I'm going to help pay off her college debt.'"

She continues, "Even if your family didn't directly enslave people, I would just say that overall, all White families are complicit in one way or another—you just have to go back and see what your family's footprint was. You need to go back and look at how your family made its wealth—whether it's that each generation gave the next generation money for a down payment or for college—somehow, wealth is getting passed from generation to generation, and that's what African American families don't have. I've actually put a webpage together called the 'Racial Wealth Gap: The Economic Basis for Reparations,' trying to show White people all the laws we've enacted that have made it impossible for African Americans to amass wealth—it's just so insidious. The idea is to transform your family's tradition of philanthropy into a tradition of engaging in repair for parties that your family has injured. For some, you can trace it back to actual people your family enslaved—in Coming to the Table, we call that forming a relationship with a linked descendant."

For people who want to do some form of individual reparations, the place to start is a conversation. "Talk to the matriarchs and patriarchs of the family," Briayna says. "You need to go and sit with the grandma, the great-grandma and ask, 'What do you wish you had the ability to give your future generations?' Some answers you might hear are a car to get to work, . . . or a lot of them have the guilt of, 'When I get older, someone will have to care for me, but they already work three jobs.'"

Individual reparations, both Briayna and Lotte acknowledge, can be awkward. A June 2020 episode of the podcast *Reply All* investigated a phenomenon that had cropped up around the time of the mass protests after George Floyd's murder: Black people receiving random Venmo payments from their White acquaintances. As the episode's host, Emmanuel Dzotsi, said, "I heard from all of these Black people who had gotten a notification that some White person had sent them cash in the weirdest form of reparations—as if to say, 'Here's a few bucks, sorry for racism.'" The recipient's reactions to these payments ranged from bemusement and confusion to feeling insulted by the gesture. A missing piece in all those stories was both the conversation and the ability of the one on the receiving end to decide whether, and how much, they wanted in reparations. But both Lotte and Briayna agree there is an awkwardness even to enacting a mutually agreed-upon plan of repair.

Unsurprisingly, they believe that HR 40, the bill to establish a commission to study and recommend redress methods for slavery and the institutional racism that followed, should be passed, but they think that there's a place for individual reparations too. "HR 40 has been introduced my entire life," Briayna reflects. (The bill is older than she is; it was first introduced five years before she was born.) "If it was going to happen, that ball could have been rolling already. I like the approach that Lotte and I err on—building that power from the individual up." In her work in local government, she's seen how local movements can become national ones. "Ask your city council person about supporting or putting in a resolution." To get White people to support HR 40, Lotte says that you can't just talk about the bill itself. "First, you have to get people to understand their family's complicity. Then supporting it becomes a no-brainer. If you try to do it the other way around, you can't even begin the conversation."

Even though Lotte's family were technically the ones who "benefited," at least financially, from their role as slaveholders, their participation in the dehumanizing systems of both slavery and all the other forms of subsequent systemic racial violence had done profound damage to the members of her family as well. "I feel like my family has been so damaged by White supremacy. I mean, we *invented* it, my family has been here since the early 1600s. But it eats you alive through the generations. Each generation in my family tried to push the others out of the way in order to get more of whatever inheritance they thought was due. There was no real love in my family. Instead of love, you were given tokens of approval—a cherished antique or piece of jewelry. Those things took the place of love, and each family member fought the others to receive as many tokens of love as possible."

One irony in their story is that Lotte didn't go to college herself. "But I just look at Briayna and I say, 'You have all the potentials that I wish I had at your age. And so, if I can do things that help power you ahead so all your potential can blossom, I'm honored to be able to do that in the context of our relationship of repair.' Part of repair is unwinding White supremacy, and part of that process is realizing how it affects those of us who are White; we need to ask ourselves, 'What do I need to be freed from?' We're talking about coliberation here.

"White supremacy is bad for White people too. I've suffered just tremendous pain because of the competition in my family for material resources, which is part of the nature of White supremacy. So, if I can heal some of that damage in myself, through being in relationship to Briayna, and applying my material resources to support her blossoming—it's my honor, and it's part of both my own atonement *and* my own healing."

Chris Moore-Backman
Oakland, CA

Chris Moore-Backman is the father of a fifteen-year-old. He has produced a radio series about mass incarceration and written a book about nonviolence; he currently works at a nonprofit doing work he describes as being "at the intersection of racial healing and climate justice." Reparations work and environmental justice work are often seen as separate and distinct projects, but Chris sees them as fundamentally intertwined, and both are at the forefront of his mind when he thinks about the question of inheritance for his daughter.

"To me," he says, "the biggest challenge as a dad has been dealing with the reality that climate change is upon us, and seeking a balance—to be honest and real about that, while recognizing the vulnerability of a child. . . . I see so many parents . . . raising their kids as if we're going to have this perpetual American future. And my parents raised me to believe in that. In large part, that was because of our privilege as White people. But it was also because none of us knew about climate change when I was growing up. Something like COVID . . . isn't going to be so unusual moving forward. We're looking at a series of compounding crises heading towards us because of what we've done to the planet, and to each other. I want my daughter to know. . . . And I feel it would be a real disservice to tell her, or to show her, something that I don't believe is true."

The many unknowns of what his daughter's adulthood will look like, and what the next generation will face, make him think differently about the question of inheritance. The traditional model, in which parents save up to pass along a lump sum of money to their children, doesn't in his view "reflect a realistic view of where we are—with climate, with race." The thing he hopes to pass down to his daughter is that "she'll be embedded in a really rich, vibrant, loving community, with all kinds of different resources and gifts. When I think of my

daughter's future and I look at the likelihood of things being drastically different a decade or two from now, I have way more confidence
in meaning and community than I do in money."

His work on a radio series about the stark racial imbalances in the
criminal justice system was what first led him to consider reparations
as a necessity to move forward. "I was reared in a set of ideas that if
we can just get all these well-meaning people together to share their
stories, then racial reconciliation *can happen*. But it didn't occur to
me that restitution was an absolutely essential piece of this process.
Restitution for harm done is a prerequisite—it's a necessary part of
what creates a pathway towards reconciliation." He began to read
about the topic: Coates's *Atlantic* essay, Raymond Winbush's *Should
America Pay? Slavery and the Raging Debate on Reparations*, the works
of Tim Wise (who most famously wrote *White Like Me: Reflections
on Race from a Privileged Son*). In 2016 Chris joined the protests at
Standing Rock against the Dakota Access Pipeline. "My conversations
deepened there," he remembers. A few months after returning from
Standing Rock, he published an essay exploring reparations. In the
opening of the essay, he describes talking to his then-eleven-year-old
daughter about his central question. "What do you do when there's
more damage than you could ever hope to repair?" Without hesitation, she offers him her thoughts: "You should repair as much as you
can. And then you should teach young people about what happened,
so it doesn't happen again. And you need to say sorry." Despite her
young age, his daughter "was ready to be in that conversation and
could help me out with her way of understanding what was going on.
It made perfect sense to her."

His views on the necessity of reparations also affects how he thinks
about inheritance. "I've thought a lot about inheritance over the course
of thinking through reparations—the basic reality that so much of the
unearned wealth in the White community lands in our bank accounts,
and in our homes in the form of inheritance that is directly traceable

to the two original sins of our country: genocide and land theft of Indigenous people, and then the enslavement and labor of the Black people who basically built this nation. And on the part of privileged, White-identifying people . . . we've yet to have a critical mass of us to take responsibility for that, as it relates to inheritance."

In the summer of 2020 Chris was deeply inspired by a project called the Reparations Procession. For forty days, White members of the Bay Area community walked from the West Berkeley Shellmound, a sacred Indigenous site, to Fruitvale station, where Oscar Grant, a young Black man, was killed by a transit police officer. They walked in black clothing and veils and called on people to offer reparations. At the end of the forty days, they had approximately $90,000, which they divided between an Indigenous-led land trust and the Black Solidarity Fund, a local organization that supports Black business owners. During the project, Chris reached out to his own father, who he knows has set aside money for him, "'Some of that money you're moving to me, how about moving it to this Reparations Procession fund?' But it wasn't where he was at. . . . My dad was raised to take care of his kids and his immediate loved ones, and for him inheritance is an integral part of that worldview. But I get to have a different analysis now—a race-class analysis shaped by people and life experiences that my dad was never exposed to."

Part of the difficulty in getting White families to think differently about inheritance is tied to our tendency to buy into a version of history that leaves out ancestors' complicity, or even direct involvement, in those "original sins." "I remember having a conversation with my aunt years ago, and she was spinning this tale that our family was more like the Quakers during the time of slavery. It's such a comforting hope that this might have been the case," he says. But for White families "chances are better that they were entrenched in that system in disturbing and shameful ways." His own mother has done research and uncovered the reality that his family was, as he puts it, "very much a slave-owning family in the south—our ancestors were wealthy sugar plantation owners in Louisiana." He, his daughter, and his mother are planning to embark on what he calls a "journey of atonement" once it's safe to travel. "There are still places standing, where we could go and reckon with the reality of that part of our family's history."

Getting privileged White people to rethink their relationship to both the past and the future is a tall order, and one that he doesn't expect to be easily solved. "We still have this incredible gravitational pull towards thinking about our nearest and dearest, without considering the whole community. Without considering that all of us are truly interconnected. That privilege—it really blocks us from seeing the deeper truth of what it means to be alive; to be a part of the human community, a part of the earth community. To feel that connection and care for all the living beings in it. Not just *my* kid, *my* aging parents. Of course, I'm going to care about them, but in the context of caring for the whole. It's not that I'm immune to the tendency of looking out for my own. But the question is, Why my kid, and not another kid?" Rather than thinking about inheritance or stockpiling for the future, he's thinking about "moving those resources now to where they're needed and encouraging other White people to do that too."

Takeaways

I struggled with my own reaction to some of the interviews I'd done for this chapter, a reaction I can best categorize as "easy for you to say." It's easy for Rachel to avoid income creep and give away her extra money. She doesn't live in Brooklyn. It's easy for Stephen to lobby for increased taxes. His children are grown, and he has more money than he could spend in his lifetime. *I'm* not likely to see anywhere close to $20 million in my lifetime, so what can I possibly have to learn from Karen, who has already given that much away? It's easy for Lotte to take on someone else's student loan debt; she isn't trying to put her own kids through college.

It's a valid reaction. But, of course, someone reading this may have had that reaction to me. I've said repeatedly in the book that I come from family wealth; I've never had student loans or faced real financial precarity.

In *Strangers Drowning: Grappling with Impossible Idealism, Drastic Choices, and the Overpowering Urge to Help*, Larissa MacFarquhar writes about a distinction between the "part-time, normal do-gooders" and "the kind of do-gooder who makes people uneasy." Some of the profiles in her book are of parents who took the challenge of living out their values to further extremes than anyone I interviewed. She spoke with Massachusetts parents with two children who give more than half of their annual income away. Some years, they've given away over 90 percent of what they make. They aren't heirs—they live with roommates and make other major lifestyle sacrifices to make that level of giving possible. Another couple in her book found themselves so disturbed by the number of children without loving homes that they adopted (and, at least according to the book, properly cared for) twenty-two children, many of them teens from the foster care system. Our reaction to people who give away so much that it affects their own standard of living, or who otherwise push doing good works to its extremes, MacFarquhar writes, is often something akin to disdain. They make us uncomfortable, and we want to dismiss them as mentally ill or as otherwise "not like us."

Another thing I grappled with was how much I should focus on voluntary giving and how much to focus on the societal changes that would make it unnecessary. In a country with universal healthcare, we wouldn't have to decide whether to donate some of our money to a stranger's life-saving surgery because people wouldn't have to rely on GoFundMe campaigns for their medical bills. And it's easy to use that fact as an excuse to justify giving less because it's painful to part with money. Shayla Griffin's framing from the schools chapter of embracing both/and solutions comes in handy when thinking about how to parse this issue. Yes, we need structural change. But also, people with more than they need must stop hoarding the wealth.

Rachel Sherman, the sociologist whose work I referenced at the beginning of this chapter, has a useful construct for thinking about wealth: no matter how much you have, you can either be "upward-oriented" or "downward-oriented." People who are upward-oriented, she writes, "tended not even to think of themselves as socially advantaged because they were focused on others around them who had the same resources or more than they did"; downward-oriented people, on the other hand "tended to have more economically diverse social networks, and to compare their own lifestyles to a broader range of other possibilities." In his article about Americans whose assets put them in the top "9.9 percent," Matthew Stewart makes a similar point. In that income bracket, which he counts himself among, he writes, "our necks get stuck in the upward position. We gaze upon the 0.1 percent with a mixture of awe, envy, and eagerness to obey."

The upward-downward construct is similarly useful for thinking about reparations work. It's easier for me to look upward and think about all the families who are *more* responsible than my own for the perpetuation of the wealth gap, and of the perpetuation of White supremacy. Lotte's family's involvement was clear-cut: she held a book in her hand that documented her family's involvement in the slave trade. In some ways, that made her task of figuring out her obligation to pay reparations easier. But in other ways, her story is more complicated. She had a neglectful, impoverished childhood herself; she has experienced a lot of suffering. But her reparations work, as she says, wasn't just about "apologizing"; it was also about her own healing from that past.

How does all this fit into what parents can reasonably put into action with their own children? I think the spend-save-give model is a useful one; we want to teach our children about all three of those options for money. But after the interviews I've done for this chapter, I'm going to think differently about how to talk about both what, and why, we give. The standard message of "giving" is that it's a nice thing to do, and that sharing is good. It's harder to communicate the more complex truth that, particularly for White families, we're not so much "sharing" as "giving back what was wrongfully taken." To say to your kids, "Yes, we have more than other people, and that's not fair or right." Finally, to teach the more radical idea that people know best for themselves; seek out the advice of the people who you want to help in how the money could be best spent.

- **Learn about your family's history**—even the unsavory parts. Lotte and Briayna's site provides a starting point. They write, "Look for signs and records of slaveholding and DNA connections to people of color. Equally important, look for ways your family may have participated in Jim Crow, or may even currently participate in behaviors that are damaging to African Americans." Learn the history of the land that you own, or that's in your family. Families with privilege like to do a lot of veneration of our ancestors. But when we talk about our histories, we need to tell the whole truths.
- **Make a plan of repair, if applicable.** Coming to the Table, Reparations4Slavery, and the Resource Generation's "Land Reparations and Indigenous Solidarity Toolkit" are all places to start. A plan of repair can't be something that you completely self-direct, nor something that I can outline. But those organizations are a place to begin that work.

    o Coming to the Table: https://comingtothetable.org/
    o Reparations4Slavery: https://reparations4slavery.com/designing-a
       -family-plan-of-repair/
    o Resource Generation: https://resourcegeneration.org/land
       -reparations-indigenous-solidarity-action-guide/

- **Think about giving away decision-making power, not just money.** To make this work, of course, we must build relationships with people in communities outside a bubble of privilege. Look for ways to model mutual aid relationships, rather than benefactor relationships, for your children with people in the community.

- **Vote and fight for policies that will lessen the need for private solutions.** In *The Sum of Us: What Racism Costs Everyone and How We Can Prosper Together*, Heather McGhee makes the argument that the reason we have a hollow middle class today is in large part because of our country's willingness to cut off its nose to spite its face. We support leaders and policies which disproportionately hurt people of color, but all but the very wealthiest Americans, no matter their racial background, pay a price. Work to elect antiracist leaders, and to shift the narrative that tells us, as McGhee puts it, "that progress for people of color has to come at white people's expense."

Further Reading

Classified: How to Stop Hiding Your Privilege and Use It for Social Change! by Karen Pittelman (SoftSkull, 2005)

Decolonizing Wealth: Indigenous Wisdom to Heal Divides and Restore Balance by Edgar Villanueva (Berrett-Koehler, 2018)

Here to Equality: Reparations for Black Americans in the 21st Century by William A. Darity Jr. and A. Kirsten Mullen (University of North Carolina Press, 2020)

Strangers Drowning: Grappling with Impossible Idealism, Drastic Choices, and the Overpowering Urge to Help by Larissa MacFarquhar (Penguin Books, 2016)

The Sum of Us: What Racism Costs Everyone and How We Can Prosper Together by Heather McGhee (One World, 2021)

The Whiteness of Wealth by Dorothy A. Brown (Penguin Random House, 2021)

CONCLUSION

—————

I N FEBRUARY 2021 a snowstorm hit Texas, causing a catastrophic humanitarian crisis in the state. Millions of people lost power and heat. Pipes froze, leaving people without access to water to drink or bathe in. A few days into the crisis, an eleven-year-old boy died of hypothermia in an unheated mobile home.

In the middle of the crisis, Ted Cruz, one of Texas's two senators, boarded a plane from Texas and traveled with his family to a Cancun resort. Pictures of Cruz boarding the plane quickly went viral across social media platforms; every major news outlet ran multiple stories about what the *Washington Post* called his "disastrous decision." He returned to Texas less than twenty-four hours after he had left. His initial statement of explanation suggested that he had planned only to escort his daughters to the resort: "With school cancelled for the week, our girls asked to take a trip with friends. Wanting to be a good dad, I flew down with them last night and am flying back this afternoon." When further details emerged that called into question his stopover story (specifically, leaked texts from his wife's friends showing that the couple had been planning to stay for the week), he changed tactics, going on a semi-apology tour. Yet he continued to reiterate that the trip was justified as a parenting decision: "In hindsight, I wouldn't have done it." But he said, "I was trying to be a dad. I think a lot of parents [would have done the same]."

The specifics of the story: a widely reviled politician, an opulent trip in the midst of a disaster—meant that his "trying to be a good dad" story got little traction. *Salon* ran an article with the headline CRUZ RIPPED TO SHREDS FOR BLAMING WIDELY CONDEMNED CANCUN VACATION ON HIS DAUGHTERS. But I could understand why Cruz thought that the excuse would garner sympathy. Culturally, we excuse all kinds of behavior from parents, from all sides of the political aisle. Privileged parenting norms give us the message that, whatever values we might say we hold, those can be left outside the threshold of our front door and abandoned as soon as it affects *our* kids.

In *Dream Hoarders*, Richard Reeves quotes one parent, a journalist who covers education inequality and saw the irony: "I spent my weekdays decrying the problem of inequality, but then I spent my evenings and weekends adding to it." We get constant message that it's fine, that there is no tension between a White parent holding a BLACK LIVES MATTER sign at a protest and then sending their child to a segregated school. That doing everything (short of paying an outright bribe) to get them in the doors of a certain college isn't corrupt, it's just what it takes to compete these days. And even if you *did* pay an outright bribe, maybe the fact that you did it for your kid makes it OK. One of the defendants in the Varsity Blues case, who paid $250,000 to gain his son admission to the University of Southern California, said at his sentencing hearing that he did it because "in my heart and soul, I wanted what was best for my son."

Some of this pattern is cultural, a product of the fear of instability discussed in the introduction. But there's also a psychological explanation. Dan Ariely, a professor of psychology who studies dishonesty, told *New York Magazine* that "the very state of being a parent obscures clear ethical reasoning, creating blinders as to what's moral and not moral." That's disturbing news if you have, as I have, looked to other parents in your social circle for signals about how to parent. People with moral blinders on are leading other people with moral blinders on, and we're taking our cues from one another.

I wrote most of this book over the course of four months, in late 2020 and early 2021. In the pandemic, we were part of the most privileged slice of families—my husband's job converted easily to work-from-home. We could survive on just his income, with me doing only a tiny smattering of income-producing work. We also did not have a school-aged child and avoided the specific hell of "remote learning." Mostly, I did what millions of parents across the country were doing, because there was no other option—taking care of my child, without any of the usual supports, activities, or community. I hated that the country had done so little to help families in that situation, while simultaneously feeling grateful every day that I *just* had to keep a three-year-old entertained rather than what I saw even the most privileged group of people around me doing (caring for multiple children while simultaneously trying to work for pay). A little after 4:00 PM, my husband would come out of our bedroom, where he'd been teaching by Zoom, and I would race in to log into Zoom myself and interview someone about a topic—equity in college, or reparations, or something—that would make me feel inspired and excited. And then I'd return once again to the day-to-day of parenting my three-year-old, where the ideas that I'd just talked about seemed very far away.

Most of parenting doesn't involve the big decisions that I've written about in this book. My day-to-day parenting life is made up of a million smaller decisions. Here are some of my current ones: If we have breakfast in the stroller, do we have a better chance of leaving the house today? What combination of bribery/games/cajoling will successfully get her to keep mittens on during the winter? How can I get her to ever eat something other than Honey Nut Cheerios? When my daughter confidently announces "Today is a day to skip bath," should I let her make that call?

There are many, many parenting books that help, or at least purport to help, with those dilemmas. And while this book is aimed at parents, it doesn't really help with any of those questions, or the others that arise when parenting a tween or teen. It's not about the millions of small decisions but the few big ones. The decisions we make about childcare and schools are really decisions about how, and with whom, our child will spend their time. The chapters about activism and wealth are about how we, the parents, decide to spend the time and money that we don't spend on just keeping our family afloat. These are the decisions that we typically make just a few times—we don't constantly revisit them. We might spend a few weeks stewing about them ourselves after bedtime, or text our partner about during our lunch hour. But those decisions then become the foundation that undergird the rest of our family life.

But part of being a privileged person is the pressure, coming both from inside and outside ourselves, to take advantage of that privilege. The Brookings Institution put out a video game that, complete with '80s graphics and cheesy music, mimics what happens when you face various crossroads as a parent of privilege. The game shows your child on a ladder and another child labeled "poor child" on a different ladder (further down). The intro tells you that you make $115,000 a year, and are thus part of the "favored fifth" of the income distribution. You face three decisions: whether you will oppose legislation that will allow more multifamily homes to move into your neighborhood, whether you'll donate and use legacy status to get your child into college, and whether you'll use your connections to garner an internship offer for your child. In perhaps the most realistic part of the whole game, if you answer "correctly" and make the choice that scootches your child down the ladder while moving the "poor child" up, another box pops up to ask, essentially, "Are you sure?" For the internship question, it asks, "It's a tough job market, and internships often lead directly to job offers. Will you call your friend?" The game thus mimics the social pressure that makes it easy to second-guess ourselves when we've made a choice for the "greater good." If you stay steadfast and answer all three questions "correctly," your own child has inched downward, but not very far. The "poor child" has moved up significantly, and the two are at roughly even spots on their respective ladders.

Holding onto your values is harder in the real world, of course. But a common thread throughout this book has been the role that organized groups can play in helping people who want to parent differently not feel like it's just them against the rest of the culture. The members of Hand in Hand help one another talk through the challenges of making their home into a workplace they can feel proud of, a concept that hasn't yet permeated the mainstream conversation about employing childcare or other domestic workers. Integrated Schools has chapters in dozens of cities and provides resources like the Awkward Conversation Guide for parents who are dealing with pushback for challenging the prevailing narrative around schools. Resource Generation gives its members a peer group who see "losing" (redistributing) millions of dollars as a good thing. Coming to the Table provides a space for people to both admit facts about their family legacies that they'd rather keep hidden and to join with people who take the project of reparations seriously, and don't debate their utility or need.

I'm an avid consumer of what one might call "burnout literature," the many books about how impossible the standards of modern parenting—and life, in general—have become. I didn't want to write another book that told parents that they were doing everything wrong or just needed to try harder. I especially didn't want to add to the guilt that's heaped on parents' shoulders that we're somehow "failing" our kids. An earlier version of the book proposal included interviews almost entirely with mothers, an imbalance I sought to at least partially correct, though mothers are still overrepresented, a reflection of who in the household often bears the responsibility for making these decisions. One publisher I met with asked if this was just another form of mental load that was being heaped disproportionately on women's shoulders. (Snacks, check; sunscreen, check; get my family to reconsider White supremacist ideas that inform school choice, check.)

I thought about the framing that Suni and Biz, the Evanston parents who changed their school district's funding structure, had used when approaching parents about making this big change: "No one has been doing anything wrong—we've all just been doing what we've been told was the right thing to do." I like that generous spirit and there's some truth to it—there is very little information, unless you know where to look, that invites you to think about childcare arrangements as an expression of your values, that invites you to think about "good schools" beyond their test scores, or that invites you to see college admissions as anything more than a zero-sum game.

But while I didn't want to necessarily add to individual parental guilt, it took writing this book before I fully appreciated the extent to which privileged parenting norms in this country are rooted in White supremacy. It doesn't mean that only White parents do these things. But White supremacy shapes the dominant societal norms around what childcare workers' labor is "worth" or what a "good school" looks like. It shapes who does and doesn't have wealth and what society tells us about who does and doesn't deserve it. I'm not the first person to use the metaphor of the fish not realizing he's in water to talk about the role that White supremacy plays in this country, but it's an apt one. White supremacy is pervasive, but to those who benefit from it, often invisible.

Also, most parents who identify themselves as valuing fairness, social justice, and the dignity of all people *know* that something is amiss when they act in ways that are unfairly advantageous to their kids. Margaret Hagerman, who wrote *White Kids: Growing Up with Privilege in a Racially Divided America*, wrote this in op-ed for the *Los Angeles Times*:

> Parents I interviewed felt conflicted about using their social status to advocate for their kids to have the "best" math teacher, because they knew other kids would be stuck with the "bad" math teacher. They registered the unfairness in leveraging their exclusive social networks to get their teenagers coveted summer internships when they knew disadvantaged kids were the ones who truly needed such opportunities. They felt guilty when they protectively removed their children from explicitly racist and contentious situations because they understood that kids of color cannot escape racism whenever they please. Still, those were the choices they made.

Hagerman and I were talking to different groups of parents, of course; I was explicitly looking for parents who, when they "registered the unfairness" in a course of action, changed their behavior or their decisions accordingly. And some parents are in such a privileged bubble that they literally don't see how their actions influence others. But Hagerman's research suggests that what differentiates the parents I talked to from the parents she talked to isn't necessarily that they *see* the world differently but that they make different choices with that information. Perhaps because she wasn't talking to parents who bucked the privileged parenting social norms, Hagerman came to the following conclusion: "In this moment when being a good citizen conflicts with being a good parent, I think that most white parents choose to be good parents, when, sometimes . . . they should choose to be good citizens."

Though Hagerman's work was an important influence on this book, I cringed to read the framing that she'd used: good parent versus good citizen. Now that I've talked to dozens of people making the "good citizen" choices, I can say with confidence: these are good parents. What exactly it means to be a "good parent" could be the subject of a whole different book, but anything it might mean—engaged, loving, thoughtful, caring—applies to the parents I interviewed. These were fiercely committed parents who had thought deeply about the project of raising a child. The only measure by which they weren't "good parents" was their failure to hoard every possible advantage for their own children.

And that, I believe, is not so much "good parenting" as it is "fear-based parenting." It seems so shortsighted to call "good parenting" only the short-term choices that directly benefit their kid when those same choices hollow out our society, cement inequality, and increase unfairness.

It's tricky because it's not like I can convincingly claim that there's nothing to fear. Unfortunately, there's a lot to lose sleep over. There's climate change, wealth inequality, our country's ongoing failure to invest in both care infrastructure and our education system, for starters. All of those compounding crises were at the backdrop, and sometimes the forefront, of the interviews I did.

The question at the center of this book is, How do we channel that anxiety? Do we only channel it into our own family? Though these structural deficiencies make it harder to live by our values, they also greatly increase the moral imperative for those who have some degree of privilege of power to *do something*. No one individual can solve our country's parental leave or daycare problem, but collective action (particularly when it's backed up by privileged people willing to both use connections and fund the work) and demands for change is how progress around these issues can actually occur.

It is a precarious time to be a parent. It is a precarious time to be alive. And yet raising a child is the ultimate expression of hope for the future. Not just *their* future, but all of ours.

ACKNOWLEDGMENTS

I AM DEEPLY GRATEFUL TO EVERYONE I interviewed for this book, including those whose interviews were not featured in the final text. This book would not exist had dozens of people not made time to speak with me in the midst of balancing their own parenting and job responsibilities, and all during the height of the pandemic. Special thanks to Courtney Everts Mykytyn, who I never got to meet but is nonetheless a huge influence on this book, and to Roman Mykytyn for his permission to write about Courtney's work.

Thank you to my own parents, Andy and Betsy, who supported this project in every possible way, from talking through ideas to providing hours of childcare while I fought my way through hundreds of endnotes. Thank you also to my in-laws: Ann, Dan, Adam, Elaina, and my niece and nephew, Sophia and Max, for providing hours (and sometimes days) of childcare so I could write this thing. Thank you to my entire extended family for the support and excitement about this project. I could not have done it without you all.

To my agents, Laura Usselman and Mackenzie Brady Watson—I can never thank you enough. Your thoughtful critiques and edits were instrumental in writing the book proposal. Through three rounds of submissions, through close calls and a lot of disappointing rejections, your belief that this book needed to exist, and someday would, never wavered. I frequently said to my writer friends that I don't know how anyone publishes a book without agents who are so optimistic, responsive, smart, and kind. I am grateful every day that I did not have to find out.

Thank you to Michelle Williams, Frances Giguette, Alayna Parsons-Valles, and everyone at Chicago Review Press for your extremely hard work to bring this book into existence.

I have had too many wonderful teachers to name—at Bryant Elementary, Assumption–St. Bridget, Seattle Prep, the Andover summer-school program, Seattle University, Whitman College, Columbia Law School, and, as of a month ago, the New School. Special thanks to Mark Oppenheimer (Andover), Gaurav Majumdar, Sharon Alker, Theresa DiPasquale, Andrew Osborn, Sam Witt, and especially Katrina Roberts (Whitman), and Philip Genty (Columbia). Thank you to everyone I lived with at the Whitman Writing House.

I have also been lucky enough to have more fabulous writing teachers through both Sackett Street and Ditmas Writing Workshops. Thank you, Jessica DuLong, Jessica Gross, Michele Filgate (Sackett Street Writers' Workshop) and Rachel Sherman (Ditmas Writing Workshops).

Thank you to the Park Slope Parents' listserv and especially to Susan Fox, who is such a champion for all parents who write. Thank you to the online communities where I've found so much support: The Binders, the One Bad Mother group, and what I think of as "parenting writer Twitter."

Thank you to my Whitman friends, including Amy, Sam, Leslie, Anna, and Berta. Thank you, Kyle, for your cover designs and your excitement about this project. Special thanks to Erin, for everything.

Thank you, Ma'am!

Thank you, Colleen, for being a source of endless support on every single step of this journey.

Thank you to the mom text group: Gabriela, Nikki, Bridgette, Georgia, Carolyn, and Diana. I would not have made it through pandemic parenting without you all. Thank you, Diana, for your insights about educational inequality and for being the most incredible publicist who is not an actual publicist. Extra thanks to Carolyn and Georgia, for your thoughtful feedback on early drafts of almost every section of this book.

Thank you, Frank and Caitlin, for your incredible enthusiasm for the project and for connecting me with interviewees.

Thank you, book club, for fun nights, commiseration, and support.

Thank you, Emily, Jessica, and other friends who said those beautiful words: "Let me know when to preorder." Thank you, Kim—I can't believe I got lucky enough to be friends with an extremely well-connected bookseller.

Thank you, Dawn, for your indefatigable work on behalf of children who have less, and for always taking me seriously as a writer and pushing me to go for it.

To the clients and colleagues I met at both A Better Childhood and the Children's Law Center—what I learned at those places forms the foundation of all of this work.

My deepest thanks go to my husband, Colin, who is three things in equal measure: a loving husband, a wonderful father, and a meticulous line editor. I could not ask for anything more.

NOTES

Prologue

In the last five years: Claire Cain Miller and Jonah E. Bromwich, "How Parents Are Robbing Their Children of Adulthood," *New York Times*, March 16, 2019, https://www.nytimes.com/2019/03/16/style/snowplow-parenting -scandal.html; Nicole Lyn Pesce, "How to Tell if You Are a 'Snowplow Parent,'" MarketWatch, March 22, 2019, https://www.marketwatch.com /story/how-to-tell-if-you-are-a-snowplow-parent-2019-03-22.

It's also called "lawnmower parenting": Sherri Gordon, "What Is Lawnmower Parenting?," Verywell Family, March 19, 2021, https://www.verywell family.com/lawnmower-parenting-4771519; Sharon Rosenfeld, "Inten- sive Parenting—Whether Helicopter, Snowplow, or Drone—Is Here to Stay," EAB, February 19, 2021, https://eab.com/insights/expert-insight /independent-school/intensive-parenting-is-here-to-stay/.

Lythcott-Haims also briefly: Julie Lythcott-Haims, *How to Raise an Adult: Break Free of the Overparenting Trap and Prepare Your Kid for Success* (New York: St. Martin's, 2015).

The idea that there is: Judith Warner, *Perfect Madness: Motherhood in the Age of Anxiety* (New York: Riverhead, 2005); Kim Brooks, *Small Animals: Parenthood in the Age of Fear* (New York: Flatiron Books, 2018).

"an endless expanse of products": Brooks, *Small Animals*, 85.

Introduction

As of this writing: Yekaterina Chzhen, Anna Gromada, Gwyther Rees, "Are the World's Richest Countries Family Friendly?," UNICEF, June 2019, https://www.unicef-irc.org/family-friendly.

In most states: Lindsey Hunter Lopez, "Yep, Child Care Officially Costs More than College—& Your Mortgage—in 30 States," *SheKnows*, October 29, 2019, https://www.sheknows.com/parenting/articles/2119734/childcare-cost-more-than-mortgage-college/.

As Anne Helen Petersen writes: Anne Helen Petersen, *Can't Even: How Millennials Became the Burnout Generation* (New York: Houghton Mifflin Harcourt, 2021).

Many academics and journalists have chronicled: Matthew Stewart, "The 9.9 Percent Is the New American Aristocracy," *Atlantic*, June 2018, https://www.theatlantic.com/magazine/archive/2018/06/the-birth-of-a-new-american-aristocracy/559130/; Richard V. Reeves, *Dream Hoarders: How the American Upper Middle Class Is Leaving Everyone Else in the Dust, Why That Is a Problem, and What to Do About It* (Washington, DC: Brookings Institution, 2017).

Accumulating wealth has been dramatically easier for White families: Dorothy A. Brown, *The Whiteness of Wealth: How the Tax System Impoverishes Black Americans—and How We Can Fix It* (New York: Crown, 2021).

In his 2015 book: Robert Putman, *Our Kids: The American Dream in Crisis* (New York: Simon & Schuster, 2015), 1.

"most of the people on the highest rung": Richard V. Reeves, "Stop Pretending You're Not Rich," *New York Times*, June 10, 2017, https://www.nytimes.com/2017/06/10/opinion/sunday/stop-pretending-youre-not-rich.html.

"mastered the old trick": Stewart, "The 9.9 Percent."

And it gets far worse: Sarah Al-Arshani, "Kids Represent a Small Fraction of Overall COVID-19 Deaths in the US but 75% of Them are Children of Color," Business Insider, February 21, 2021, https://www.businessinsider.com/majority-kids-died-covid-19-children-of-color-2021-2.

Philip Cohen, a sociologist: Claire Cain Miller, "The Relentlessness of Modern Parenting," *New York Times*, December 25, 2018, https://www.nytimes.com/2018/12/25/upshot/the-relentlessness-of-modern-parenting.html.

"One either allows racial inequalities to persevere": Ibram X. Kendi, *How to Be an Antiracist* (New York: One World, 2019), 9.

But, as Richard V. Reeves: Reeves, *Dream Hoarders*, 22; "Most of us think of the upper class as the thin slice at the very top, but the tectonic plates are separating lower down. It is not just the top 1 percent pulling away, but the top 20 percent."

Two of the parents involved: Christopher Rim, "The Money Lori Loughlin Used to Allegedly Bribe USC Coaches Could've Made Olivia Jade an Olympian," *Forbes*, March 16, 2019, https://www.forbes.com/sites/christoph errim/2019/03/16/the-money-lori-loughlin-used-to-allegedly-bribe-usc -coaches-couldve-made-olivia-jade-an-olympian/?sh=1d3e33d016ba.

At the beginning of the pandemic: Nikita Stewart, "She's 10, Homeless, and Eager to Learn. But She Has No Internet," *New York Times*, March 26, 2020, https://www.nytimes.com/2020/03/26/nyregion/new-york-homeless -students-coronavirus.html.

She added, "I didn't want my daughter": Kasha Philips-Lewis, Facebook messages to author, June 2, 2020.

"What if, instead, what is healthy": Courtney E. Martin, "The Benefits of Sending Your Privileged Child to an 'Underperforming' School," *On Being*, June 20, 2018, https://onbeing.org/blog/courtney-martin-the-benefits-of -sending-your-privileged-child-to-an-underperforming-school/.

1. Childcare

Is this the most demanding ad: Poppy Noor, "Must Ski, Cook and Know Excel: Is This the Most Demanding Ad for a Nanny Ever?," *Guardian*, January 24, 2020, https://www.theguardian.com/lifeandstyle/2020/jan/24 /nanny-viral-ad-california-ceo.

Jezebel suggested that the mother: Emily Alford, "Silicon Valley CEO Family Looks to Disrupt Living by Outsourcing Their Entire Existence to Contract Laborer," *Jezebel*, January 24, 2020, https://jezebel.com/silicon -valley-ceo-family-looks-to-disrupt-living-by-ou-1841202888.

Almost a quarter of children: "Religion and Living Arrangements Around the World," *Pew Research Center*, December 12, 2019, https://www.pewforum .org/2019/12/12/religion-and-living-arrangements-around-the-world/.

a report from the Center for American Progress: Leila Schochet and Rasheed Malik, "2 Million Parents Forced to Make Career Sacrifices Due to Problems with Child Care," Center for American Progress, September

13, 2017, https://www.americanprogress.org/issues/early-childhood
/news/2017/09/13/438838/2-million-parents-forced-make-career-sacrifices
-due-problems-child-care/.

"affordable" childcare: US Department of Health and Human Services Administration for Children and Families, "Child Care and Development Fund
(CCDF) Program," *Federal Register* 81, no. 190 (2016): 67438–67595,
https://www.govinfo.gov/content/pkg/FR-2016-09-30/pdf/2016-22986.pdf.

There has been no state: "Child Care Access and Affordability," Child Care
Aware, https://www.childcareaware.org/our-issues/public-policy/child
-care-access-and-affordability/.

"is a problem for the three-quarters": Elliot Haspel, *Crawling Behind: America's
Childcare Crisis and How to Fix It* (Montreal: Black Rose Books, 2019), 5.

The Economic Policy Institute found: "Childcare Costs in the United States,"
Economic Policy Institute, https://www.epi.org/child-care-costs-in-the
-united-states/.

The median hourly wage: US Bureau of Labor Statistics, last modified April 9,
2021, https://www.bls.gov/ooh/personal-care-and-service/childcare
-workers.htm.

"The roots of domestic work are deeply connected": Sheila Bapat, "History
of Exploitation: From Slavery to Domestic Work," interview by Preeti
Shekar, *RadioRPE*, https://www.reimaginerpe.org/20-1/shekar-bapat.

The experience of employing: Megan K. Stack, *Women's Work: A Reckoning
with Work and Home,* (New York: Doubleday, 2019), 203.

Low-income families who both: Stephanie Thomson, "Parents Are Desperate for Day Care. Yet N.Y. Centers Have Empty Spots," *New York Times*,
March 30, 2021, https://www.nytimes.com/2021/03/30/nyregion/child-care
-vouchers.html.

The childcare system is thus: Linda Jacobson, "Study: Early-Childhood
Programs More Segregated than K-12," K–12 Dive, October 1, 2019,
https://www.k12dive.com/news/study-early-childhood-programs-more
-segregated-than-k-12/563945/.

In Seattle, for instance: Paige Cornwell, "'You Should Get on a Waiting List':
Seattle's Child-Care Crunch Takes Toll on Parents, Providers," *Seattle
Times*, December 9, 2018, https://www.seattletimes.com/seattle-news/you
-should-get-on-a-waiting-list-seattles-child-care-crunch-takes-toll-on-parents
-providers/.

"Parents can't pay more": Rhian Evans Allvin, "Why Aren't We Paying Early Childhood Educators What They're Worth?," EdSurge, February 14, 2020, https://www.edsurge.com/news/2020-02-14-why-aren-t-we-paying-early -childhood-educators-what-they-re-worth.

Domestic help is a poorly regulated industry: "MacArthur 'Genius' Ai-jen Poo, Organizing America's Domestic Workers," NBC News, September 16, 2014, https://www.nbcnews.com/feature/in-plain-sight/macarthur -genius-Ai-jen-poo-organizing-americas-domestic-workers-n204996.

For the past decade: Hand in Hand, The Domestic Employers Network, "About Us," https://domesticemployers.org/about/.

"Most of us want to do the right thing": Hand in Hand, The Domestic Employers Network, "Resources and Education," https://domesticemployers.org/.

The organization has extensive: "FAQs and Templates," https://domestic employers.org/resources-and-faqs/templates/.

New York State passed: "Passed Legislation: States and Cities with Domestic Workers Bill of Rights," National Domestic Workers Alliance, https://www.domestic workers.org/programs-and-campaigns/developing-policy-solutions/bill -of-rights/passed-legislation/.

"Does this mean a living wage?": Phyllis Palmer, "Black Domestics During the Depression," *Federal Records and African American History* 29, no. 2 (Summer 1997), https://www.archives.gov/publications/prologue/1997 /summer/domestics-in-the-depression.

Enclosed with the letter: Rebecca Sharpless, *Cooking in Other Women's Kitchens: Domestic Workers in the South, 1865-1960* (Chapel Hill: University of North Carolina Press, 2010), 83.

The racist motivation: Larry DeWitt, "The Decision to Exclude Agricultural and Domestic Workers from the 1935 Social Security Act," *Social Security Bulletin* 70, no. 4 (2010), https://www.ssa.gov/policy/docs/ssb/v70n4 /v70n4p49.html.

The omission famously led: Derrick Johnson, "Viewing Social Security Through a Civil Rights Lens," NAACP, August 4, 2020, https://naacp.org/articles /viewing-social-security-through-civil-rights-lens.

"ask, diplomatically, for vacation": Daniel Slotnick, "Overlooked No More: Dorothy Bolden, Who Started a Movement for Domestic Workers," *New York Times*, February 20, 2019, https://www.nytimes.com/2019/02/20 /obituaries/dorothy-bolden-overlooked.html.

Care.com offers: Care.com, "Nanny Tax and Payroll Calculator," HomePay, https://www.care.com/homepay/nanny-paycheck-calculator.

Even though employers who: Laura Saunders, "You're Not the Only One Who's Not Paying Your 'Nanny Tax,'" *Wall Street Journal*, October 28, 2018, https://www.wsj.com/articles/youre-not-the-only-one-whos-not -paying-your-nanny-tax-1539336600.

One mother wrote in Slate: Leslie Forde, "Paying Nannies Under the Table Is the Norm," *Slate*, May 18, 2018, https://slate.com/human-interest/2018/05 /child-care-man-nannies-feel-forced-into-under-the-table-pay.html.

The requirement to pay: "What Should Be Included on Your Nanny's Pay Stub?," GTM Payroll Services, March 6, 2020, https://gtm.com /household/nanny-pay-stub/.

The Nevada Domestic Workers' Bill of Rights: "SB 232 Fact Sheet," National Domestic Workers Alliance, https://www.leg.state.nv.us/Session/79th2017 /Exhibits/Assembly/CL/ACL1017K.pdf.

Seattle's bill of rights: Ordinance SMC 14.23, https://www.seattle.gov /laborstandards/ordinances/domestic-workers.

Eilis, a Rhode Island: Comment on Slate Parenting Facebook group, June 28, 2019.

Caitlin, also from the Northeast: Comment on Slate Parenting Facebook group, June 28, 2019.

Amy, a mother in Georgia: Comment on Slate Parenting Facebook group, June 28, 2019.

"providing regular childcare": Paula Span, "When Grandparents Help Hold It All Together," *New York Times*, July 23, 2019, https://www.nytimes .com/2019/07/23/well/family/when-grandparents-help-hold-it-all -together.html.

The US's au pair program: Glenn Collins, "Au Pair in America: First Group Arrives," *New York Times*, June 11, 1986, https://www.nytimes.com/1986 /06/11/garden/au-pair-in-america-first-group-arrives.html.

They typically live with their families: Sabine Hess and Annette Puckhaber, "'Big Sisters' Are Better Domestic Servants?! Comments on the Booming Au Pair Business," *Feminist Review* no. 77 (2004): 65–78, https://journals.sagepub.com/doi/abs/10.1057/palgrave.fr .9400177?journalCode=fera.

Instead, the fifteen au pair: Zach Kopplin, "'They Think We Are Slaves,'" *Politico Magazine*, March 27, 2017, https://www.politico.com/magazine/story /2017/03/au-pair-program-abuse-state-department-214956/.

"Working as an au pair": Rachel Micah-Jones, "Au Pair Program Is No 'Cultural Exchange,'" *Baltimore Sun*, August 29, 2018, https:// digitaledition.baltimoresun.com/tribune/article_popover.aspx?guid =83e24abd-a6d7-4adb-b11e-45bdd448f008.

An employee of Centro de los Derechos: Evy Pena, email to author, September 11, 2019.

In 2019 a federal court judge: Kate Taylor, "A Court Said Au Pairs Deserve Minimum Wage. Some Families Are Protesting," *New York Times*, January 8, 2020, https://www.nytimes.com/2020/01/08/us/au-pair-massachusetts -ruling.html.

"But what about everybody else": Cristina Quinn, "Families with Au Pairs Struggle to Comply with Court Ruling," GBH News, December 18, 2019, https://www.wgbh.org/news/local-news/2019/12/18/families-with-au -pairs-struggle-to-comply-with-court-ruling.

Several Republican members of Congress: Paul Waldman, "GOP Claims About 'Real Infrastructure' Are Silly. Why Are Media Playing Along?," *Washington Post*, April 5, 2021, https://www.washingtonpost.com/opinions/2021/04/05 /gop-claims-about-real-infrastructure-are-silly-why-are-media-playing -along/.

even the left-leaning website: Ryan Lizza, Tara Palmeri, and Eugene Daniels, "POLITICO Playbook: The Question That's About to Dominate Politics," *Politico*, April 12, 2021, https://www.politico.com/newsletters /playbook/2021/04/07/the-question-thats-about-to-dominate-politics -492386.

But the idea of care as infrastructure: Moira Donegan, "How Domestic Labor Became Infrastructure," *Atlantic*, April 14, 2021, https://www.theatlantic .com/ideas/archive/2021/04/why-care-work-infrastructure/618588/.

"Caregiving," she has said: Ai-jen Poo, "Care Package with Ai-jen Poo," interview by Kate Spencer and Doree Shafrir, *Forever 35*, October 28, 2020, https://forever35podcast.com/episode-archive/episode-144-with -ai-jen-poo.

As of this writing , it's still unclear: Elliot Haspel, "American Parents Don't Get How Much Life Is About to Improve," *Atlantic*, October 31, 2021,

https://www.theatlantic.com/ideas/archive/2021/10/child-care-biden
-congress-build-back-better/620558/.

Poo has urged both: Poo, "Care Package."

When Poo appeared on the podcast: Poo, "Care Package."

2. Schools

Regardless of the parent's own race: David Washburn, "The Price of Punishment—New Report Shows Students Nationwide Lost 11 Million School Days Due to Suspensions," EdSource, August 31, 2018, https://edsource.org/2018/the-price-of-punishment-new-report-shows-students-nationwide-lost-11-million-school-days-due-to-suspensions/601889.

Mann had several ideas: Jonathan Messerli, *Horace Mann, A Biography* (New York: Knopf, 1972).

Mann believed that uneducated citizens: Horace Mann, *Report of the Massachusetts Board of Education* (1848), https://wps.ablongman.com/wps/media/objects/28/29256/timeline/docs/sources/theme_primarysources_Reform_4.html.

Horace Mann School, a private school: Tuition, Costs & Financial Aid, https://www.horacemann.org/admissions/tuition-financial-aid.

The school provides financial aid: "Financial Aid Frequently Asked Questions," Horace Mann School, https://www.horacemann.org/admissions/tuition-financial-aid; "For the 2020–2021 academic year, over 270 students, or approximately 15% of our enrollment, received more than $11,200,000 in Financial Aid."

Another namesake school: Catherine Brown, Scott Sargrad, and Meg Benner, "Hidden Money: The Outsized Role of Parent Contributions in School Finance," Center for American Progress, April 2017, 1, https://cdn.americanprogress.org/content/uploads/2017/04/18074902/ParentFundraising-report-corrected.pdf; "Not surprisingly, Horace Mann is one of the most affluent schools in the city, with only 6 percent of students coming from low-income families."

Its PTA raises nearly: Brown, Sargrad, and Benner, "Hidden Money," 1.

Caitlin Flanagan, in a biting: Caitlin Flanagan, "Private Schools Have Become Truly Obscene," *Atlantic*, March 11, 2021, https://www.theatlantic.com/magazine/archive/2021/04/private-schools-are-indefensible/618078/.

Only 10 percent of US students: "Private School Enrollment," National Center for Education Statistics, May 2020, https://nces.ed.gov/programs/coe /indicator/cgc.

The public DC elementary school: "Mann Elementary School," SchoolDigger, https://www.schooldigger.com/go/DC/schools/0003000035/school.aspx.

But it's located within: D.C. Hunger Solutions, "D.C. Public Schools School Breakfast Scorecard, School Year 2017–2018," https://www.dchunger. org/wp-content/uploads/2019/SY1718-DCPS-school-breakfast-score card.pdf.

The remainder of the piece: Grant Matthews as told to Marianne Hayes, "Confessions of a Six-Figure Father: Why I'd Never Send My Kids to Private School," *Forbes*, September 25, 2014, https://www.forbes.com /sites/learnvest/2014/09/25/confessions-of-a-six-figure-father-why-id -never-send-my-kids-to-private-school/?sh=ad870365278b.

They pay more taxes: Stephen J. Carroll and Emre Erkut, "How Taxpayers Benefit When Students Attain Higher Levels of Education," RAND Corporation, 2009, https://www.rand.org/pubs/research_briefs/RB9461.html.

"For those families that do enjoy": David F. Labaree, "Public Schools for Private Gain: The Declining American Commitment to Serving the Public Good," *Phi Delta Kappan*, October 22, 2018, https://kappanonline .org/labaree-public-schools-private-gain-decline-american-commitment -public-good/.

She reflects on those years: Nikole Hannah-Jones, "Choosing a School for My Daughter in a Segregated City," *New York Times Magazine*, June 9, 2016, https://www.nytimes.com/2016/06/12/magazine/choosing-a-school-for -my-daughter-in-a-segregated-city.html.

But the court's 1974: Jon Hale, "The Supreme Court Decision That Kept Suburban Schools Segregated," The Conversation, July 24, 2019, https:// theconversation.com/the-supreme-court-decision-that-kept-suburban- schools-segregated-120478.

In 1988 I was two: "Brown v. Board: Timeline of School Integration in the U.S.," *Learning for Justice* no. 25 (Spring 2004), https://www.learning forjustice.org/magazine/spring-2004/brown-v-board-timeline-of-school -integration-in-the-us.

And schools have never: Ta-Nehisi Coates, "The Case for Reparations," *Atlantic*, June 2014, https://www.theatlantic.com/magazine/archive/2014/06/the -case-for-reparations/361631/.

In New York 65 percent: Erica Frankenberg, Jongyeon Ee, Jennifer B. Ayscue, and Gary Orfield, "Harming Our Common Future: America's Segregated Schools 65 Years After Brown," Civil Rights Project, May 10, 2019, 5, https:// www.civilrightsproject.ucla.edu/research/k-12-education/integration -and-diversity/harming-our-common-future-americas-segregated -schools-65-years-after-brown/Brown-65-050919v4-final.pdf.

California is the most segregated: Frankenberg et al., "Harming Our Common Future."

72 percent of US cities: Ryan W. Coughlan, "Divergent Trends in Neigh- borhood and School Segregation in the Age of School Choice," *Pea- body Journal of Education* 93, no. 4 (2018): 349–366; Matt Barnum, "In Most U.S. Cities, Neighborhoods Have Grown More Integrated. Their Schools Haven't," Chalkbeat, November 19, 2018, https://www .chalkbeat.org/2018/11/19/21106185/in-most-u-s-cities-neighborhoods -have-grown-more-integrated-their-schools-haven-t.

One of the findings: Eric Torres and Richard Weissbourd, "Do Parents Really Want School Integration?," Making Caring Common Project, Har- vard Graduate School of Education, January 2020, 15, https://mcc.gse .harvard.edu/reports/do-parents-really-want-school-integration.

For Black and Latino parents: Steven Glazerman and Dallas Dotter, "Market Signals: A Deep-Dive Analysis of Parental School Choice in Washington, DC," Mathematica Policy Research, June 15, 2016, https://mathematica .org/publications/market-signals-how-do-dc-parents-rank-schools-and -what-does-it-mean-for-policy; Dana Goldstein, "One Reason School Seg- regation Persists," *Slate*, July 15, 2016, https://slate.com/human-interest /2016/07/when-white-parents-have-a-choice-they-choose-segregated -schools.html.

The Denver library page: "Park Hill Neighborhood History," Denver Public Library, https://history.denverlibrary.org/park-hill-neighborhood-history.

"through its actions": Keyes v. Denver School District No. 1, 413 US 189 (1973).

"the vestiges of past discrimination": Catherine L. Horn and Michal Kurlaender, "The End of Keyes—Resegregation Trends and Achievement in Denver Public Schools," Civil Rights Project, April 1, 2006, https://civilrights

project.ucla.edu/research/k-12-education/testing-and-assessment/the
-end-of-keyes2014resegregation-trends-and-achievement-in-denver
-public-schools.

The podcast hasn't shied: Chris Stewart, "Our Obsession with Integration Is
Hurting Kids of Color," *Washington Post*, June 10, 2016, https://www
.washingtonpost.com/news/in-theory/wp/2016/06/10/our-obsession
-with-integration-is-hurting-kids-of-color/.

This second wave of desegregation: Hannah-Jones, "Choosing a School."

there are no "all White" schools: Kyle Stokes, "LA's Schools Are Segregated.
LAUSD Says There's Only So Much They Can Do", *LAist*, July 3,
2018, https://laist.com/news/las-schools-are-segregated-lausd-says
-theres-only-so-much-they-can-do-about-it; "School Diversity in NYC,"
New York City Council, 2018–2019 school year, https://council.nyc.gov
/data/school-diversity-in-nyc/.

In New York, Hannah-Jones: Hannah-Jones, "Choosing a School."

"As a parent who supports the premise": Integrated Schools, Families Choosing Integration, "Two Tour Pledge—2021," https://integratedschools
.org/two-tour-pledge/.

Another useful resource: "Talking About Race Toolkit," *Center for Social Inclusion*,
https://www.cityofmadison.com/humanresources/documents/Leadership
DevConf/2016/AffirmCounterTransformScenarios.pdf.

The school was desegregated: Amanda Lewis and John Diamond, *Despite the
Best Intentions: How Racial Inequality Thrives in Good Schools* (Oxford:
Oxford University Press, 2015).

When Black parents attempted: Lewis and Diamond, *Best Intentions*, 231.

One senior official at the school: Lewis and Diamond, *Best Intentions*, 260.

During the Obama administration: Case Summaries, The United States
Department of Justice, https://www.justice.gov/crt/case-summaries.

It's also become a hot-button issue: Karol Markowicz, "Kids Will Pay a
Steep Price for This War on Merit in Schools," *New York Post*, May
10, 2021, https://nypost.com/2021/05/10/kids-will-pay-a-steep-price-for
-this-war-on-merit-in-schools/; David Frum, "The Left's War on Gifted
Kids," *Atlantic*, June 29, 2021, https://www.theatlantic.com/politics/archive
/2021/06/left-targets-testing-gifted-programs/619315/.

"too many Americans": Vanessa Siddle Walker, *The Lost Education of Horace Tate: Uncovering the Hidden Heroes Who Fought for Justice in Schools* (New York: New Press, 2018), 8.

she shared some of the questions: "Conversation with Parent Advocates on School Integration," *Everyday Race Blog*, July 19, 2017, https://everydayraceblog.com/2017/07/19/conversation-with-parent-advocates-on-school-integration/.

"advantage is a relative term": "Parenting to Win: Who Pays for the Helicopter?," *Integrated Schools* (podcast), November 27, 2019, https://integrated schools.org/podcast/calarco/.

bitter enemies for nearly thirty years: Arianna Prothero, "Why, and Where, Charter School Teachers Unionize," *Education Week*, March 22, 2019, https://www.edweek.org/policy-politics/why-and-where-charter-school-teachers-unionize/2019/03.

Teachers' unions opposed: Zachary Jason, "The Battle over Charter Schools," *Harvard Ed. Magazine* (Summer 2017), https://www.gse.harvard.edu/news/ed/17/05/battle-over-charter-schools.

Today, twenty-nine states automatically exempt: National Center for Education Statistics, "Table 3.3. States with Charter School Caps, Automatic Exemptions, Required Teacher Certification, and Identification of Special Education Responsibilities for Charter Schools, by State: 2017–18," State Education Practices, https://nces.ed.gov/programs/statereform/tab3_3.asp.

Advocates for public schools: Matt Barnum, "Critics of Charter Schools Say They're Hurting School Districts. Are They Right?," Chalkbeat, June 11, 2019, https://www.chalkbeat.org/2019/6/11/21108318/critics-of-charter-schools-say-they-re-hurting-school-districts-are-they-right.

Charter school advocates contend: Valerie Strauss, "Yes, Some Charter Schools Do Pick Their Students. It's Not a Myth," *Washington Post*, January 17, 2021, https://www.washingtonpost.com/education/2021/01/17/yes-some-charter-schools-do-pick-their-students-its-not-myth/.

Charter schools are just one component: James Foreman Jr., "The Secret History of School Choice: How Progressives Got There First," *Georgetown Law Journal* 93 (2005), https://digitalcommons.law.yale.edu/cgi/viewcontent.cgi?article=4146&context=fss_papers.

One such form is "voucher programs": Josh Cunningham, "School Choice: Vouchers," National Conference of State Legislatures, December 1, 2016, https://www.ncsl.org/research/education/school-choice-vouchers.aspx.

Voucher programs exist in only sixteen: "School Vouchers," EdChoice, 2021, https://www.edchoice.org/school-choice/types-of-school-choice/what-are-school-vouchers-2/; Alyssa Rafa, Ben Erwin, Bryan Kelley, and Micah Ann Wixom, "50-State Comparison: Charter School Policies," Education Commission of the States, January 28, 2020, https://www.ecs.org/charter-school-policies/.

"Both sides say they're the underdog": "Mo' Charters Mo' Problems," *School Colors* (podcast), Brooklyn Deep, November 8, 2019, https://www.school colorspodcast.com/episodes/episode-6-mo-charters-mo-problems.

Ember emphasizes mental health treatment: "Our Design," Ember Charter School, https://www.embercs.org/our-design.

A story that's played out in many states: Will Huntsberry, "Charter School Case Exposes Big Loopholes in How the State Funds Schools," *Voice of San Diego*, July 17, 2019, https://www.voiceofsandiego.org/topics/education/charter-school-case-exposes-big-loopholes-in-how-the-state-funds-schools/; Noliwe Rooks, *Cutting School: The Segrenomics of American Education* (New York: New Press, 2017).

Charters have also served: Valerie Strauss, "The 5 Most Serious Charter School Scams in 2019—and Why They Matter," *Washington Post*, January 27, 2020, https://www.washingtonpost.com/education/2020/01/27/5-most-serious-charter-school-scandals-2019-why-they-matter/.

Only about 7 percent: "Public School Charter Enrollment," National Center for Education Statistics, May 2021, https://nces.ed.gov/programs/coe/indicator/cgb.

New Orleans essentially doesn't: David Osborne, "Reinventing the New Orleans Public Education System," *New England Journal of Public Policy* 32, no. 1 (2020), https://scholarworks.umb.edu/nejpp/vol32/iss1/10/.

"did not have everything they needed": Derek W. Black, *Schoolhouse Burning: Public Education and the Assault on American Democracy* (New York: PublicAffairs, 2020).

"redefine their commitment": Black, *Schoolhouse Burning*.

"pulling the levers": Black, *Schoolhouse Burning*.

A 2012 study found: Jonathan Rothwell, "Housing Costs, Zoning, and Access to High Scoring Schools," Brookings Metropolitan Policy Program, April 2021, https://www.brookings.edu/wp-content/uploads/2016/06/0419_school_inequality_rothwell.pdf.

today's divisions are between affluent: Richard Florida, "The Persistent Inequality of Neighborhoods," Bloomberg CityLab, December 9, 2016, https://www.bloomberg.com/news/articles/2016-12-09/the-persistent -inequality-of-neighborhoods.

Precise school funding structures: Cory Turner, "Why America's Schools Have a Money Problem," NPR, April 18, 2016, https://www.npr .org/2016/04/18/474256366/why-americas-schools-have-a-money-problem.

In the early 1970s: Laura Isensee, "How a Dad Helped Start the Fight for Better Public School Funding In Texas," Houston Public Media, September 7, 2015, https://www.houstonpublicmedia.org/articles/news /2015/09/07/59720/how-a-dad-helped-start-the-fight-for-better-public -school-funding-in-texas-2/.

"Equal Protection Clause does not require": San Antonio Indep. Sch. Dist. v. Rodriguez, 411 US 1, 24 (1973).

"You cannot pretend that we": Dale Mezzacappa and Bill Hangley Jr., "At Board Hearing, Speakers Seek Fewer Police and More Support Services," Chalkbeat Philadelphia, June 18, 2020, https://philadelphia.chalkbeat .org/2020/6/18/22186746/board-hearing-report-speakers-seek-fewer -police-more-support-services.

"segregation academies": Valerie Strauss, "The Big Problem with Education 'Pandemic Pods' Suddenly Cropping Up," *Washington Post*, July 22, 2020, https://www.washingtonpost.com/education/2020/07/22/ huge-problem-with-education-pandemic-pods-suddenly-popping-up/.

"whatever parents ultimately decide": Clara Totenberg Green, "The Latest in School Segregation: Private Pandemic 'Pods,'" *New York Times*, July 22, 2020, https://www.nytimes.com/2020/07/22/opinion/pandemic-pods -schools.html.

"Well, what if our pod falls apart": Dan Kois, "When Learning Pods Came to Greenbrier Elementary," *Slate*, October 22, 2020, https://slate.com /human-interest/2020/10/learning-pods-greenbrier-elementary charlottes ville-divided-racial-lines.html.

"Many will read this article": Green, "Latest in School Segregation."

"I don't know that we can handle": "So . . . You Want to Be a Home Schooler?," *Mom and Dad Are Fighting* (podcast), *Slate*, July 30, 2020, https:// slate.com/podcasts/mom-and-dad-are-fighting/2020/07/slates-parenting -podcast-before-homeschool.

In a blog post on Medium: Shayla R. Griffin, "Some Students Should Go to School, Most Should Stay Home," *Medium*, July 16, 2020, https:// medium.com/@shaylargriffin/some-students-should-go-to-school-most -should-stay-home-8a57894b8487.

"The biggest social justice risk": Shayla R. Griffin, "If 'Most Students Should Stay Home,' What Do I Do with My Kids?: The Social Justice Dilemma of Pandemic Pod Schools for Privileged Parents," *Justice Leaders Collaborative*, August 11, 2020, https://www.justiceleaderscollaborative .com/blog/if-most-students-should-stay-home-what-do-i-do-with-my -kids-the-social-justice-dilemma-ofnbsppandemicnbsppod-schools-for -privileged-parents.

In an interview with Andrew Lefkowits: "Reopening Schools and Equity," *Integrated Schools* (podcast), August 5, 2020, https://integratedschools .simplecast.com/episodes/griffin.

"who in your circles of privilege": "Reopening Schools and Equity."

A rising number of Black and Hispanic families: Jessica Huseman, "The Rise of Homeschooling Among Black Families," *Atlantic*, February 17, 2015, https://www.theatlantic.com/education/archive/2015/02/the-rise-of -homeschooling-among-black-families/385543/.

3. College

"ultimate suburban legend": Jim Jump, "Ethical College Admissions: The Real Victims," Inside Higher Ed, September 16, 2019, https://www .insidehighered.com/admissions/views/2019/09/16/there-were-real-victims -admissions-scandal-opinion.

In her hometown of Palo Alto: Jacqueline Lee, "CDC Report: Youth Suicide Rates in Santa Clara County Highest in Palo Alto, Morgan Hill," *Mercury News*, March 3, 2017, https://www.mercurynews.com/2017/03/03/cdc -report-youth-suicide-rates-in-county-highest-in-palo-alto-morgan-hill/.

"We love our kids fiercely": Julie Lythcott-Haims, *How to Raise an Adult: Break Free of the Overparenting Trap and Prepare Your Kid for Success* (New York: Griffin, 2016).

"real chances": Lythcott-Haims, *How to Raise an Adult*.

"Tell your friends": Lythcott-Haims, *How to Raise an Adult*.

She does raise the possibility: Lythcott-Haims, *How to Raise an Adult*.

Melissa Korn and Jennifer Levitz: Jennifer Levitz and Melissa Korn, *Unacceptable: Privilege, Deceit & the Making of the College Admissions Scandal* (New York: Portfolio, 2020).

George Washington didn't go: Valerie Strauss, "Which U.S. Presidents Didn't Earn a College Degree? (Two of Them Are on Mount Rushmore)," *Washington Post*, February 12, 2015, https://www.washingtonpost.com /news/answer-sheet/wp/2015/02/12/which-u-s-presidents-didnt-earn-a -college-degree-two-of-them-are-on-mount-rushmore/.

College just wasn't very common: "History of College Education," Britannica ProCon.org, January 14, 2021, https://college-education.procon.org /history-of-college-education/.

exclusively wealthy, White, and Christian: Annika Neklason, "Elite-College Admissions Were Built to Protect Privilege," *Atlantic*, March 18, 2019, https://www.theatlantic.com/education/archive/2019/03/history -privilege-elite-college-admissions/585088/.

"grizzled, battle-hardened soldiers": Philo A. Hutcheson, "The Truman Commission's Vision of the Future," *Thought & Action* (Fall 2007): 107–115.

Black servicemembers, however: Erin Blakemore, "How the GI Bill's Promise Was Denied to a Million Black WWII Veterans," History.com, June 21, 2019, https://www.history.com/news/gi-bill-black-wwii-veterans -benefits.

Three years after the GI Bill: "Statement by the President Making Public a Report of the Commission on Higher Education," American Presidency Project, December 15, 1947, https://www.presidency.ucsb.edu/documents /statement-the-president-making-public-report-the-commission-higher -education.

In his book on college: Paul Tough, *The Inequality Machine: How College Divides Us* (Boston: Houghton Mifflin Harcourt, 2019), 25.

But a college degree: Tough, *Inequality Machine*, 26.

Adults who have a high school: Colleen Campbell, "Those Left Behind: Gaps in College Attainment by Race and Geography," Center for American Progress, June 17, 2019, https://www.americanprogress.org/issues /education-postsecondary/reports/2019/06/27/471242/those-left-behind/.

It is also a shield: Preston Cooper, "Job Losses Hit Workers Without College Degrees the Hardest," *Forbes*, May 12, 2020, https://www.forbes

.com/sites/prestoncooper2/2020/05/12/job-losses-hit-workers-without
-college-degrees-the-hardest/.

"elicit murmurs of agreement": David Leonhardt, "College for the Masses,"
New York Times, April 24, 2015, https://www.nytimes.com/2015/04/26
/upshot/college-for-the-masses.html.

"dinged everywhere": Howard Gold, "Rich Parents Keep Behaving Badly to Get
Their Children into College," MarketWatch, August 29, 2019, https://
www.marketwatch.com/story/rich-parents-keep-behaving-badly-to-get
-their-children-into-college-2019-08-22.

They aren't nearly as expensive: Jennifer Ma, Matea Pender, and CJ Libassi,
"Trends in College Pricing and Student Aid 2020," October 2020, https://
research.collegeboard.org/pdf/trends-college-pricing-student-aid-2020
.pdf#page=17.

In a parenting group: Slate Parenting Facebook group, 2020.

"America's best kept secret": Darlene Superville, "Jill Biden Pushes Free Access
to Community College, Training," *AP News*, February 11, 2021, https://
apnews.com/article/joe-biden-jill-biden-coronavirus-pandemic-economy
-850496234e66e5f21c9af50a75509a77.

Instead of going to community colleges: Thomas Peele, "California Community
Colleges Lose Students to More Expensive For-Profit Colleges," EdSource,
June 15, 2021, https://edsource.org/2021/california-community-colleges
-must-address-why-students-are-opting-for-more-expensive-for-profit
-schools/656436.

In the past twenty years: Ariel Gelrud Shiro and Richard V. Reeves, "The For-
Profit College System Is Broken and the Biden Administration Needs
to Fix It," Brookings, January 12, 2021, https://www.brookings.edu/blog
/how-we-rise/2021/01/12/the-for-profit-college-system-is-broken-and-the
-biden-administration-needs-to-fix-it/.

Kendra's hardships were extreme: Ashley A. Smith, "For-Profit Graduate Schools Popular with Black Women," Inside Higher Ed, July 25,
2017, https://www.insidehighered.com/news/2017/07/25/black-women
-graduate-students-enroll-higher-numbers-profits.

"legitimize the education gospel": Tressie McMillan Cottom, *Lower Ed: The
Troubling Rise of For-Profit in the New Economy* (New York: New Press,
2017), 11.

For-profit colleges, however: Patrick Cohen, "For-Profit Colleges Accused of Fraud Still Receive U.S. Funds," *New York Times*, October 12, 2015, https://www.nytimes.com/2015/10/13/business/for-profit-colleges-accused-of-fraud-still-receive-us-funds.html.

for-profit schools "too often tether": Caitlin Zaloom, *Indebted: How Families Make College Work at Any Cost* (Princeton: Princeton University Press, 2019), 192.

For-profit schools charge: Andrew Josuweit, "For-Profit Schools Can Cost $466 More Per Credit—But Rarely Pay Off," *Forbes*, February 28, 2017, https://www.forbes.com/sites/andrewjosuweit/2017/02/28/for-profit-schools-can-cost-466-per-credit/?sh=46b5bb41e769.

Every year thousands of students: "In an Extraordinary Year, Princeton Offers Admission to 1,498 Students for the Class of 2025," *Princeton University*, April 6, 2021, https://www.princeton.edu/news/2021/04/06/extraordinary-year-princeton-offers-admission-1498-students-class-2025; "1,968 Total Accepted to the Class of 2025 as Regular-Decision Letters Go Out," *Harvard Gazette*, April 6, 2021, https://news.harvard.edu/gazette/story/2021/04/harvard-college-accepts-1968-to-class-of-2025/.

Most colleges despise it: Tough, *Inequality Machine*, 276.

But, for many families: Tough, *Inequality Machine*, 70.

For example, colleges get a bump: William Deresiewicz, *Excellent Sheep: The Miseducation of the American Elite and the Way to a Meaningful Life* (New York: Free Press, 2014), 68.

"some families making more than $80,000": Tough, *Inequality Machine*, 200.

Among liberal arts colleges: Economic Diversity, National Universities, *U.S. News & World Report*, https://www.usnews.com/best-colleges/rankings/national-universities/economic-diversity.

"merit aid curtails": Zaloom, *Indebted*, 112.

Merit aid students, Zaloom writes: Zaloom, *Indebted*, 112.

More than one-fifth: Kenneth Tran, "At Dartmouth, an Environment of Wealth Not Eliminated by Scholarships," *Concord Monitor*, July 8, 2021, https://www.concordmonitor.com/At-Dartmouth-College-an-environment-of-wealth-and-privilege-might-be-changing-in-campus-life-but-certainly-not-in-the-lecture-halls-41362156.

During her older son's application process: Liz Willen, "Ten Things Not to Do When Your Child Is Applying to College," *Washington Post*, October 15, 2014,

https://www.washingtonpost.com/news/answer-sheet/wp/2014/10/15
/ten-things-not-to-do-when-your-child-is-applying-to-college/.

"can't produce more college graduates": Liz Willen, "Testing Abuses, Legacy Preferences and Bad Parent Behavior All Influence Who Gets into College: What Must Change?," Hechinger Report, June 20, 2019, https:// hechingerreport.org/testing-abuses-legacy-preferences-and-bad-parent -behavior-all-influence-who-gets-into-college-what-must-change/.

The researchers were then able: Gregor Aisch, Larry Buchanan, Amanda Cox, and Kevin Quealy, "Some Colleges Have More Students from the Top 1 Percent than the Bottom 60. Find Yours," *New York Times*, January 18, 2017, https://www.nytimes.com/interactive/2017/01/18/upshot /some-colleges-have-more-students-from-the-top-1-percent-than-the -bottom-60.html.

The list of the ten colleges: David Leonhardt, "America's Great Working-Class Colleges," *New York Times*, January 18, 2017, https://www.nytimes .com/2017/01/18/opinion/sunday/americas-great-working-class-colleges .html.

Thirty-eight highly selective: Aisch et al., "Some Colleges."

However, they found that: Caroline M. Hoxby and Christopher Avery, "The Missing 'One-Offs': The Hidden Supply of High-Achieving, Low-Income Students," Brookings, Spring 2013, https://www.brookings.edu/bpea -articles/the-missing-one-offs-the-hidden-supply-of-high-achieving-low -income-students/.

Daniel Golden's 2005 book: Daniel Golden, *The Price of Admission: How America's Ruling Class Buys Its Way into Elite Colleges—and Who Gets Left Outside the Gates* (New York: Broadway Books, 2006), 14.

As Golden writes: Golden, *Price of Admission*, 25.

Though The Price of Admission: Jeffrey Selingo, *Who Gets In and Why: A Year Inside College Admissions* (New York: Scribner, 2020), 233.

The sports for which Amherst: Selingo, *Who Gets In*, 222; Golden, *Price of Admission*, 147.

"far cry from the origins": Selingo, *Who Gets In*, 324.

"College leaders talk about pricing": Selingo, *Who Gets In*, 324.

"students we'd like to turn down": Tough, *Inequality Machine*, 278.

"the parents make too much money": Zaloom, *Indebted*, 15.

Students for Fair Admissions: Sarah Hinger, "Meet Edward Blum, the Man Who Wants to Kill Affirmative Action in Higher Education," ACLU, October 18, 2018, https://www.aclu.org/blog/racial-justice/affirmative-action /meet-edward-blum-man-who-wants-kill-affirmative-action-higher.

Many commenters noted that: Katherine Hu, "The Real Affirmative Action Dominating Admission to Elite Colleges Benefits Privileged White Kids," *Los Angeles Times*, August 27, 2020, https://www.latimes.com/opinion /story/2020-08-27/affirmative-action-yale-harvard-admissions-legacies.

In May 2021 Colorado: Jon Marcus, "Colorado Leads the Way in Closing the Door on Legacy Admission at Public Universities," *Washington Post*, July 16, 2021, https://www.washingtonpost.com/local/education /colorado-legacy-admissions-public-colleges/2021/07/15/2dfef94a-e4b8 -11eb-a41e-c8442c213fa8_story.html.

"For underrepresented Black": Ashton Lattimore, "Ending Legacy Admissions Is the Right Thing to Do. But for Black Alums, It Stings," *Washington Post*, August 6, 2018, https://www.washingtonpost.com/outlook/2018/08/06 /aaa7db6e-968d-11e8-80e1-00e80e1fdf43_story.html.

whether the Supreme Court will hear the case: Vivi E. Lu and Dekyi T. Tsotsong, "Supreme Court Delays Decision on Reviewing Harvard Admissions Lawsuit," *Harvard Crimson*, June 14, 2021, https://www.thecrimson.com /article/2021/6/14/supreme-court-delays-hearing-admissions-lawsuit/.

"how-to" guide: Daniel Golden, "How the Rich Really Play, 'Who Wants to Be an Ivy Leaguer?,'" ProPublica, March 12, 2019, https://www.propublica .org/article/college-admission-bribe-rich-parents-ivy-league-how-to.

"ever-shrinking club": Selingo, *Who Gets In*, 22.

"adversity index": "Frequently Asked Questions: Environmental Context Dashboard," College Board (2019), https://secure-media.collegeboard .org/pdf/environmental-context-dashboard-faqs.pdf.

"view a student's academic accomplishment": Scott Jaschik, "New SAT Score: Adversity," Inside Higher Ed, May 20, 2019, https://www .insidehighered.com/admissions/article/2019/05/20/college-board -will-add-adversity-score-everyone-taking-sat.

"storm of criticism": Anemona Hartocollis, "SAT 'Adversity Score' Is Abandoned in Wake of Criticism," *New York Times*, August 27, 2019, https://www .nytimes.com/2019/08/27/us/sat-adversity-score-college-board.html.

One innovative program: Erica L. Green, "A College Program for Disadvantaged Teens Could Shake Up Elite Admissions," *New York Times*, February 18, 2021, https://www.nytimes.com/2021/02/18/us/politics/college-admissions-poor-students.html.

Leslie Cornfeld, the founder: Erica L. Green, "A College Program for Disadvantaged Teens Could Shake Up Elite Admissions," *New York Times*, February 18, 2021, https://www.nytimes.com/2021/02/18/us/politics/college-admissions-poor-students.html.

In 2019 Representative: S.2640—Students Not Profits Act of 2019, Congress.gov, October 17, 2019, https://www.congress.gov/bill/116th-congress/senate-bill/2640/all-info.

$6.6 billion less in 2018: Michael Mitchell, Michael Leachman, and Matt Saenz, "State Higher Education Funding Cuts Have Pushed Costs to Students, Worsened Inequality," Center on Budget and Policy Priorities, October 24, 2019, https://www.cbpp.org/research/state-budget-and-tax/state-higher-education-funding-cuts-have-pushed-costs-to-students.

Jerry Lucido, the executive director: Jerry Lucido, email to author, July 10, 2019.

College Advising Corps, Nicole Hurd's: "How It Works," CollegePoint, 2021, https://www.collegepoint.info/what-we-do/.

4. Activism, Mutual Aid, and Grassroots Organizing

"Trayvon's murder spoke to": Nefertiti Austin, *Motherhood So White: A Memoir of Race, Gender, and Parenting in America* (Naperville: Sourcebooks, 2019), 18.

"an unwilling participant": Will Drabold, "Read What the Mothers of the Movement Said at the Democratic Convention," *Time*, July 26, 2016, https://time.com/4424704/dnc-mothers-movement-transcript-speech-video/.

She has since become: About Page, U.S. Representative Lucy McBath, https://mcbath.house.gov/about.

"that you want to help others": Jordan Flaherty, *No More Heroes: Grassroots Challenges to the Savior Mentality* (Chico: AK Press, 2016), 211.

"Because who wants to shoot a mom?": Vanessa Friedman, "What Does It Mean to 'Look Like a Mom'?," *New York Times*, July 28, 2020, https://www.nytimes.com/2020/07/28/style/wall-of-moms-image.html.

Numerous news outlets published lengthy pieces: Fabiola Cineas, "How
  Portland's Wall of Moms Collapsed—and Was Reborn Under Black
  Leadership," *Vox*, August 4, 2020, https://www.vox.com/21353939
  /portland-wall-of-moms-collapses-to-form-moms-united-for-black-lives.
"Black moms formed": Cineas, "Portland's Wall of Moms."
Portland's own deeply divided: Alana Semuels, "The Racist History of Port-
  land, the Whitest City in America," *Atlantic*, July 22, 2016, https://www
  .theatlantic.com/business/archive/2016/07/racist-history-portland/492035/.
In one of the Wall of Moms postmortems: Jagger Blaec, "The Complicated Rise
  and Swift Fall of Portland's Wall of Moms Protest Group," *Portland
  Monthly*, August 3, 2020, https://www.pdxmonthly.com/news-and-city
  -life/2020/08/the-complicated-rise-and-swift-fall-of-portland-s-wall-of
  -moms-protest-group.
Of the ten charities: "10 Incredible Charities Started by Kids," Buzzfeed,
  September 10, 2013, https://www.buzzfeed.com/nakedjuice/incredible
  -charities-started-by-children.
"too many people assume": Craig Kielburger, "Don't Start a Charity," *Medium*,
  January 23, 2020, https://medium.com/swlh/dont-start-a-charity
  -569d55b79be8.
Deep involvement in mutual: Dean Spade, *Mutual Aid: Building Solidarity
  During this Crisis (and the Next)* (London: Verso, 2020), 26.
Its Social Justice Standards: "Social Justice Standards," *Teaching Tolerance*,
  https://www.learningforjustice.org/sites/default/files/2017-06/TT_Social
  _Justice_Standards_0.pdf.
Lydia wrote, in an essay: Lydia Kiesling, "Can I Talk to You About Preschool for
  All?," *Cut*, November 12, 2020, https://www.thecut.com/2020/11/oregon
  -universal-preschool.html.
Then, the group faced two: Don McIntosh, "Universal Preschool Drive Seeks Signatures," *Northwest Labor Press*, May 13, 2020, https://nwlaborpress.org
  /2020/05/universal-preschool-drive-seeks-signatures/.
"one of the most progressive": Claire Cain Miller, "How an Oregon Measure for Universal Preschool Could Be a National Model," *New York
  Times*, November 6, 2020, https://www.nytimes.com/2020/11/06/upshot
  /oregon-universal-preschool-election.html.
"parent revolt": Helaine Olen, "What Happens When Petulant Parents Won't
  Share? School Funding Inequities, That's What," *Slate*, November 10,

2011, https://slate.com/human-interest/2011/11/school-funding-equality
-what-happens-when-well-off-parents-won-t-share.html.

"stormy, high-profile divorce": Zahira Torres, "Malibu Wants Its Own
School District, but a Split from Santa Monica Might Require 'Ali-
mony,'" *Los Angeles Times*, March 11, 2016, https://www.latimes.com/local
/education/la-me-santa-monica-malibu-20160311-story.html.

One of the *"secrets"*: Bruce Feiler, *The Secrets of Happy Families* (New York:
William Morrow, 2013), 87.

That horrific history: Rukmini Callimachi, "Lost Lives, Lost Culture: The For-
gotten History of Indigenous Boarding Schools," *New York Times*, July
19, 2021, https://www.nytimes.com/2021/07/19/us/us-canada-indigenous
-boarding-residential-schools.html.

"ICE pulling children from their mothers": Hayley DeRoche, "It's Time to Abolish Foster Care," SheKnows, October 12, 2020, https://www.sheknows
.com/parenting/articles/2356957/abolish-foster-care/.

"vodka as my co-pilot": Rachel Hollis, *Girl, Wash Your Face: Stop Believing
the Lies About Who You Are So You Can Become Who You Were Meant
to Be* (Thomas Nelson, 2018), 274.

"psychological mechanism": JPB Gerald, "Combatting the Altruistic Shield in
English Language Teaching," *NYS Tesol Journal* 7, no. 1, January 2020,
http://journal.nystesol.org/jan2020/3_AP.pdf.

5. Money, Wealth, and Legacy

The system suggests: Ron Lieber, *The Opposite of Spoiled: Raising Kids Who
Are Grounded, Generous, and Smart About Money* (New York: Harper,
2015).

In the United States, "legitimate privilege": Rachel Sherman, *Uneasy Street: The
Anxieties of Affluence* (Princeton: Princeton University Press, 2017), 25.

She found a pervasive belief: Sherman, *Uneasy Street*, 25.

"They want their children": Sherman, *Uneasy Street*, 24.

"the hollow middle class": Anne Helen Petersen, "The Hollow Middle Class,"
Vox, December 15, 2020, https://www.vox.com/the-goods/22166381
/hollow-middle-class-american-dream.

operated his factories "non-stop": Paul Vallely, *Philanthropy: From Aristotle
to Zuckerberg* (London: Bloomsbury, 2020), 735.

"sliding scale": Vallely, *Philanthropy*, 735.

Likewise, in the oil industry: Vallely, *Philanthropy*, 751.

"no amount of charities": Dylan Matthews, "The Case Against Billionaire Philanthropy," *Vox*, December 17, 2018, https://www.vox.com/future -perfect/2018/12/17/18141181/foundation-charity-deduction-democracy -rob-reich.

Reverend John Haynes Holmes: Yoni Appelbaum, "Is Big Philanthropy Compatible with Democracy?," *Atlantic*, June 28, 2017, https://www .theatlantic.com/business/archive/2017/06/is-philanthrophy-compatible -democracy/531930/.

criticisms did not stop Rockefeller: Vallely, *Philanthropy*, 788.

When the WHO was formed: Catherine Cheney, "'Big Concerns' over Gates Foundation's Potential to Become Largest WHO Donor," Devex, June 5, 2020, https://www.devex.com/news/big-concerns-over-gates-foundation -s-potential-to-become-largest-who-donor-97377.

"taking on the problems": Anand Giridharadas, *Winners Take All: The Elite Charade of Changing the World* (New York: Knopf Doubleday, 2019).

In the comments section: Aaron (Orange County, CA), November 27, 2018, comment on David Bornstein, "A Call to Modernize American Philanthropy," *New York Times*, November 27, 2018, https://www .nytimes.com/2018/11/27/opinion/philanthropy-minorities-charities .html#commentsContainer.

Family foundations are required: David Bornstein, "A Call to Modernize American Philanthropy," *New York Times*, November 27, 2018, https://www .nytimes.com/2018/11/27/opinion/philanthropy-minorities-charities .html.

The rich don't feed and house: Stephen Prince, "Why I Am a Patriotic Millionaire," Patriotic Millionaires, April 28, 2016, https://patrioticmillionaires .org/2016/04/28/why-i-am-a-patriotic-millionaire-stephen-prince/.

The group's original name was Comfort Zone: Anna Altman, "The Millennials Who Want to Get Rid of Their Class Privilege," *Washington Post Magazine*, March 2, 2020, https://www.washingtonpost.com/magazine/2020/03 /02/their-families-built-fortunes-these-millennials-are-trying-figure-out -how-undo-their-class-privilege/.

When the group has been: Abby Aguirre, "Easy Come, Easy Go for Idealistic Heirs," *New York Times*, March 9, 2008, https://www.nytimes.com/2008 /03/09/fashion/09rich.html.

White families are equally: Dorothy A. Brown, *The Whiteness of Wealth: How the Tax System Impoverishes Black Americans—and How We Can Fix It* (New York: Crown, 2021), 18.

As Nikole Hannah-Jones wrote: Nikole Hannah-Jones, "What Is Owed," *New York Times Magazine*, June 30, 2020, https://www.nytimes.com/inter active/2020/06/24/magazine/reparations-slavery.html.

The word wealth, *she said*: "'Sum of Us' Examines the Hidden Cost of Racism—for Everyone," NPR Fresh Air, February 17, 2021, https:// www.npr.org/2021/02/17/968638759/sum-of-us-examines-the-hidden -cost-of-racism-for-everyone.

The first case of reparations: Roy Finkbine, "Belinda's Petition: Reparations for Slavery in Revolutionary Massachusetts," *William and Mary Quarterly* 64, no. 1 (2007): 95–104.

In April 2021, thirty-two years: Juana Summers, "House Lawmakers Advance Historic Bill to Form Reparations Commission," NPR News, April 15, 2021, https://www.npr.org/2021/04/14/986853285/house-lawmakers-advance -historic-bill-to-form-reparations-commission.

practicalities *of reparations*: Ta-Nehisi Coates, "The Case for Reparations," *Atlantic*, June 15, 2014, https://www.theatlantic.com/magazine/archive /2014/06/the-case-for-reparations/361631/.

As the episode's host: "The Least You Could Do," *Reply All* (podcast), Gimlet Media, June 18, 2020, https://gimletmedia.com/shows/reply-all/ z3h94o.

In the opening of the essay: Chris Moore-Backman, "How I Can Offer Repa-rations in Direct Proportion to My White Privilege," *Yes!*, October 25, 2017, https://www.yesmagazine.org/issue/just-transition/2017/10/25 /how-i-can-offer-reparations-in-direct-proportion-to-my-white -privilege.

Our reaction to people: Larissa MacFarquhar, *Strangers Drowning: Grappling with Impossible Idealism, Drastic Choices, and the Overpowering Urge to Help* (New York: Penguin, 2016), 20.

People who are upward-oriented: Sherman, *Uneasy Street*, 20.

Matthew Stewart makes a similar point: Stewart, "The 9.9 Percent."

Work to elect antiracist leaders: "Sum of Us."

Conclusion

Pictures of Cruz boarding: Ashley Parker, "One Night in Cancun: Ted Cruz's Disastrous Decision to Go on Vacation During Texas Storm Crisis," *Washington Post*, February 19, 2021, https://www.washingtonpost.com /politics/ted-cruz-cancun-storm/2021/02/19/ce1dc25e-7252-11eb-93be -c10813e358a2_story.html.

His initial statement of explanation: Oma Seddiq, "Ted Cruz Explains Away Cancun Trip with Family During Severe Winter Storm in Texas as Him 'Wanting to Be a Good Dad,'" *Business Insider*, February 18, 2021, https://www.businessinsider.com/ted-cruz-defends -mexico-trip-good-dad-winter-storm-2021-2.

Yet he continued to reiterate: "Ted Cruz Claims He Was Being a 'Good Dad' for Leaving Texas While Millions Were Left Without Power," *Telegraph*, February 18, 2021, https://www.youtube.com/watch?v=6qOQOcroyiY.

Salon *ran an article*: Travis Gettys, "Cruz Ripped to Shreds for Blaming Widely Condemned Cancun Vacation on His Daughters," *Salon*, February 18, 2021, https://www.salon.com/2021/02/18/cruz-ripped-to-shreds-for -blaming-widely-condemned-cancun-vacation-on-his-daughters_partner/.

One of the defendants: Joey Garrison, "LA Businessman Sentenced to 4 Months in Prison for Paying $250K to Get Son into USC as Water Polo Recruit," *USA Today*, September 25, 2019, https://www.usatoday.com/story/news /nation/2019/09/24/usc-college-admissions-scandal-dad-faces-prison -paying-250-k/2373143001/.

Dan Ariely, a professor of psychology: Lisa Miller, "Ethical Parenting," *New York Magazine*, October 4, 2013, https://nymag.com/news/features /ethical-parenting-2013-10/.

The game shows your child: Carrie Engel, "Play the Dream Hoarders Game," Brookings, July 13, 2017, https://www.brookings.edu/blog /brookings-now/2017/07/13/play-the-dream-hoarders-game/.

"Parents I interviewed felt conflicted": Margaret A. Hagerman, "White Progressive Parents and the Conundrum of Privilege," *Los Angeles Times*, September 30, 2018, https://www.latimes.com/opinion/op-ed/la-oe-hagerman -white-parents-20180930-story.html.

Perhaps because she wasn't talking: Hagerman, "White Progressive Parents."

INDEX